CHAPTER 4

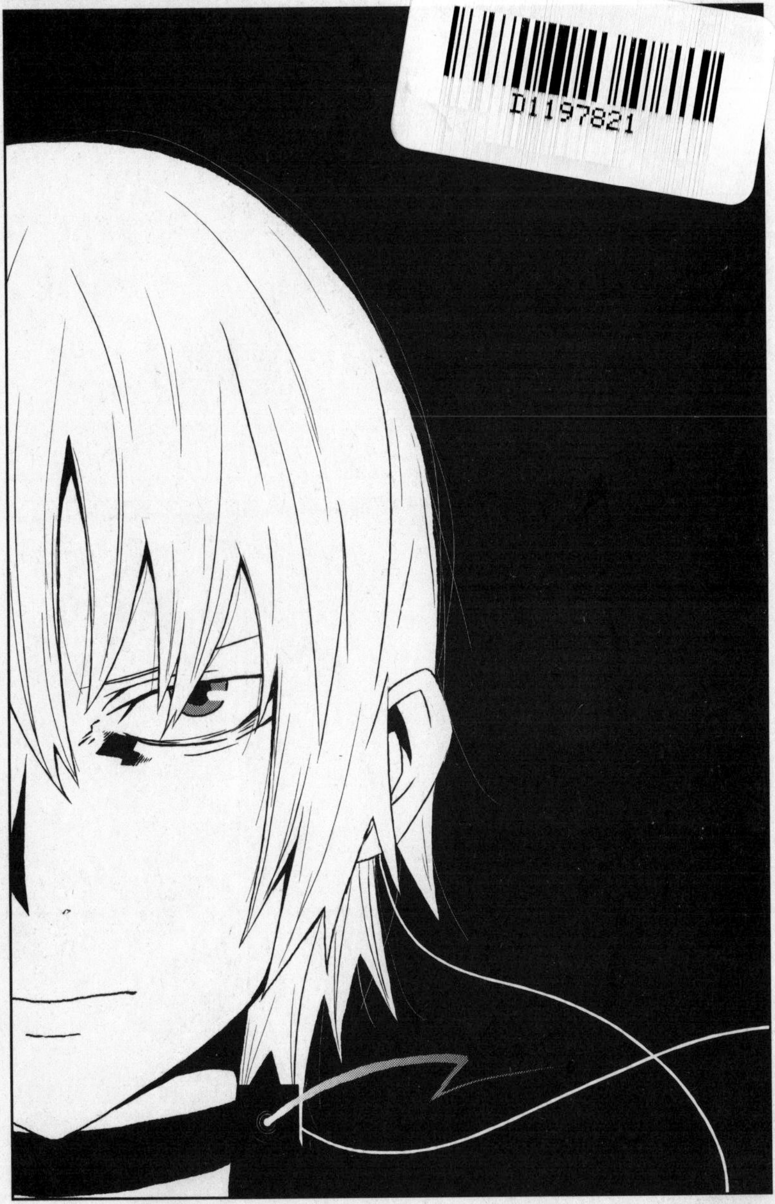

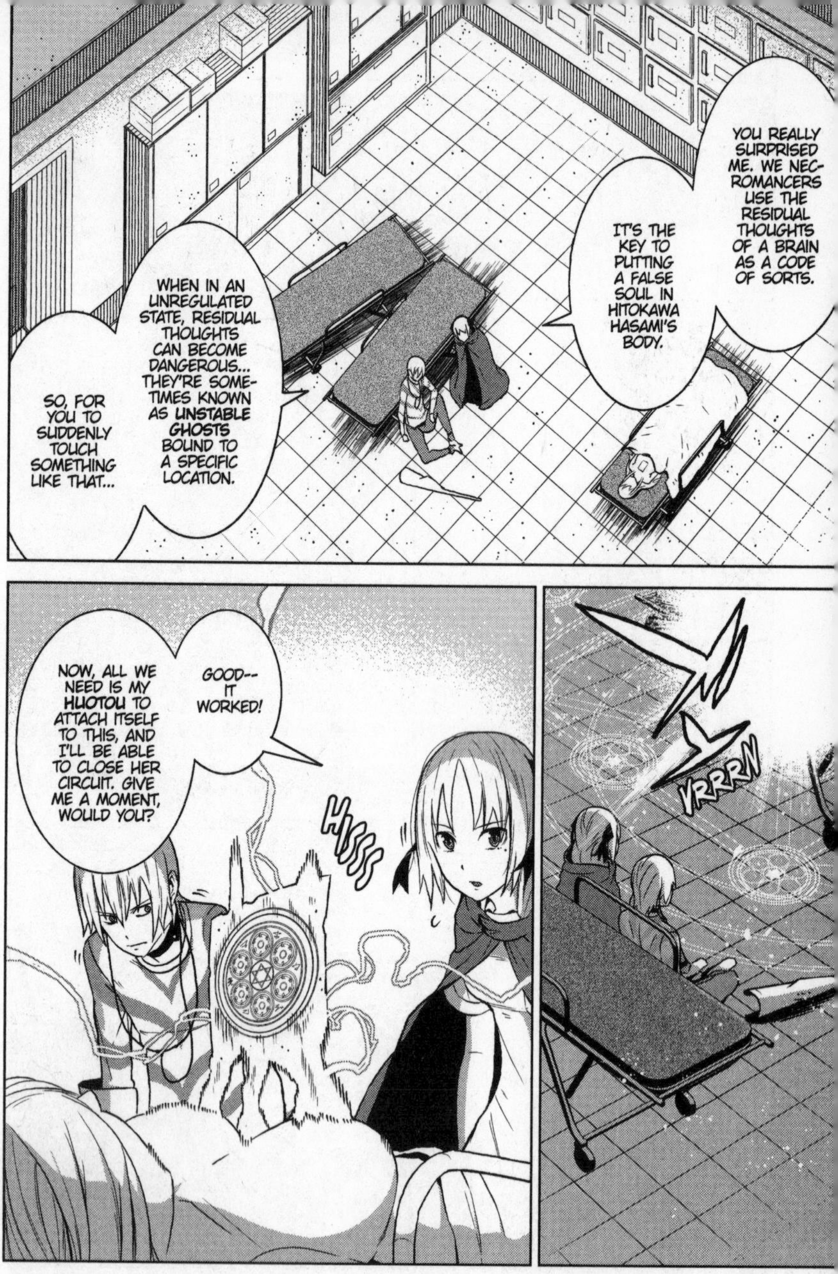
YOU REALLY SURPRISED ME. WE NECROMANCERS USE THE RESIDUAL THOUGHTS OF A BRAIN AS A CODE OF SORTS.
IT'S THE KEY TO PUTTING A FALSE SOUL IN HITOKAWA HASAMI'S BODY.
WHEN IN AN UNREGULATED STATE, RESIDUAL THOUGHTS CAN BECOME DANGEROUS... THEY'RE SOMETIMES KNOWN AS **UNSTABLE GHOSTS** BOUND TO A SPECIFIC LOCATION.
SO, FOR YOU TO SUDDENLY TOUCH SOMETHING LIKE THAT...
VRRRN
GOOD-- IT WORKED!
NOW, ALL WE NEED IS MY **HUOTOU** TO ATTACH ITSELF TO THIS, AND I'LL BE ABLE TO CLOSE HER CIRCUIT. GIVE ME A MOMENT, WOULD YOU?
HISSS

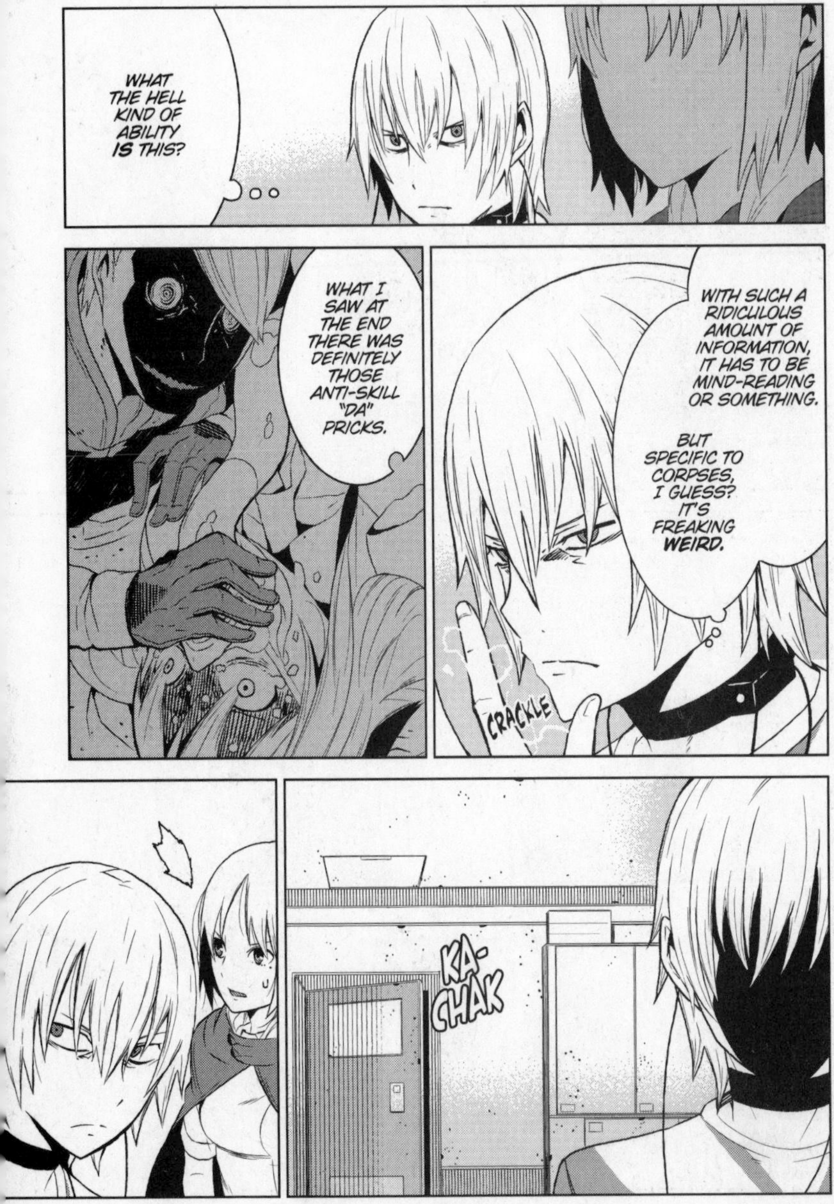
WHAT THE HELL KIND OF ABILITY IS THIS?
...
WITH SUCH A RIDICULOUS AMOUNT OF INFORMATION, IT HAS TO BE MIND-READING OR SOMETHING.
BUT SPECIFIC TO CORPSES, I GUESS? IT'S FREAKING WEIRD.
CRACKLE
WHAT I SAW AT THE END THERE WAS DEFINITELY THOSE ANTI-SKILL "DA" PRICKS.
KA-CHAK

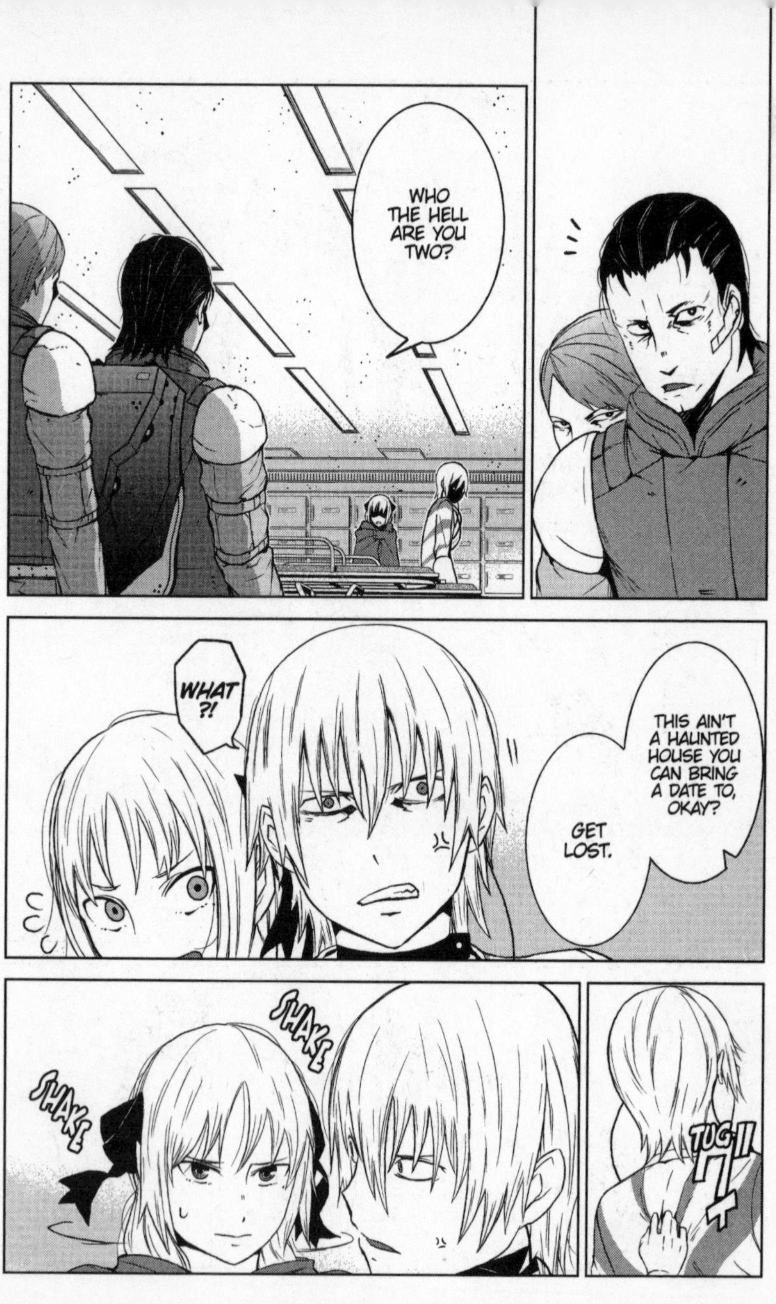
WHO THE HELL ARE YOU TWO?
THIS AIN'T A HAUNTED HOUSE YOU CAN BRING A DATE TO, OKAY?
GET LOST.
WHAT?!
TUG
SHAKE
SHAKE

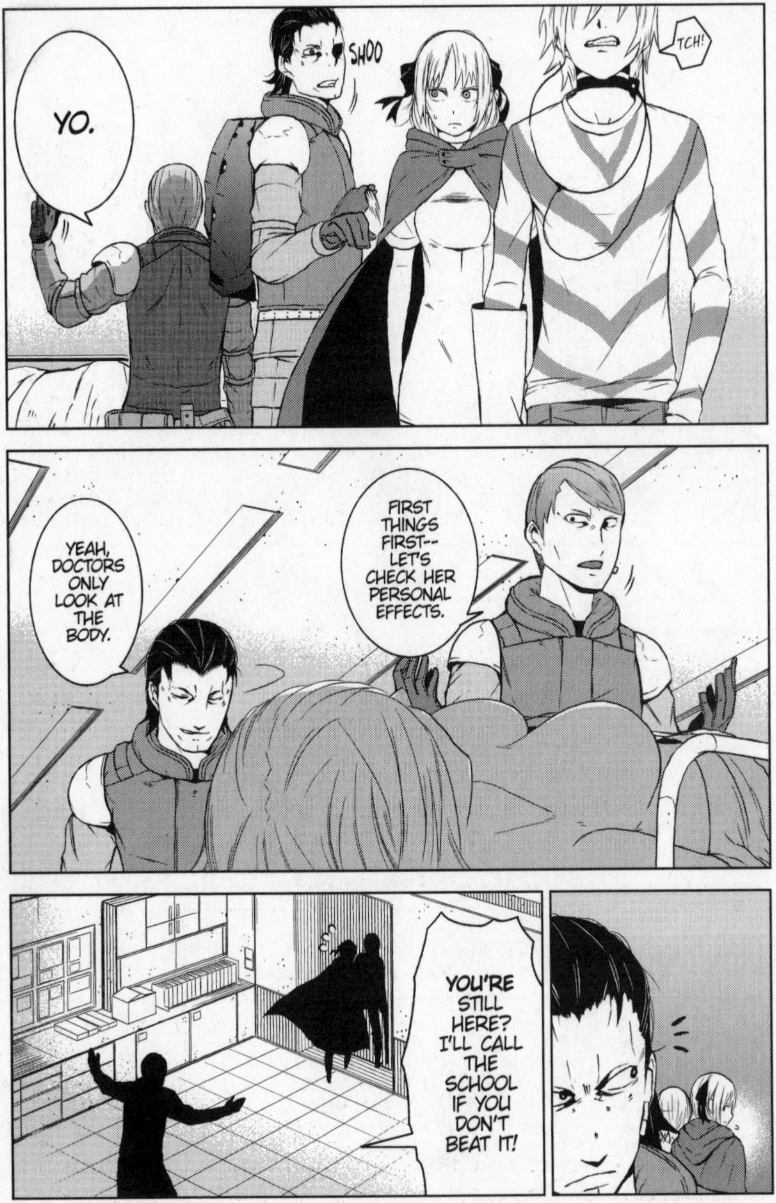
TCH!
SHOO
YO.
FIRST THINGS FIRST-- LET'S CHECK HER PERSONAL EFFECTS.
YEAH, DOCTORS ONLY LOOK AT THE BODY.
YOU'RE STILL HERE? I'LL CALL THE SCHOOL IF YOU DON'T BEAT IT!

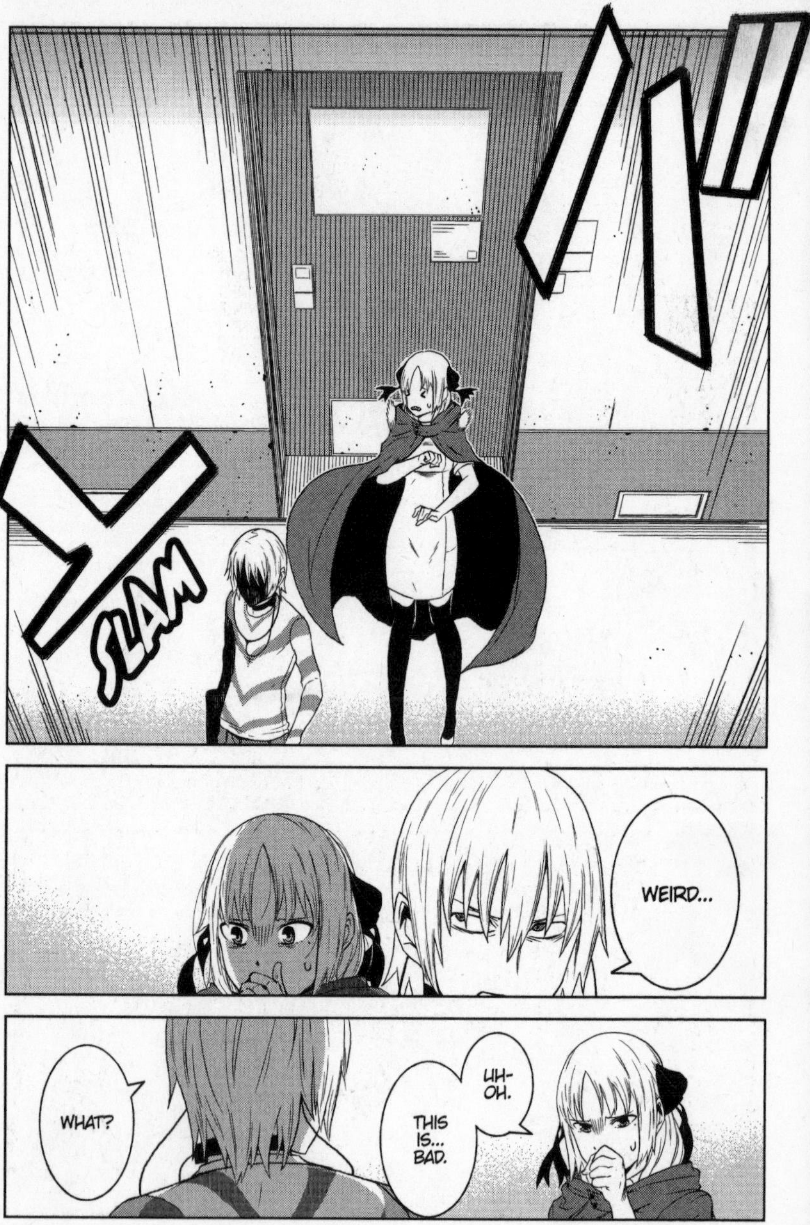
SLAM
WEIRD...
UH-OH.
THIS IS... BAD.
WHAT?

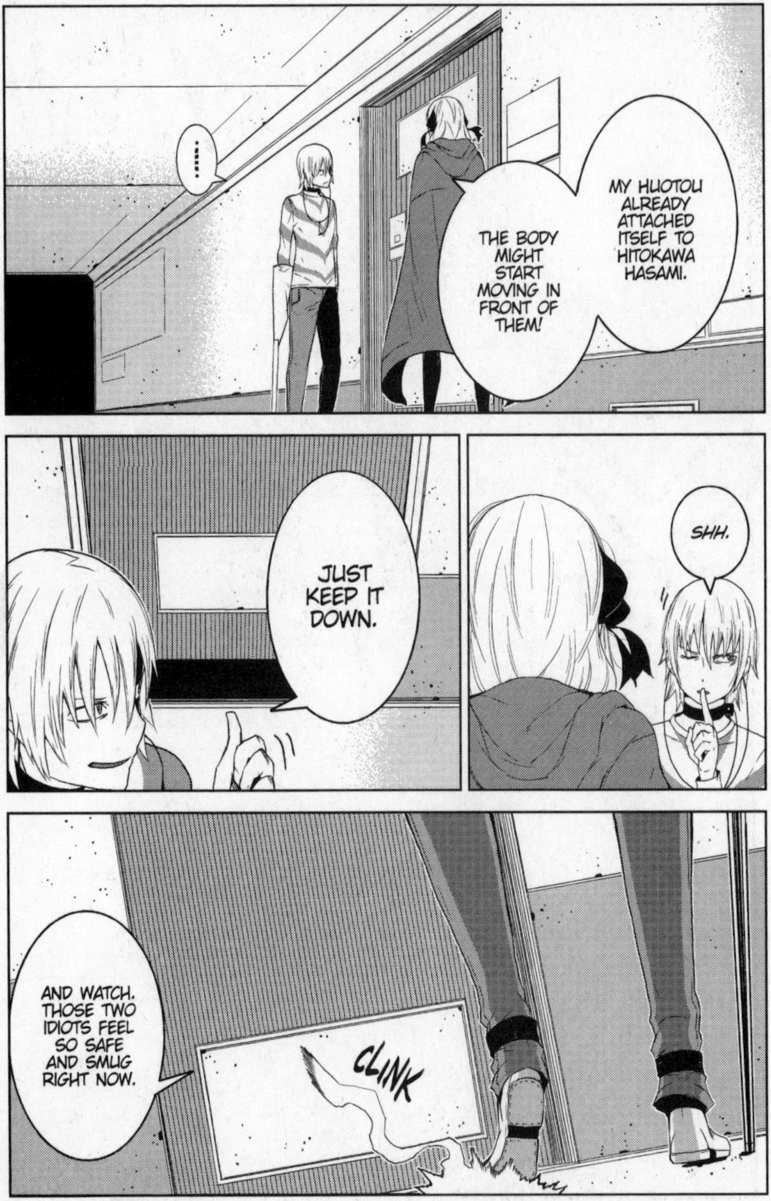
MY HUOTOU ALREADY ATTACHED ITSELF TO HITOKAWA HASAMI.
THE BODY MIGHT START MOVING IN FRONT OF THEM!
......
SHH.
JUST KEEP IT DOWN.
AND WATCH. THOSE TWO IDIOTS FEEL SO SAFE AND SMUG RIGHT NOW.
CLINK

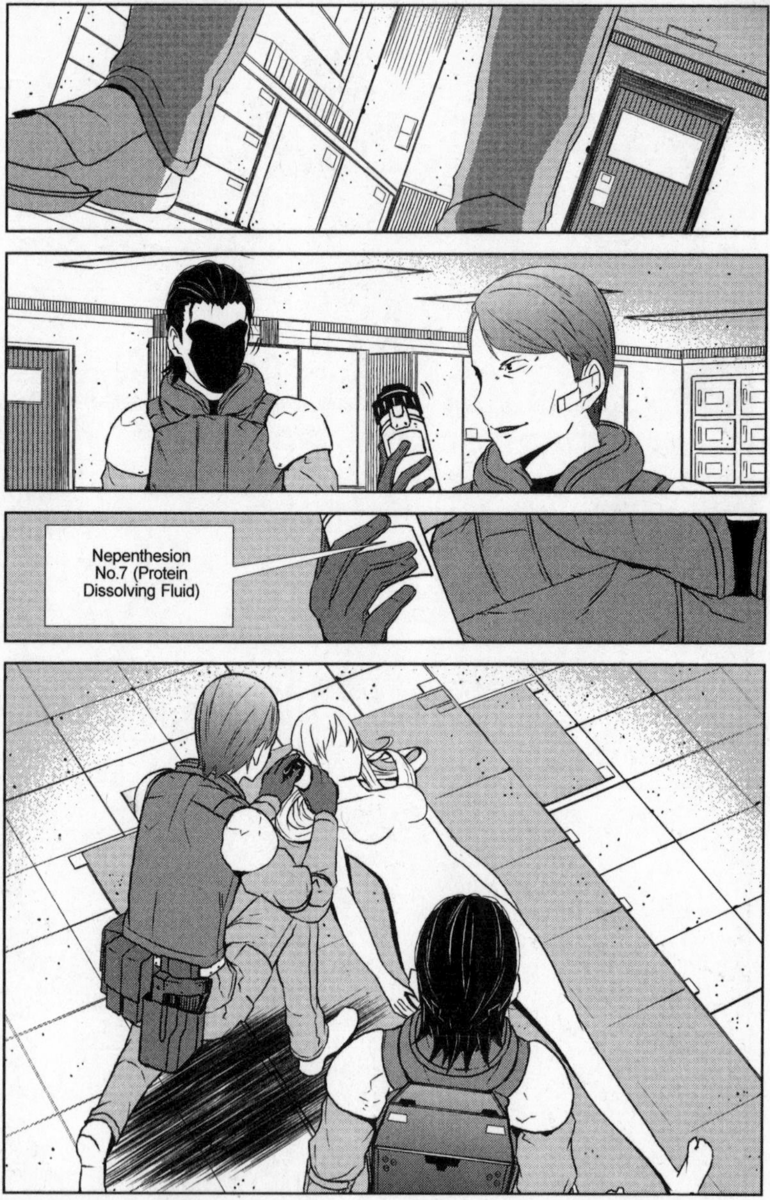
Nepenthesion No.7 (Protein Dissolving Fluid)

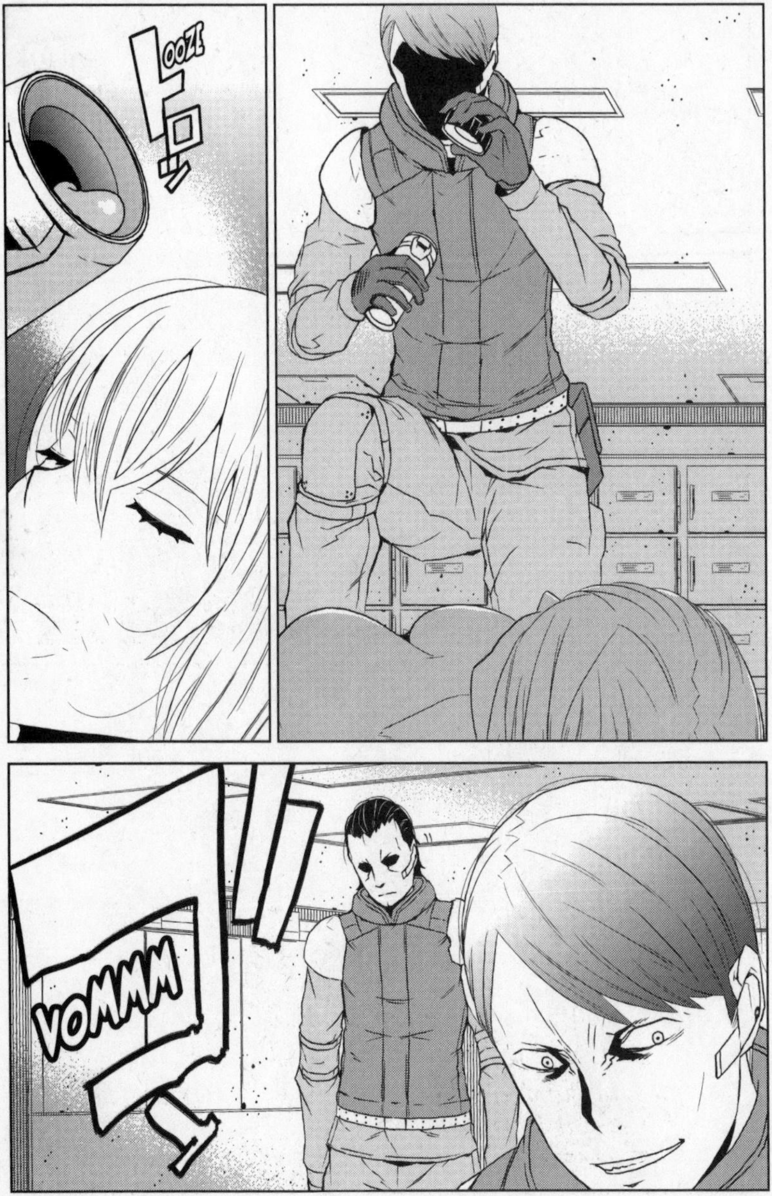
LOOZE
トロッ
VOMMM

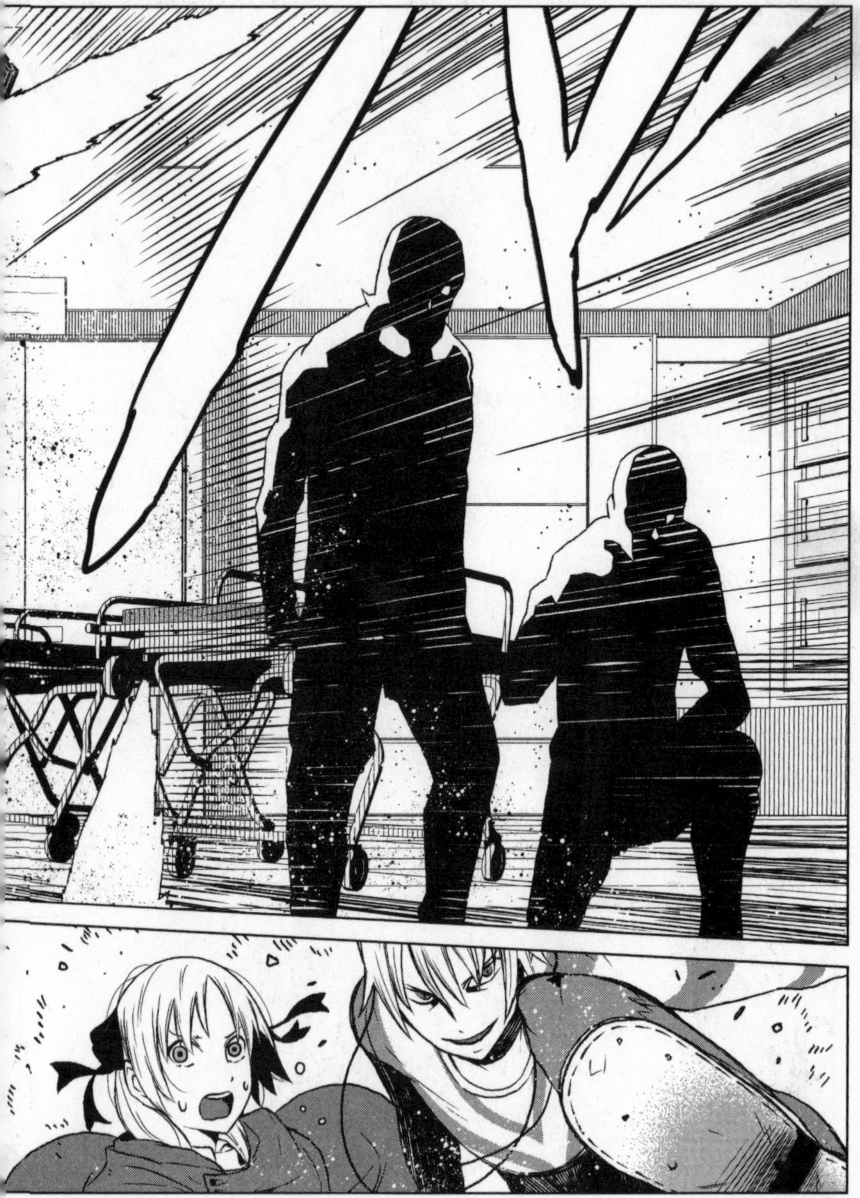

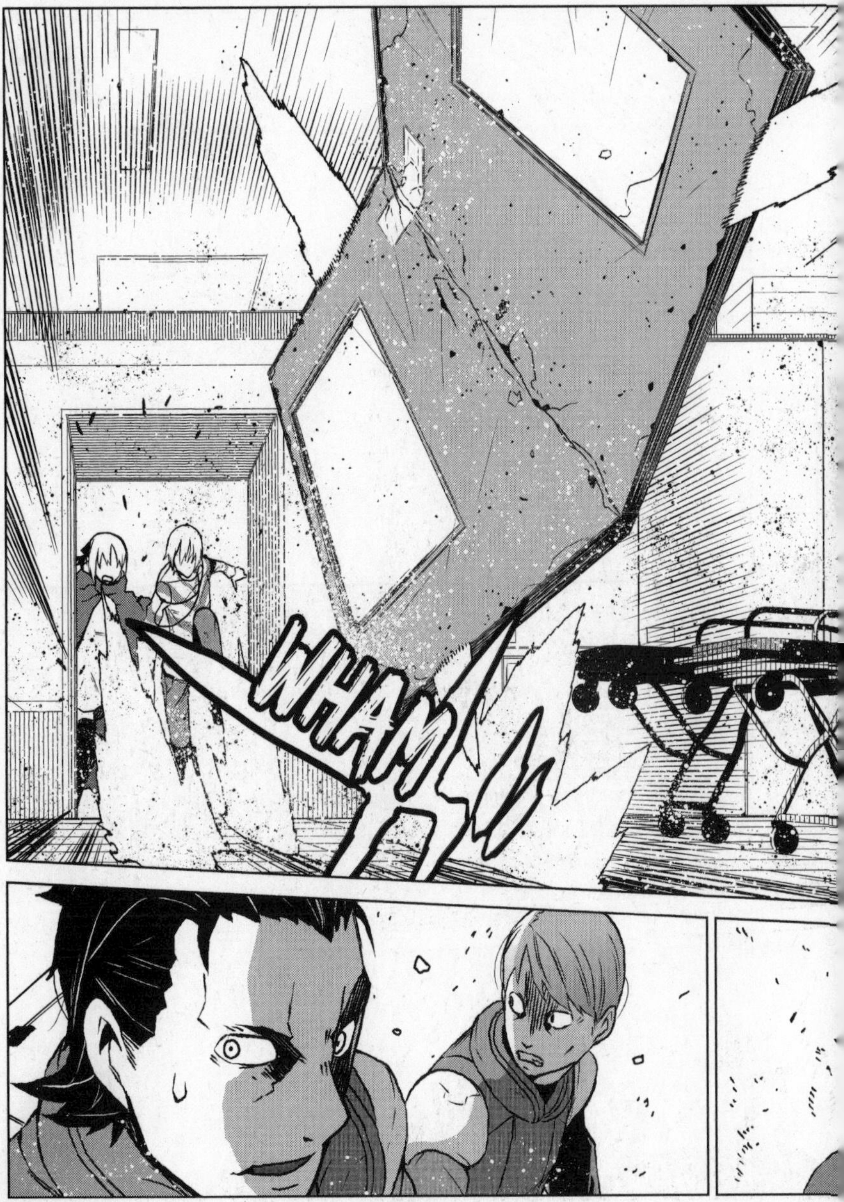
WHAM

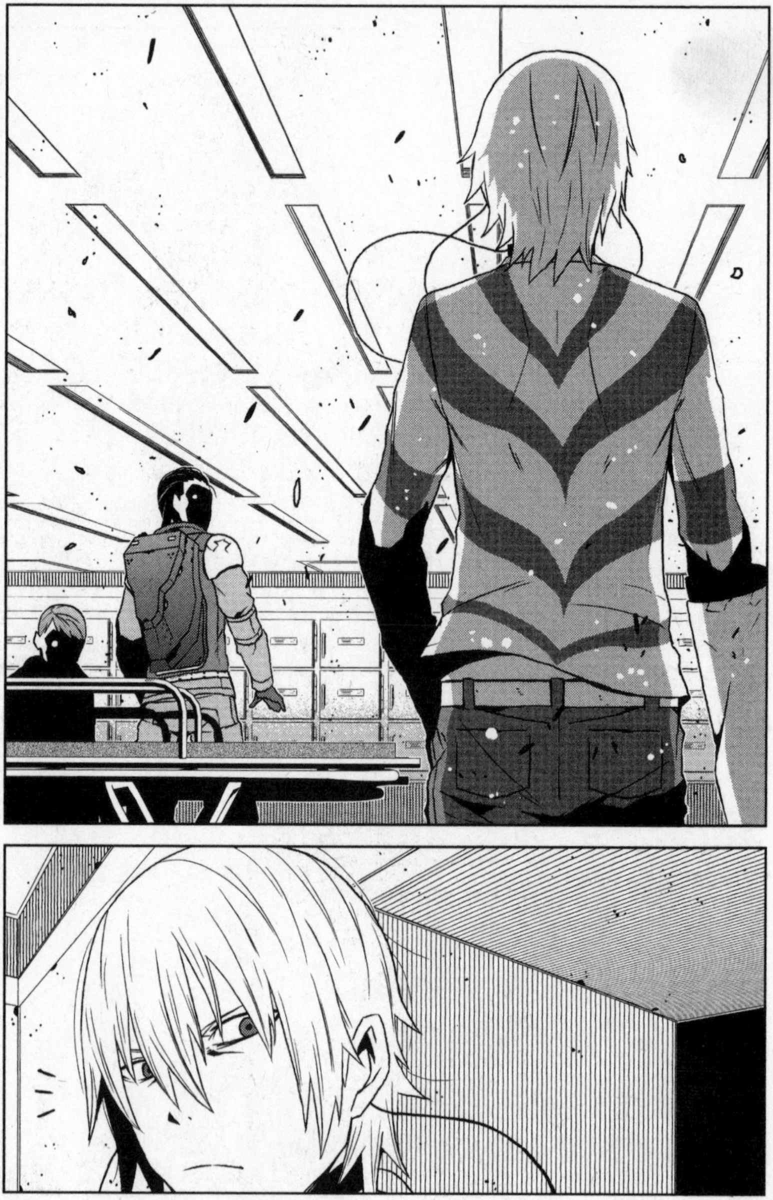

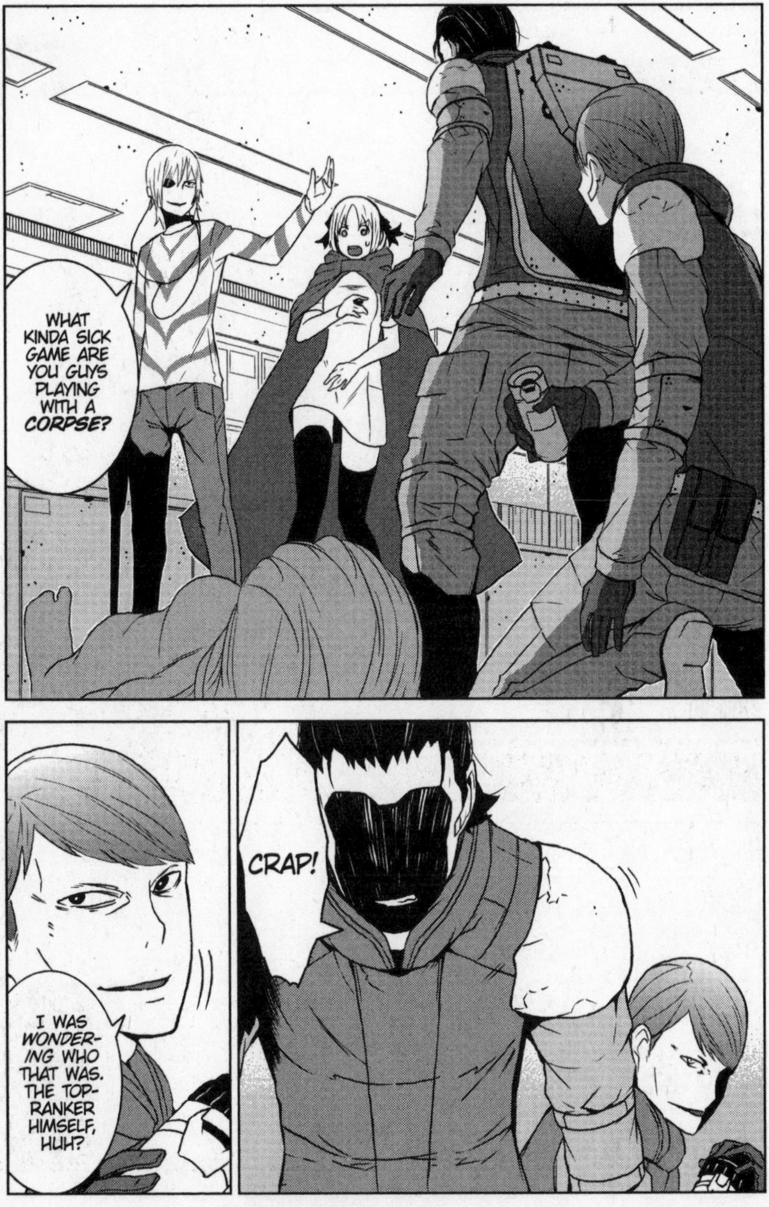
WHAT KINDA SICK GAME ARE YOU GUYS PLAYING WITH A CORPSE?
CRAP!
I WAS WONDERING WHO THAT WAS. THE TOP-RANKER HIMSELF, HUH?

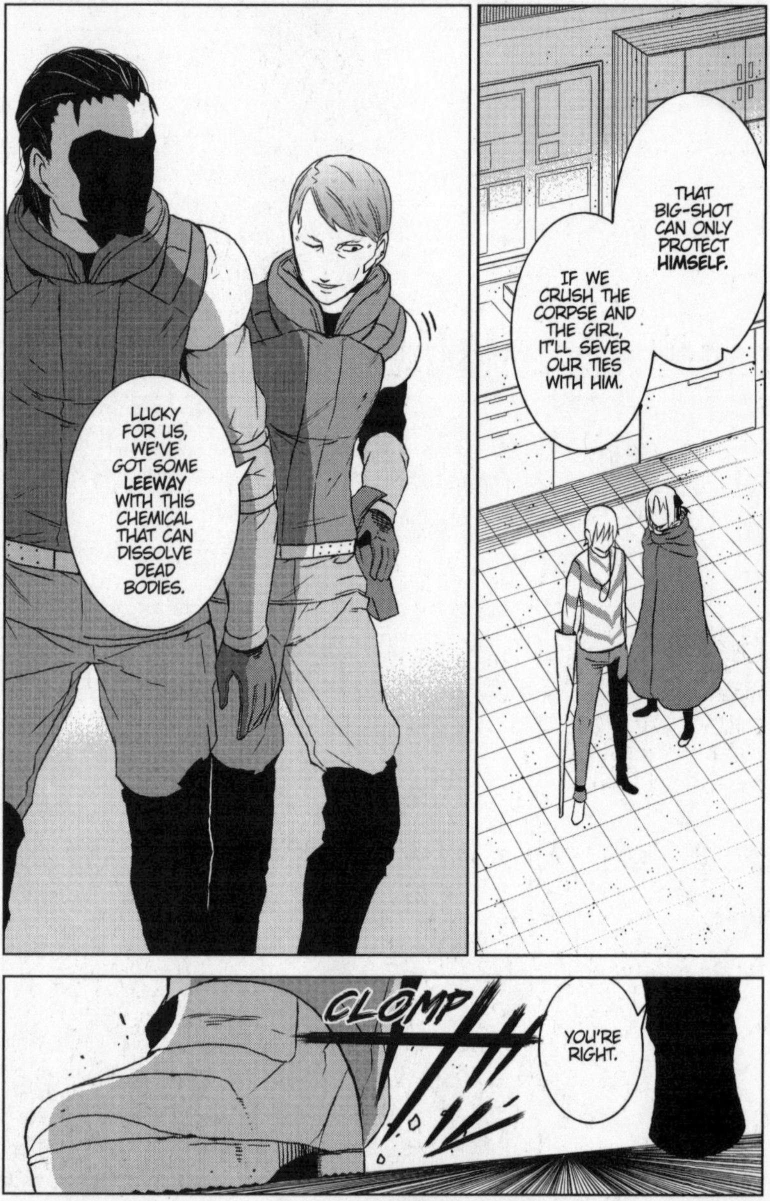
THAT BIG-SHOT CAN ONLY PROTECT HIMSELF.
IF WE CRUSH THE CORPSE AND THE GIRL, IT'LL SEVER OUR TIES WITH HIM.
LUCKY FOR US, WE'VE GOT SOME LEEWAY WITH THIS CHEMICAL THAT CAN DISSOLVE DEAD BODIES.
YOU'RE RIGHT.
CLOMP

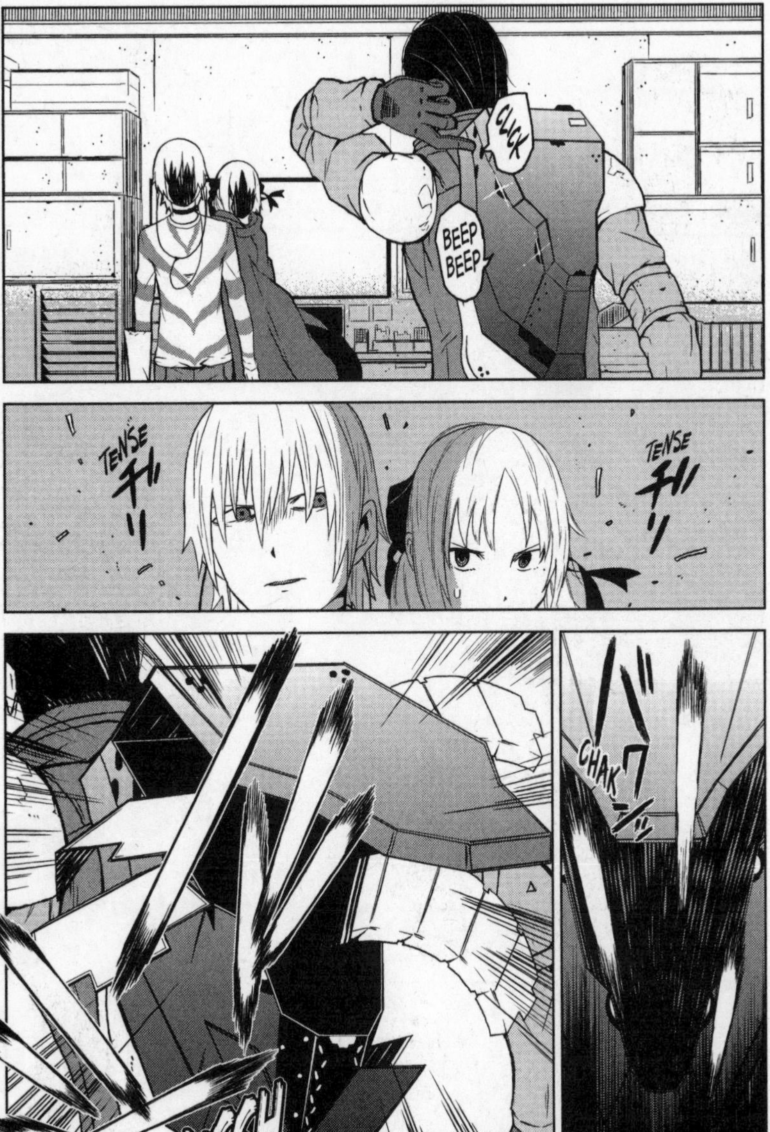
CLICK
BEEP BEEP
TENSE
TENSE
CHAK
VSSH

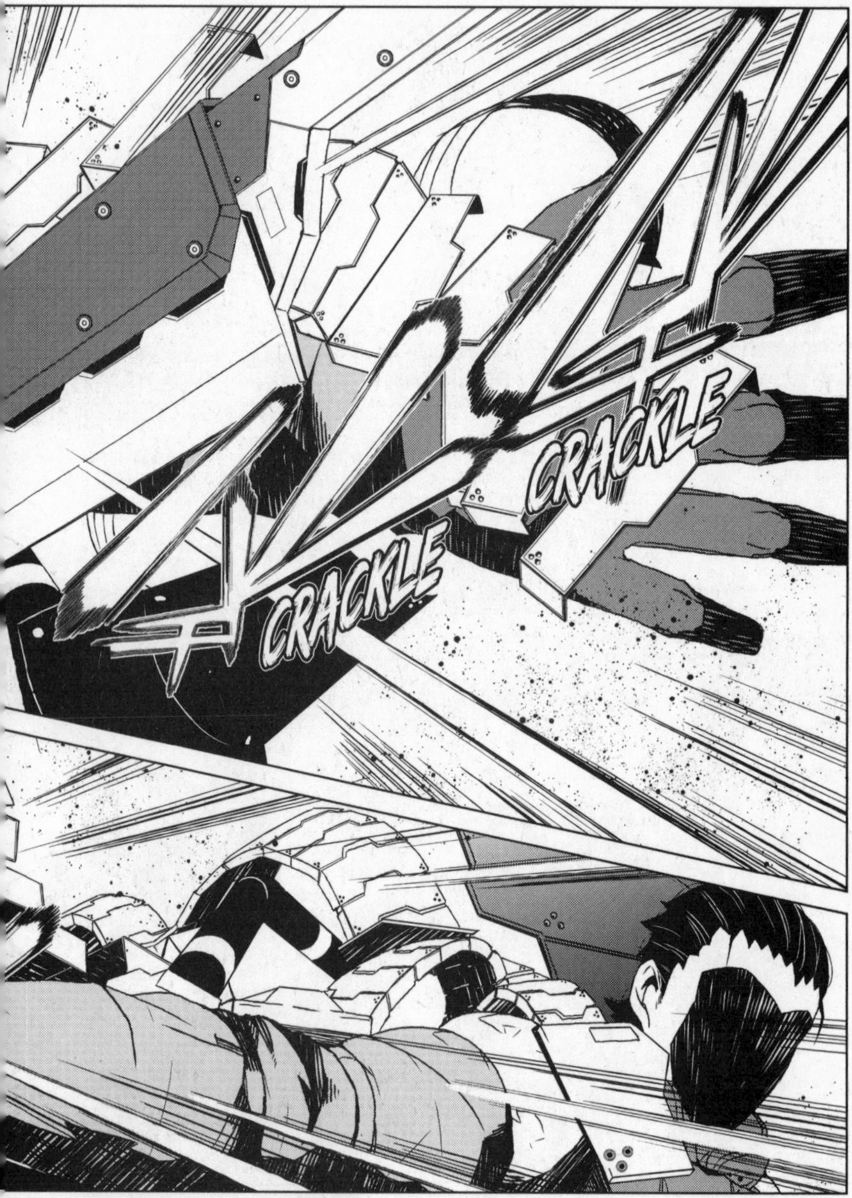
CRACKLE
CRACKLE

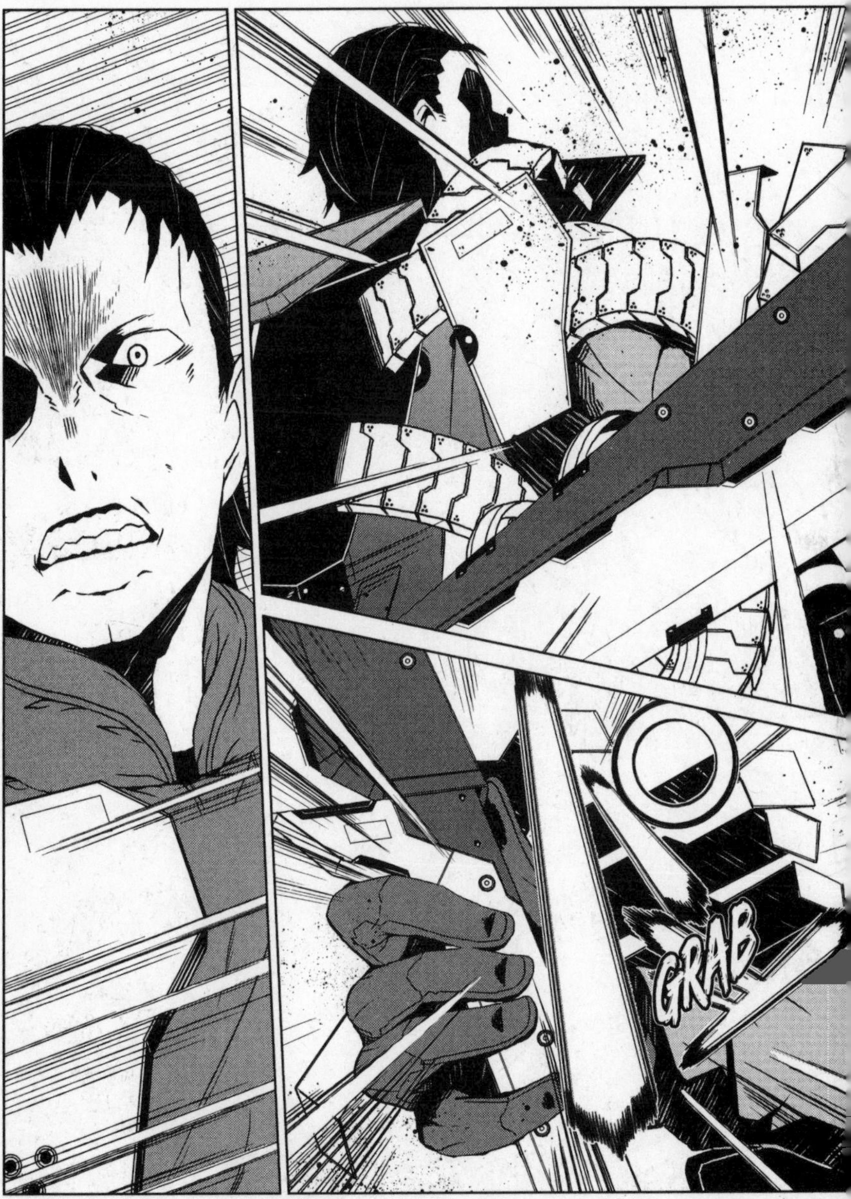
GRAB

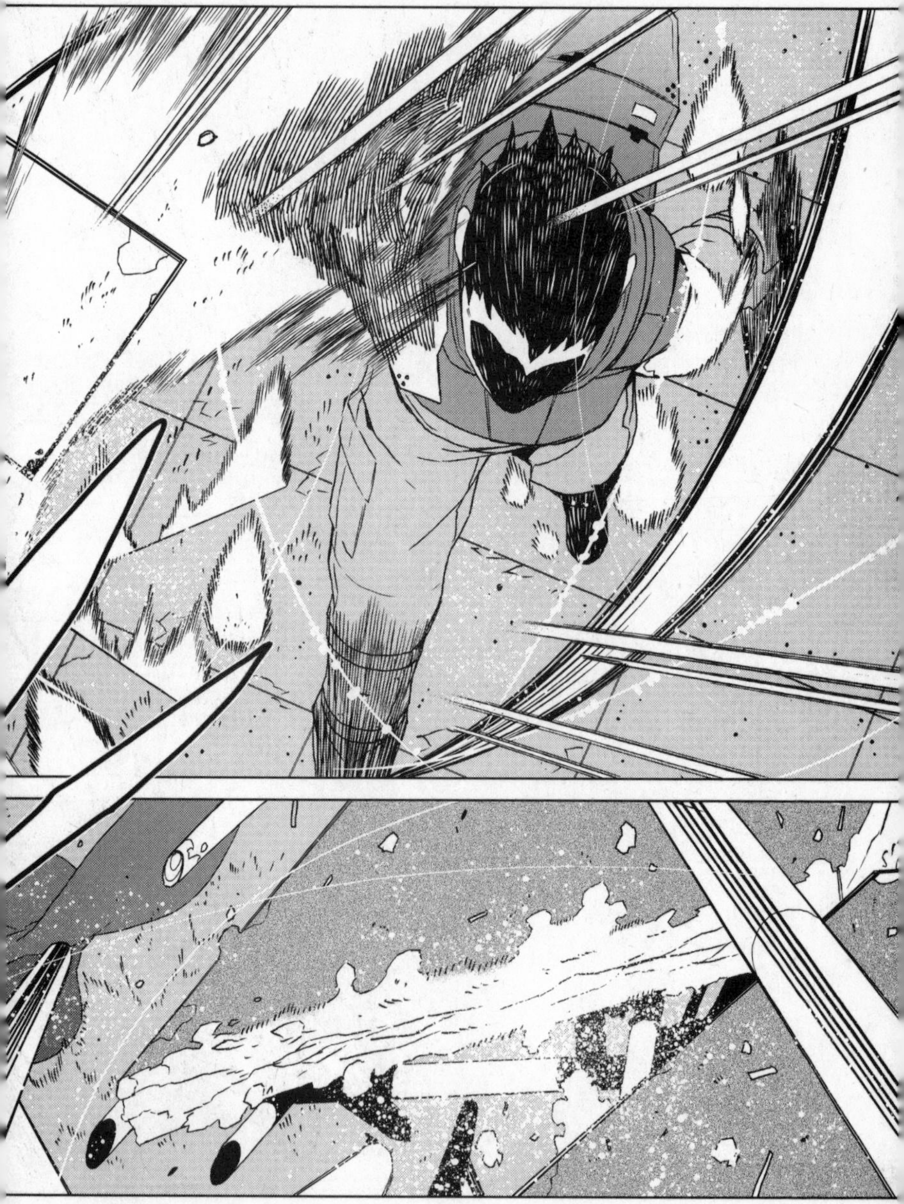

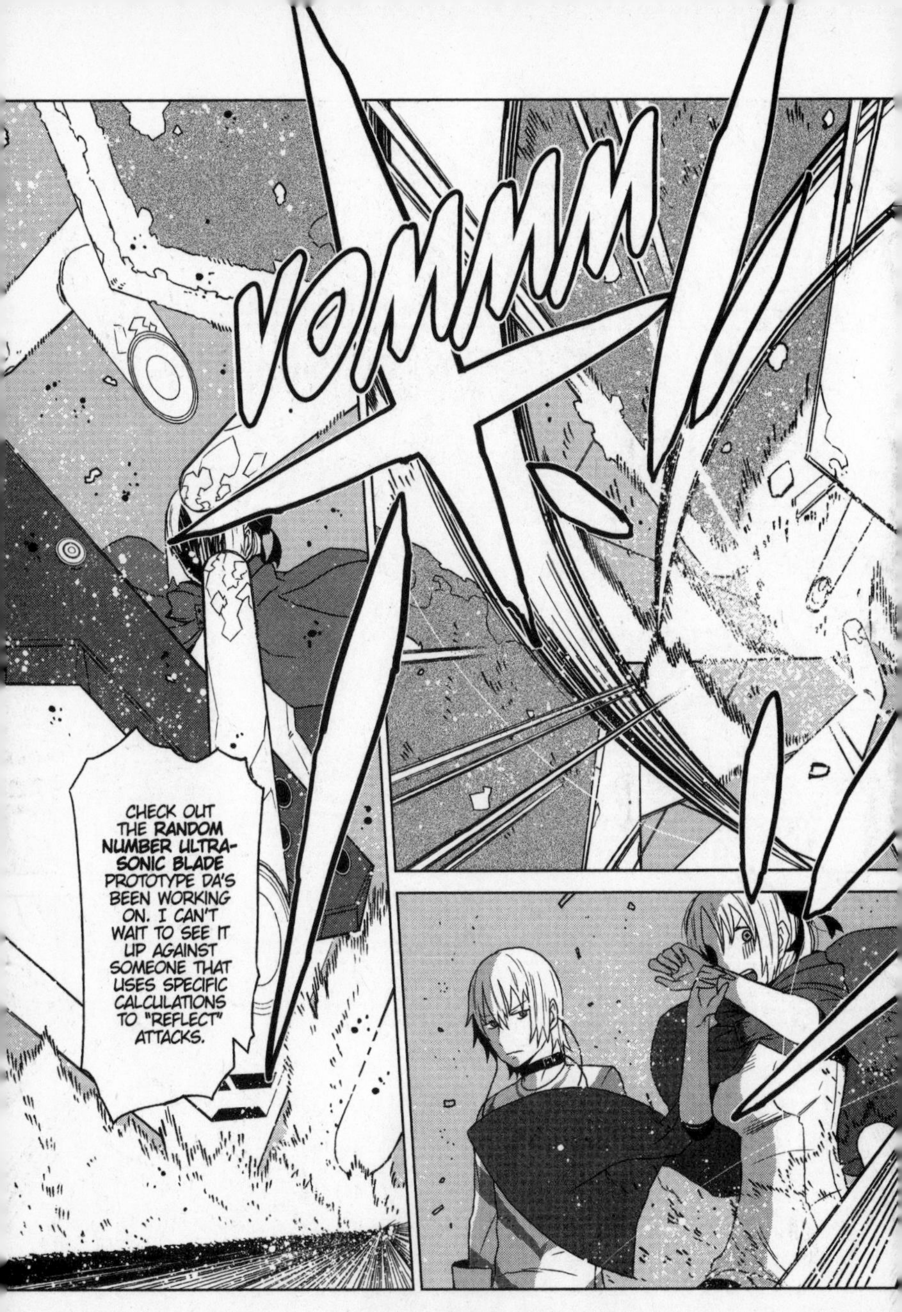
VOMMM
CHECK OUT THE RANDOM NUMBER ULTRA-SONIC BLADE PROTOTYPE DA'S BEEN WORKING ON. I CAN'T WAIT TO SEE IT UP AGAINST SOMEONE THAT USES SPECIFIC CALCULATIONS TO "REFLECT" ATTACKS.

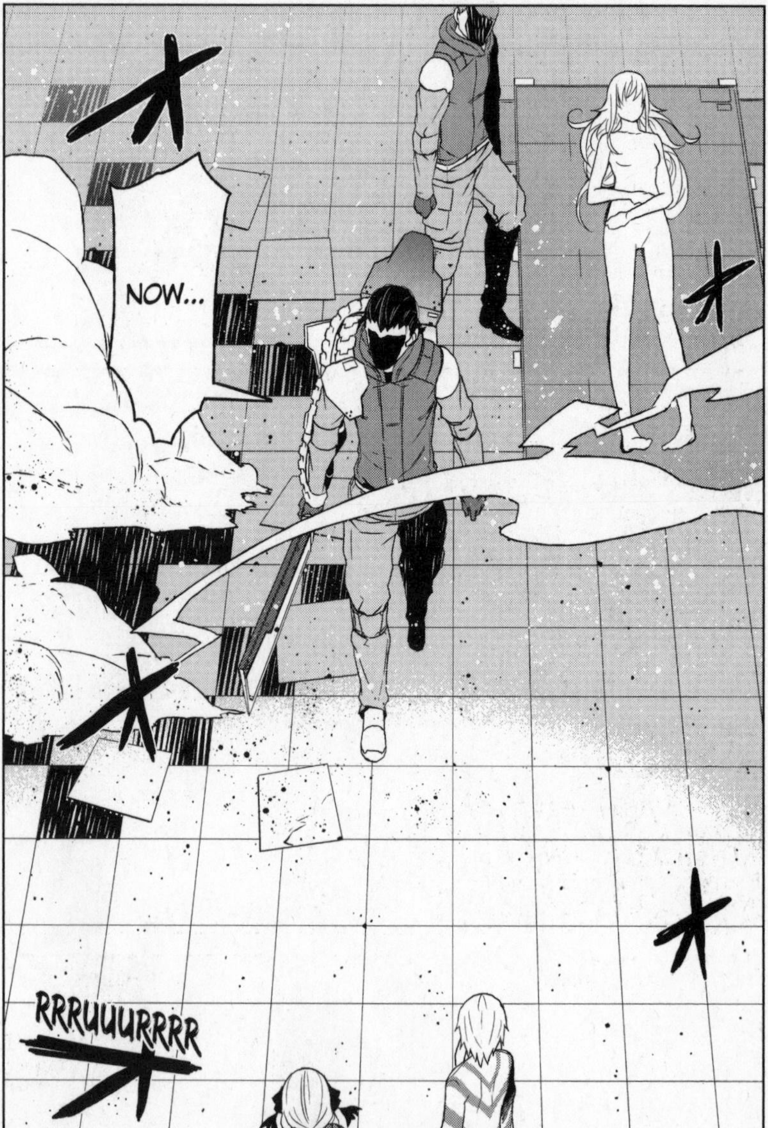
NOW...
RRRUUURRRR

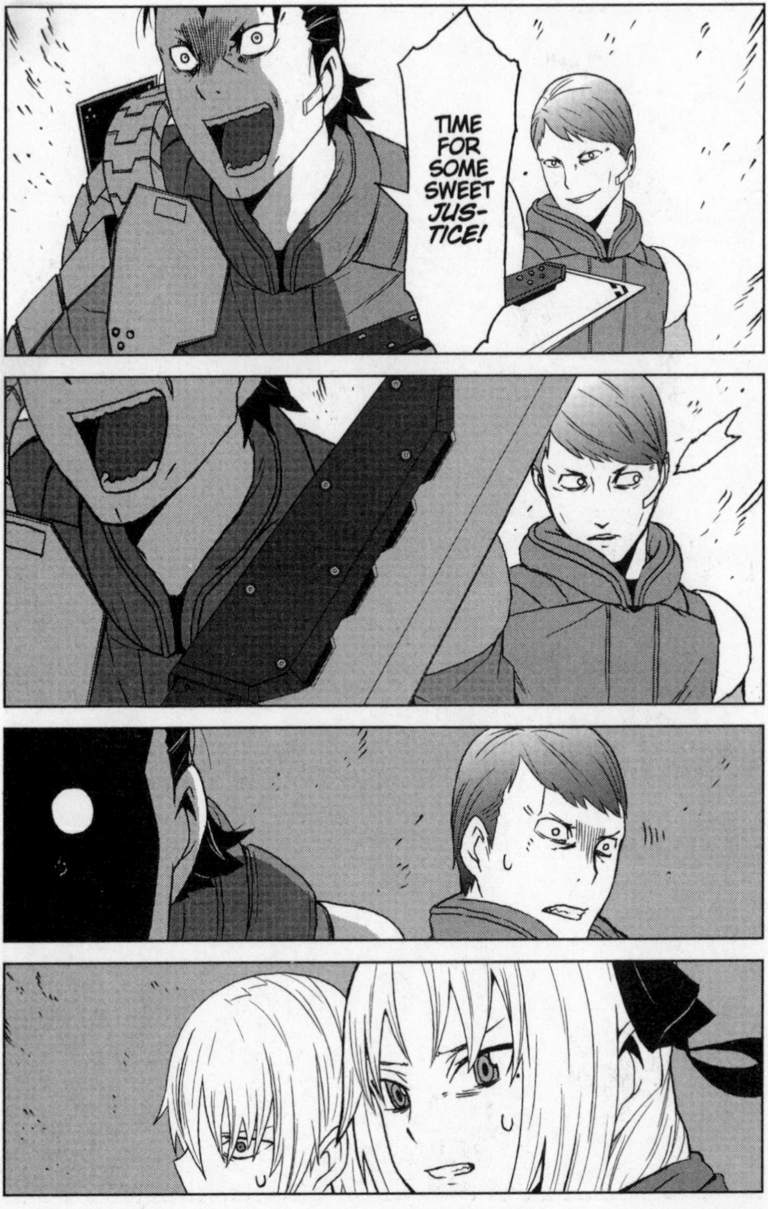
TIME FOR SOME SWEET JUS-TICE!

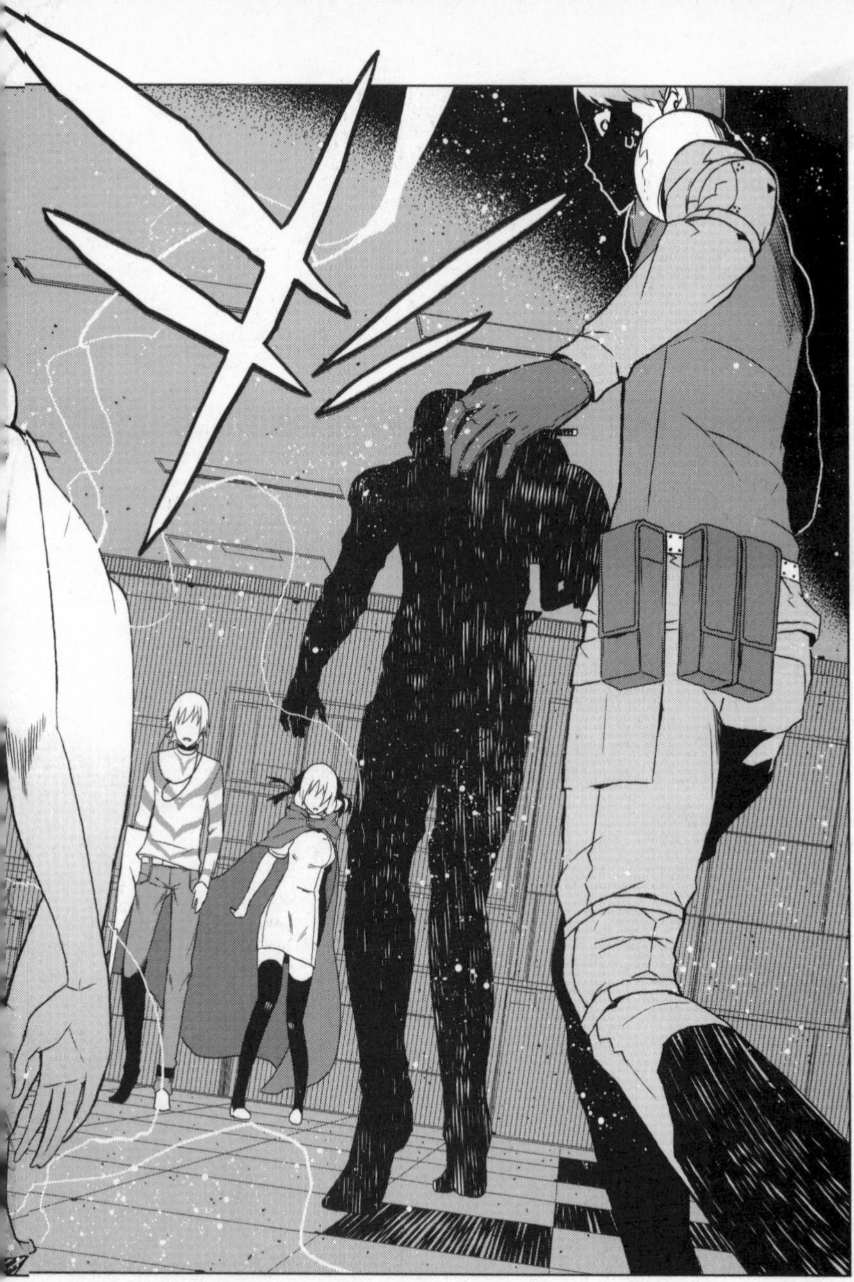

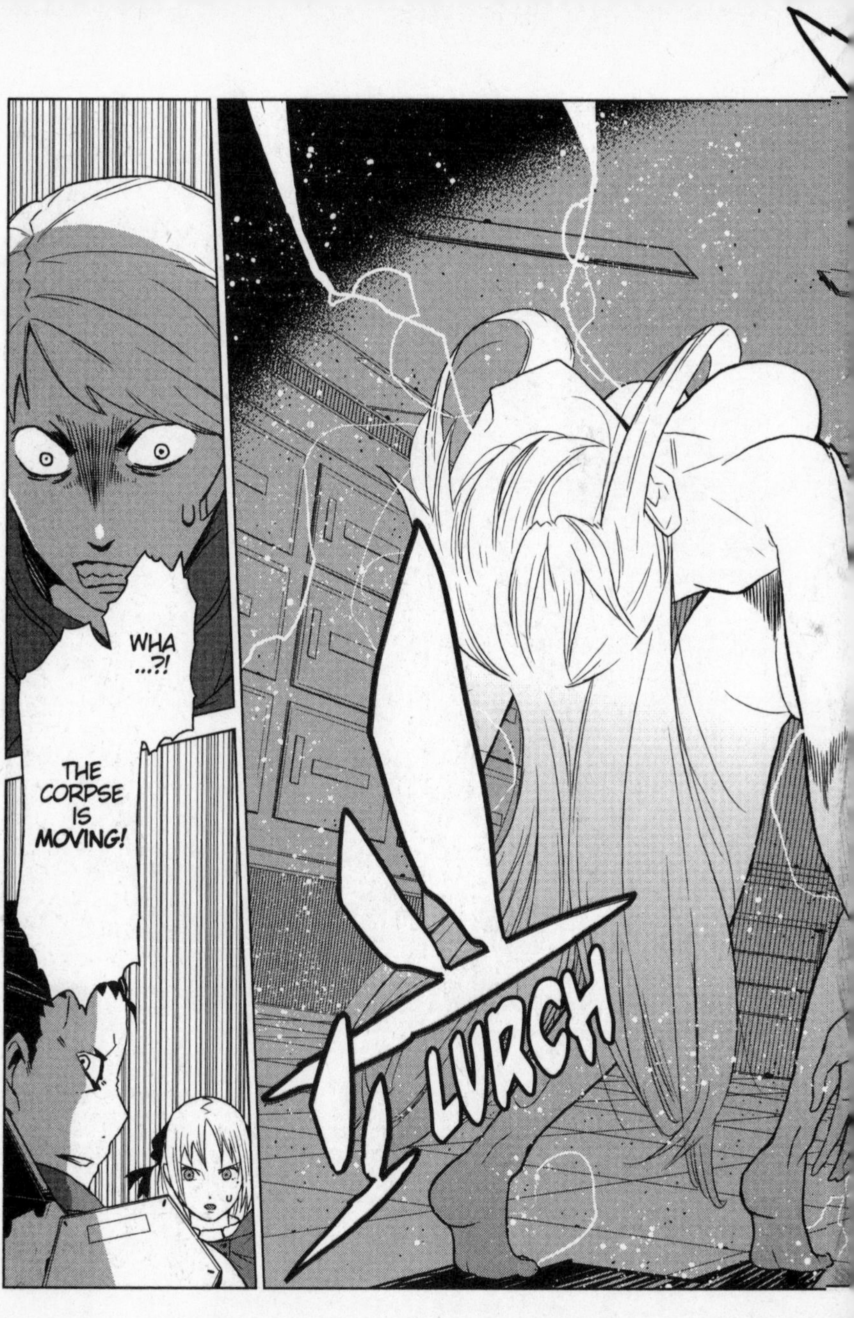
WHA ...?!
THE CORPSE IS MOVING!
LURCH

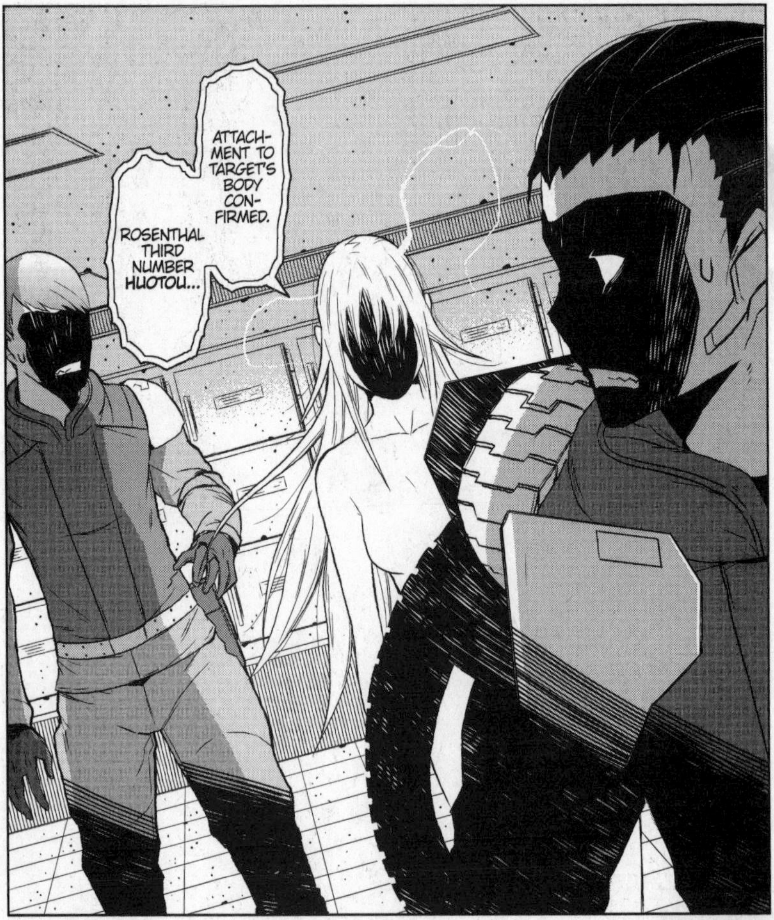
ATTACHMENT TO TARGET'S BODY CONFIRMED.
ROSENTHAL THIRD NUMBER HUOTOU...

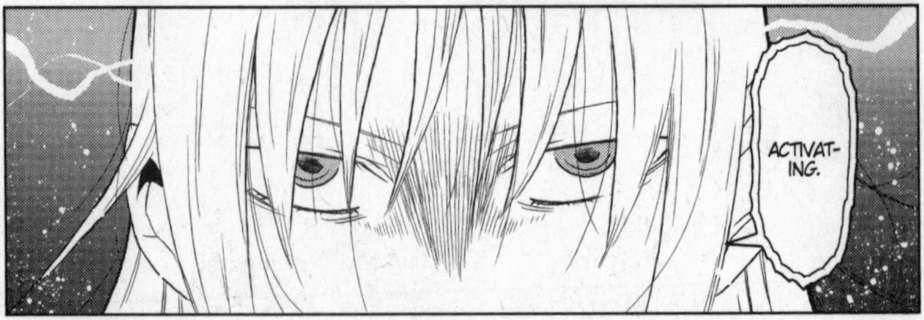
ACTIVATING.

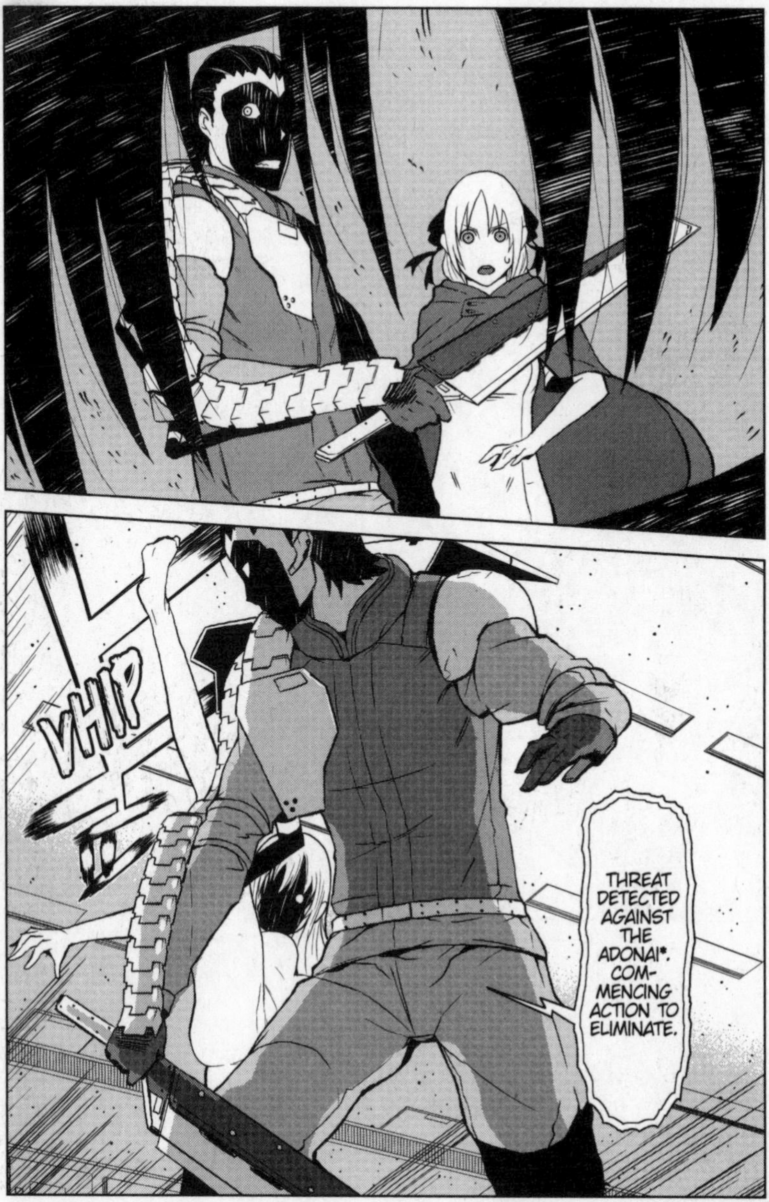
VHIP
THREAT DETECTED AGAINST THE ADONAI*. COMMENCING ACTION TO ELIMINATE.

*Hebrew for "lord" or "master."

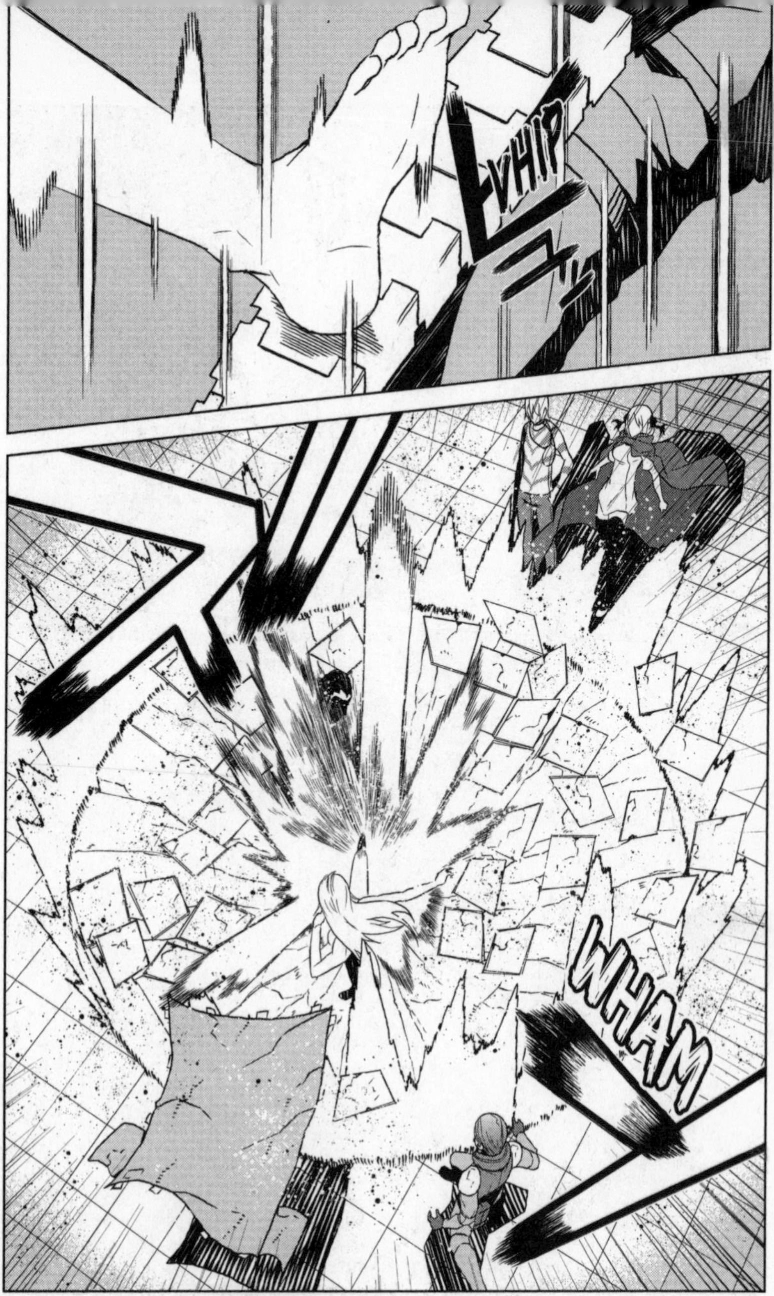
WHIP
WHAM

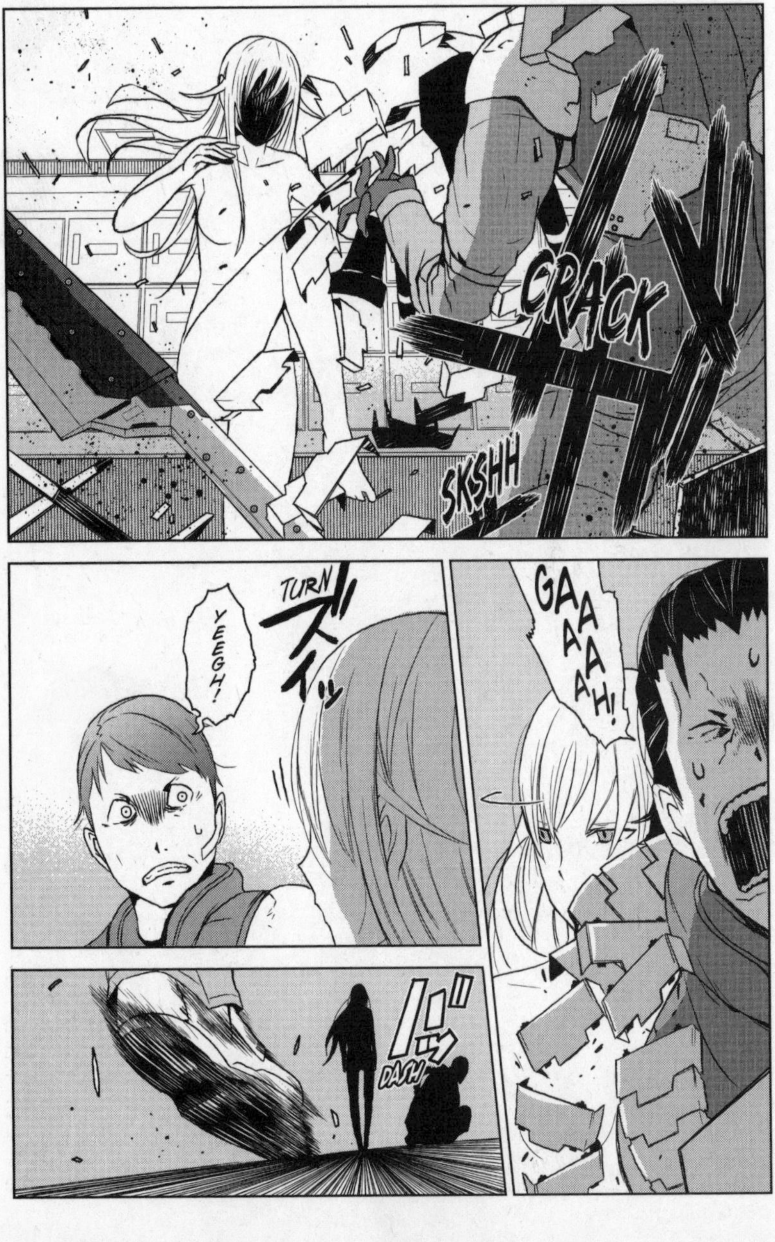
CRACK
SKSHH
GAAAAAH!
TURN
YEEGH!
DASH

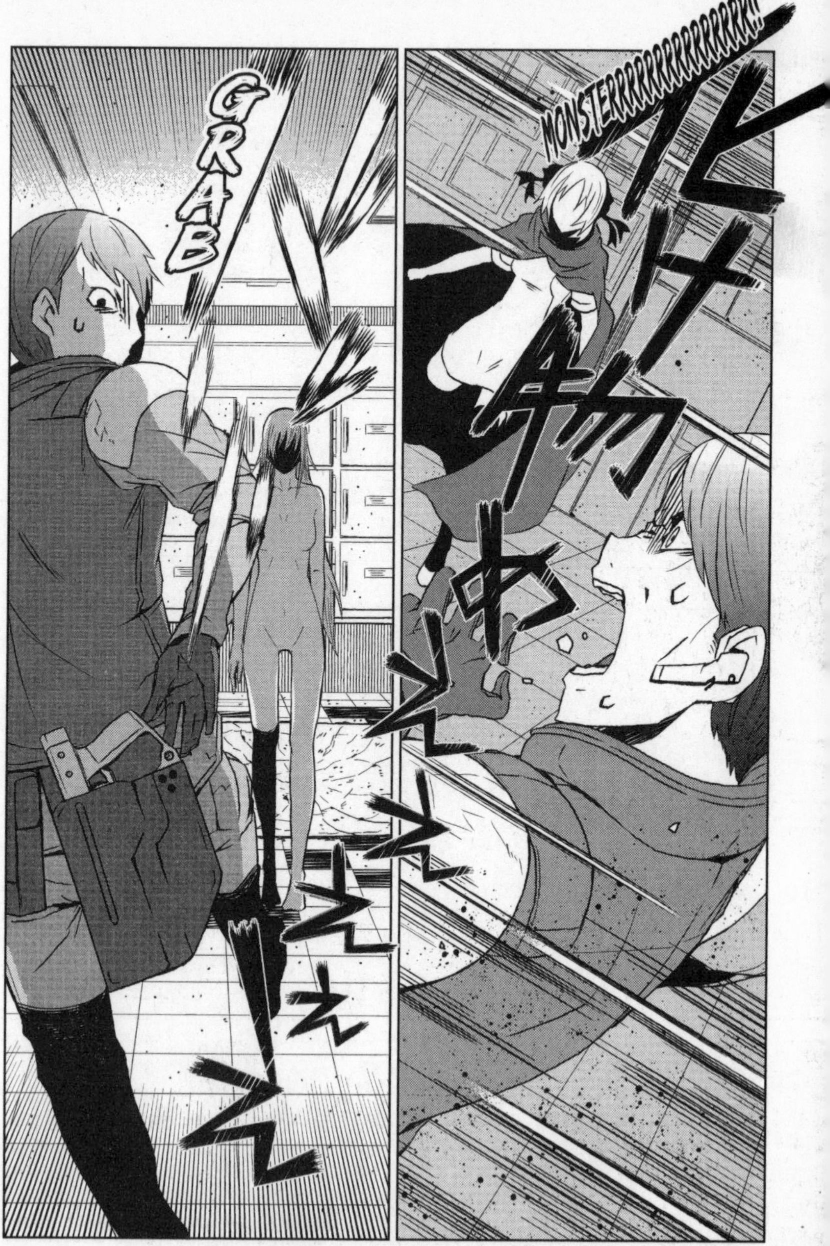
MONSTERRRRRRRRRRRRRRR!!
GRAB

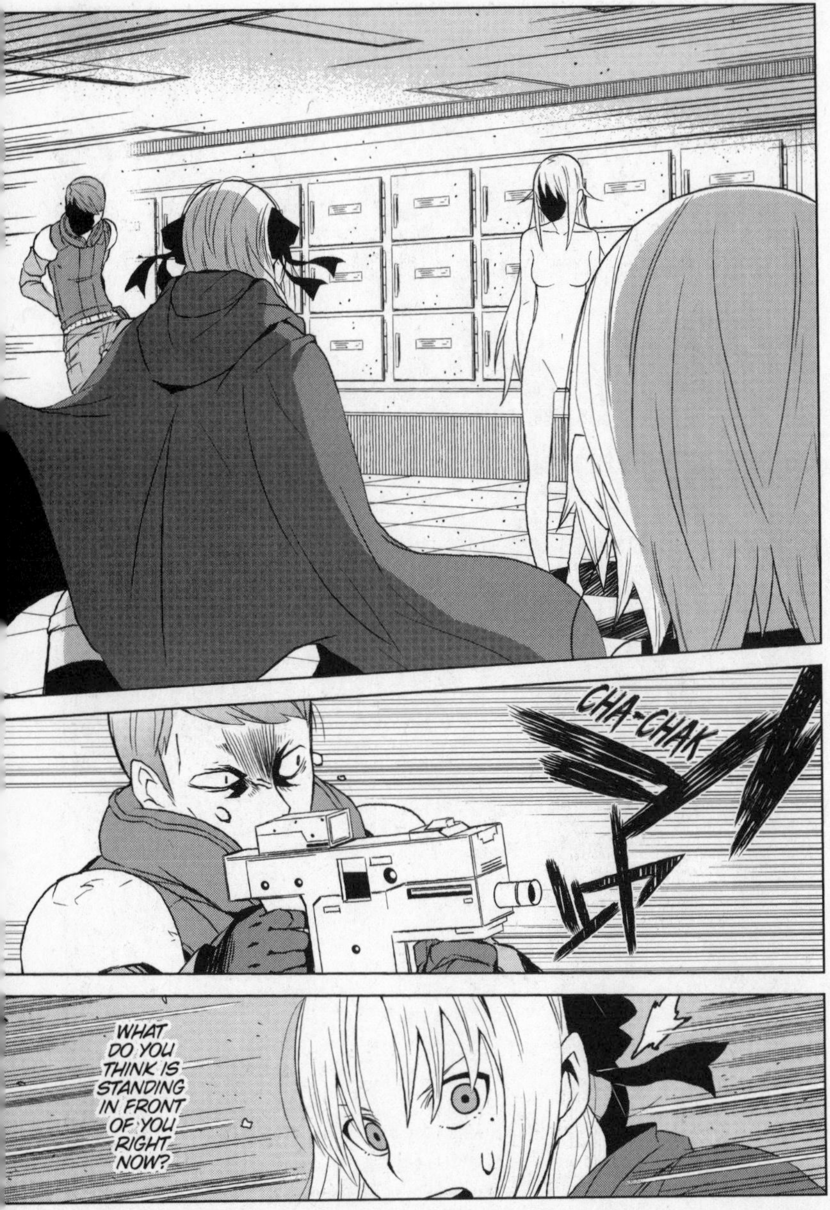
CHA-CHAK
WHAT DO YOU THINK IS STANDING IN FRONT OF YOU RIGHT NOW?

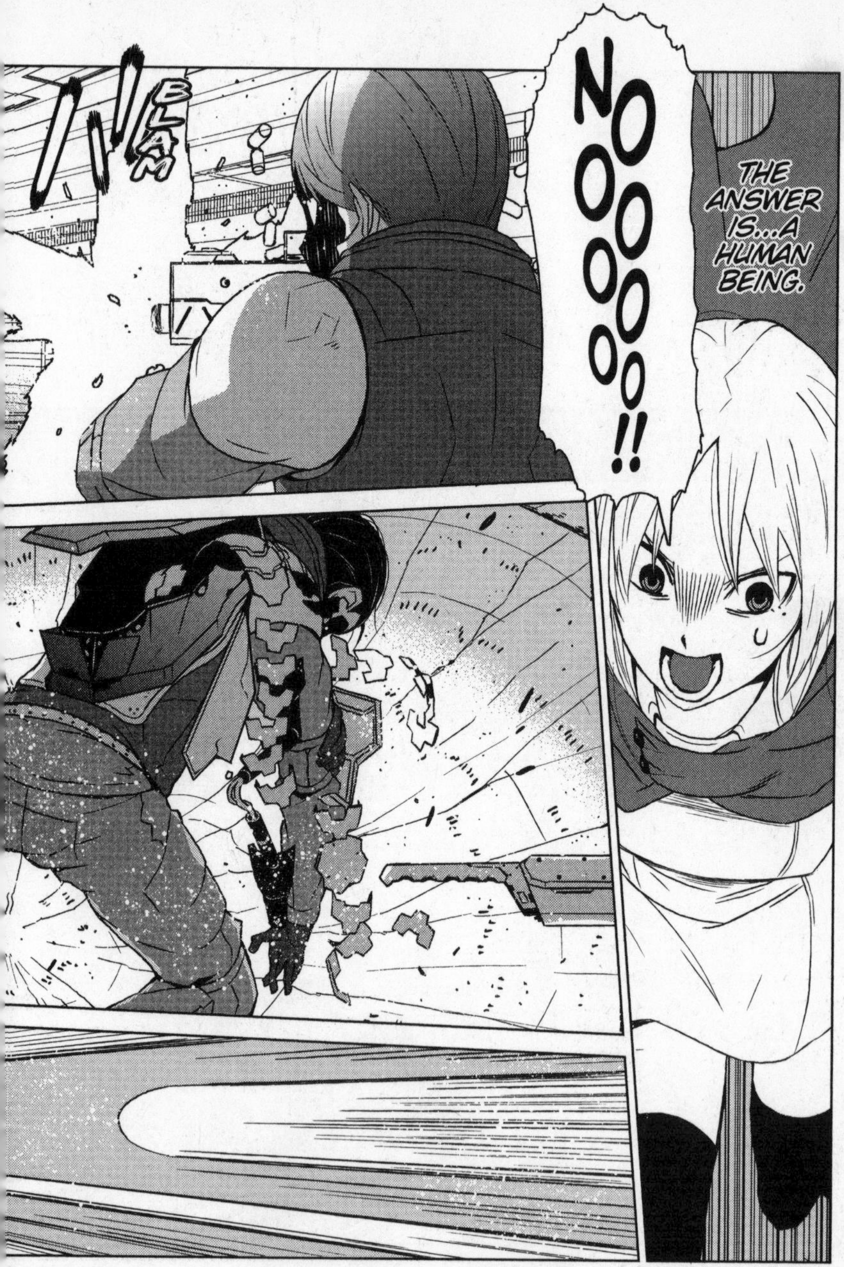
THE ANSWER IS...A HUMAN BEING.
NOOOOOOO!!
BLAM

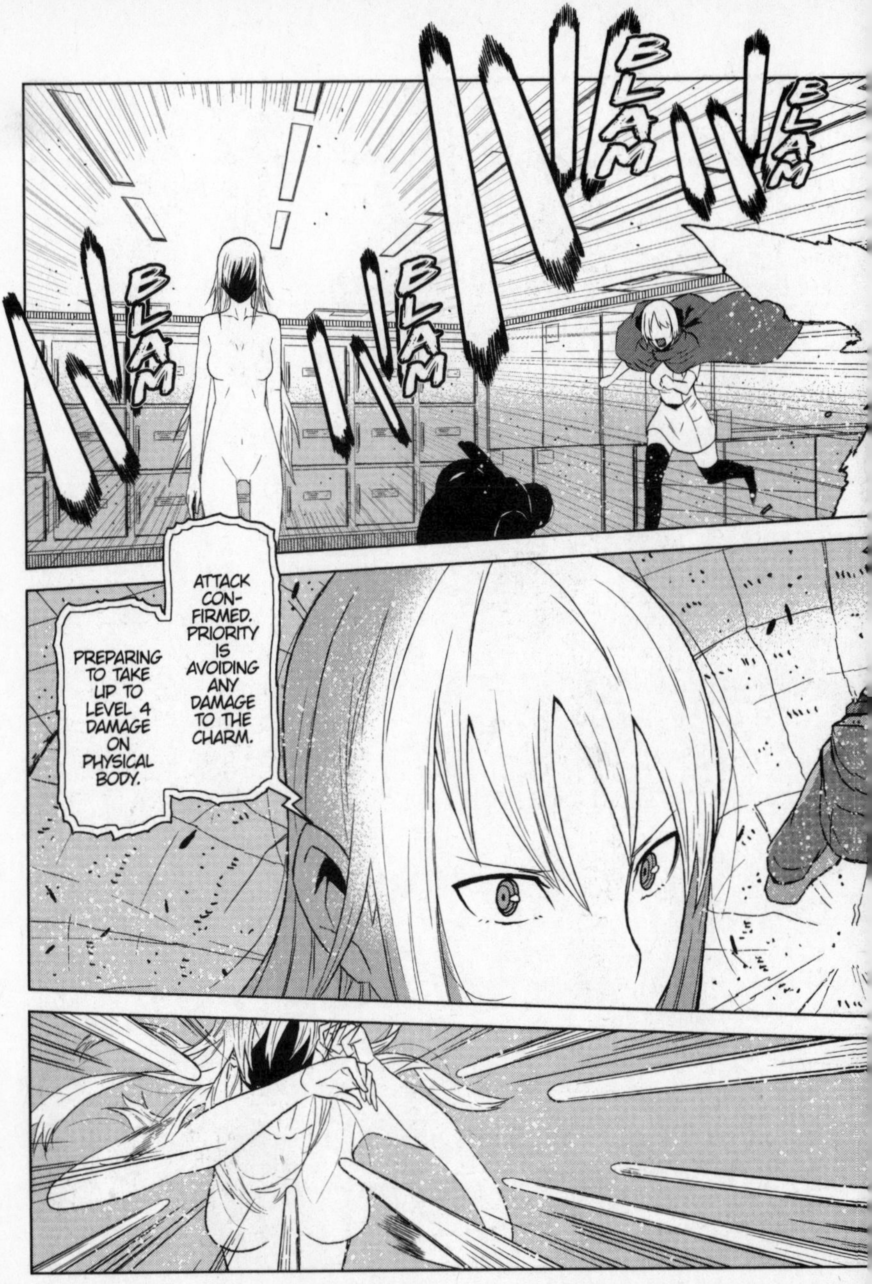
BLAM
BLAM
BLAM
BLAM
ATTACK CON-FIRMED. PRIORITY IS AVOIDING ANY DAMAGE TO THE CHARM.
PREPARING TO TAKE UP TO LEVEL 4 DAMAGE ON PHYSICAL BODY.

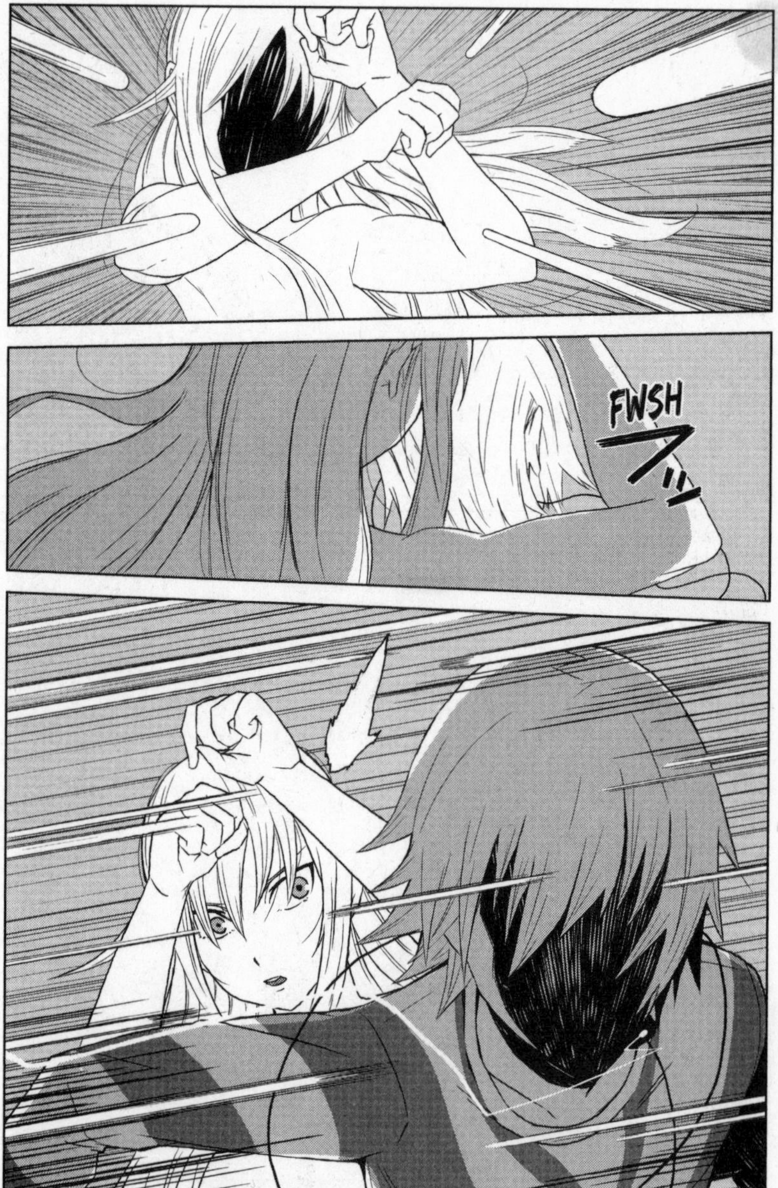
FWSH

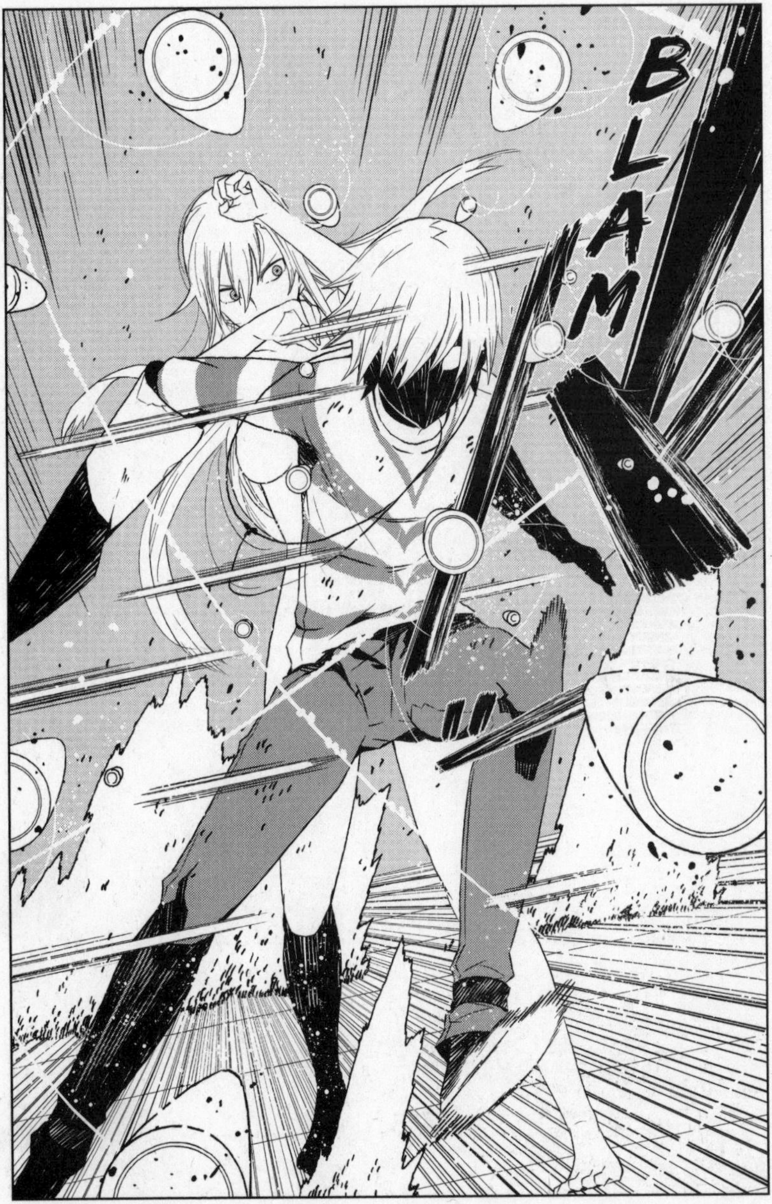
BLAM

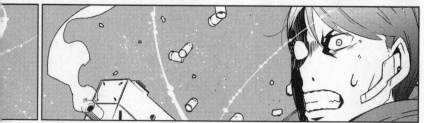

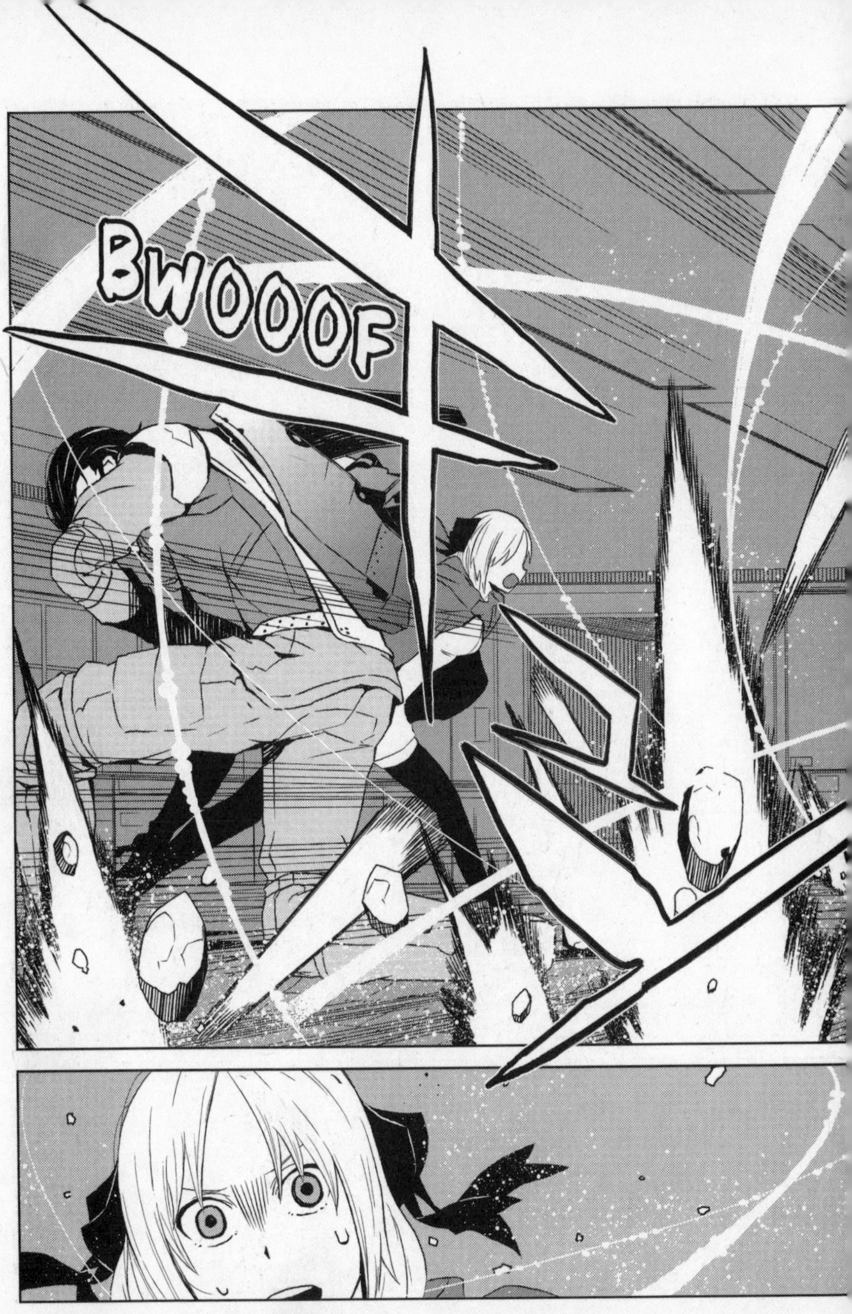
BWOOOF

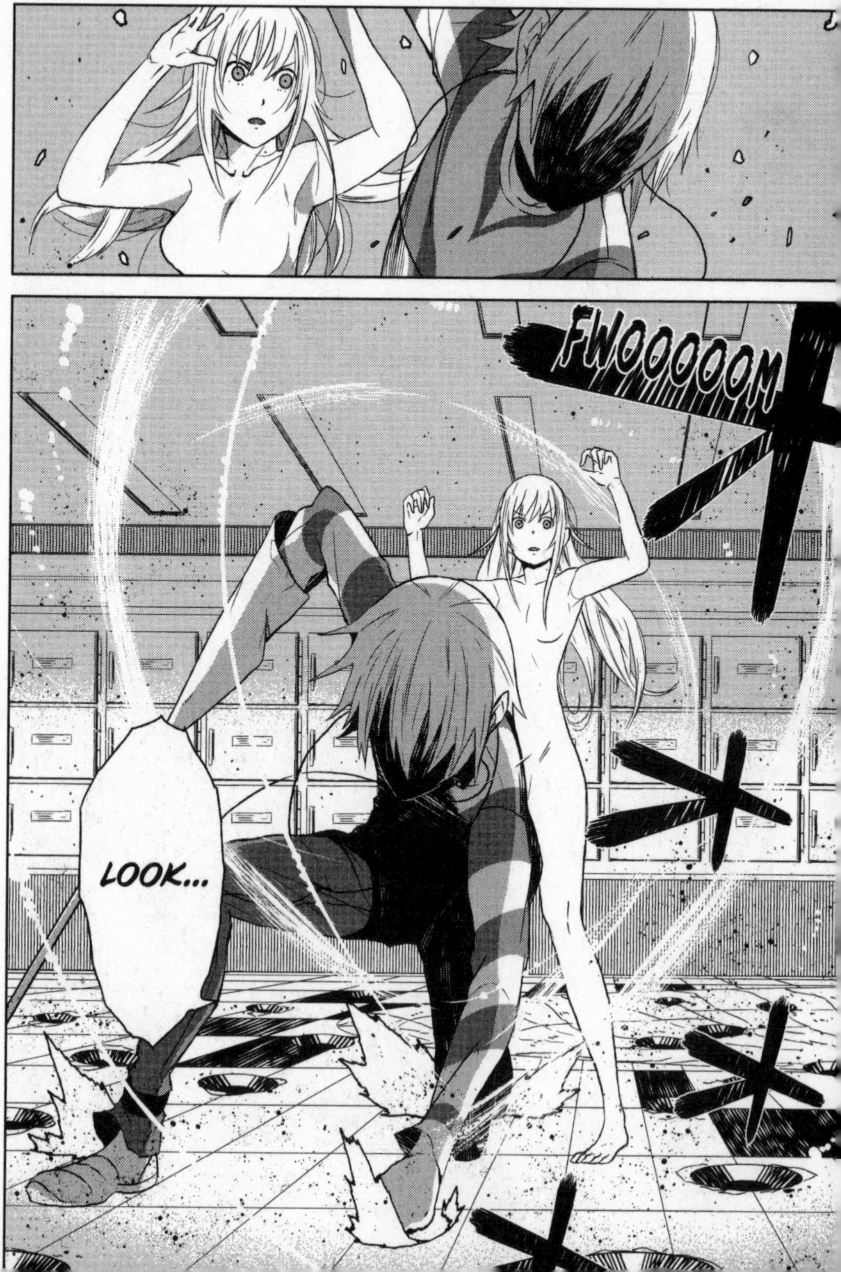
FWOOOOOM
LOOK...

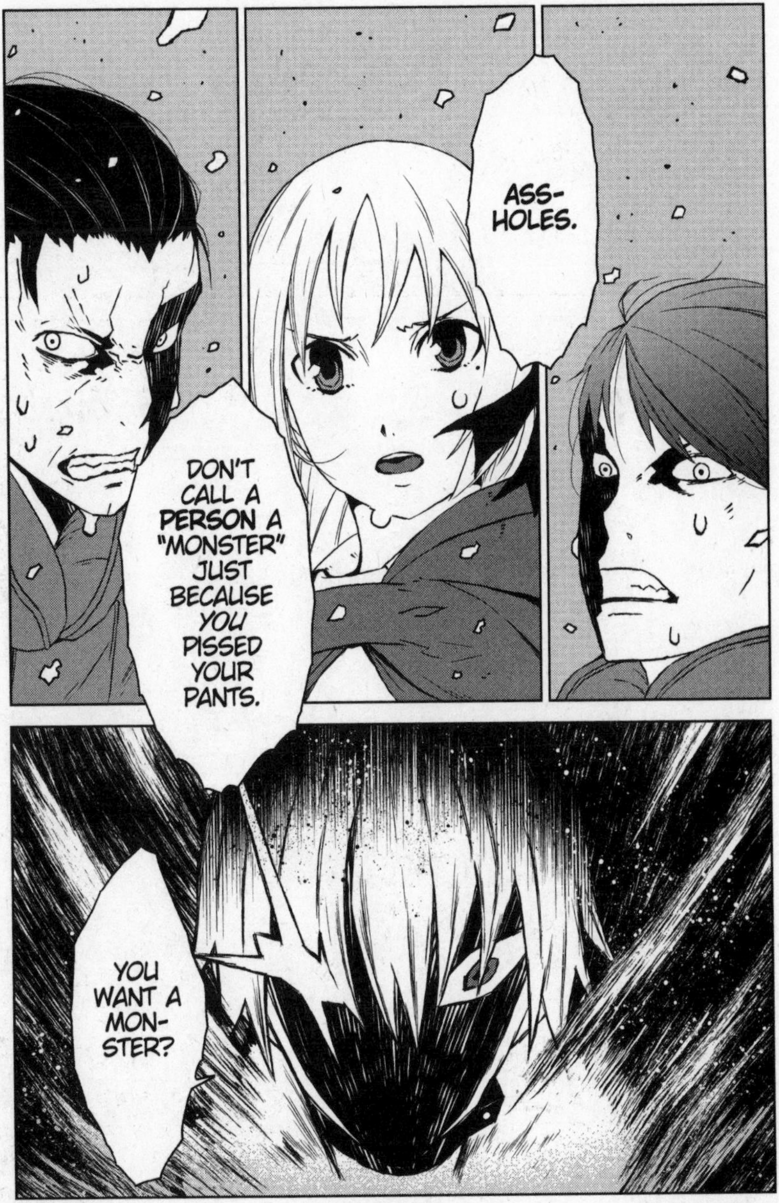
ASS-
HOLES.
DON'T CALL A PERSON A "MONSTER" JUST BECAUSE YOU PISSED YOUR PANTS.
YOU WANT A MON-STER?

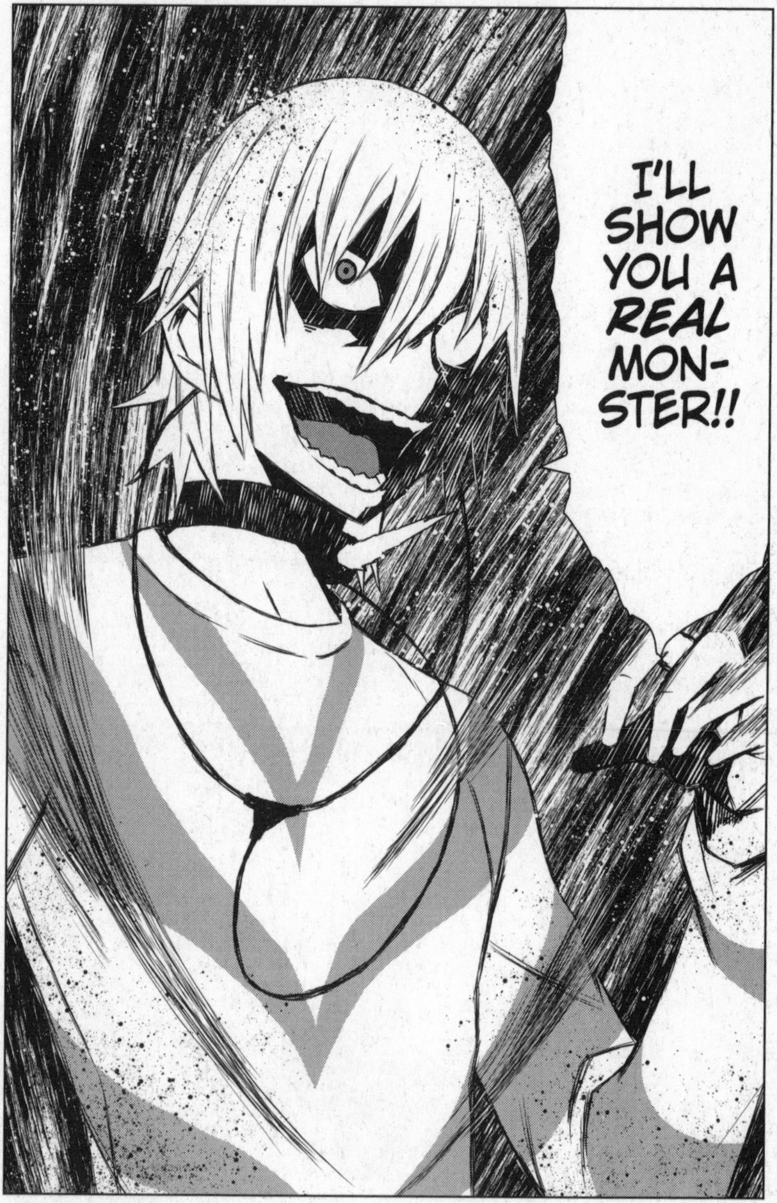
I'LL SHOW YOU A *REAL* MON-STER!!

a certain SCIENTIFIC ACCELERATOR

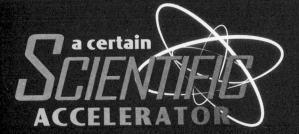

とある科学の一方通行

とある魔術の禁書目録外伝

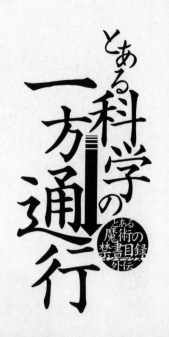

CHAPTER 5

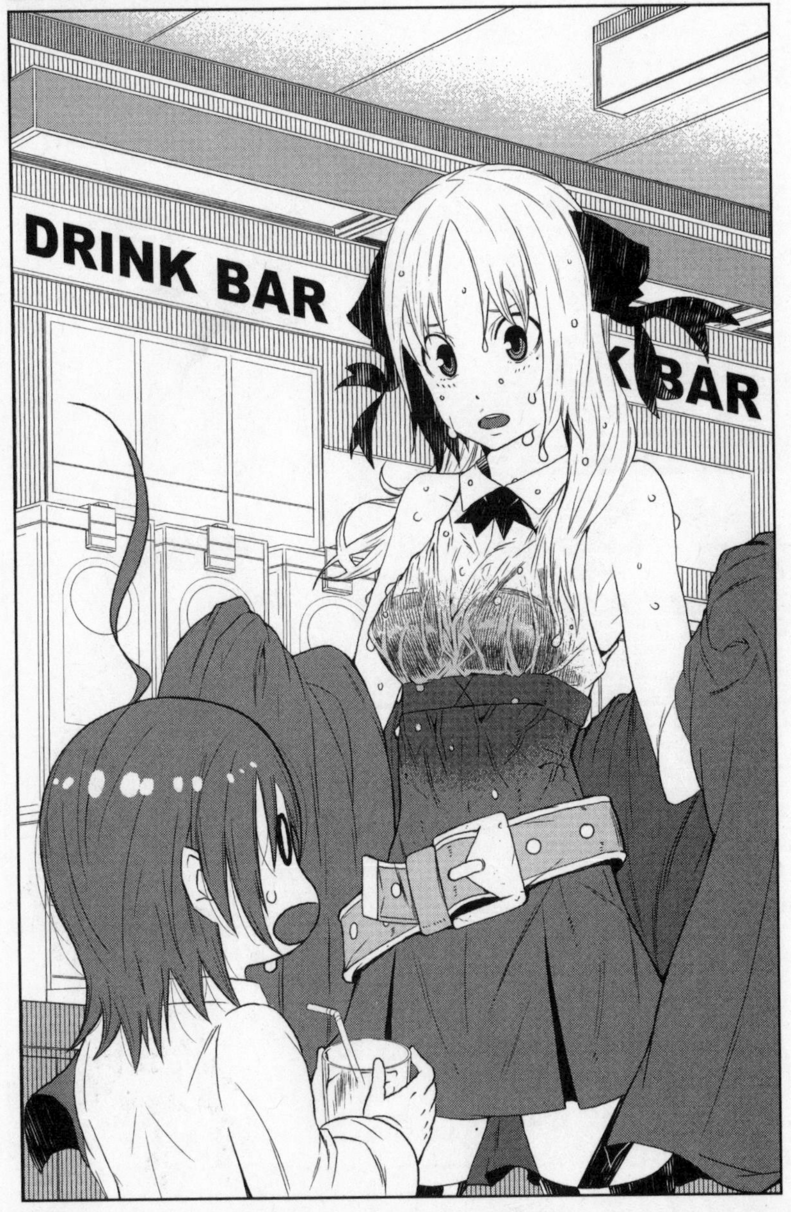
DRINK BAR
BAR

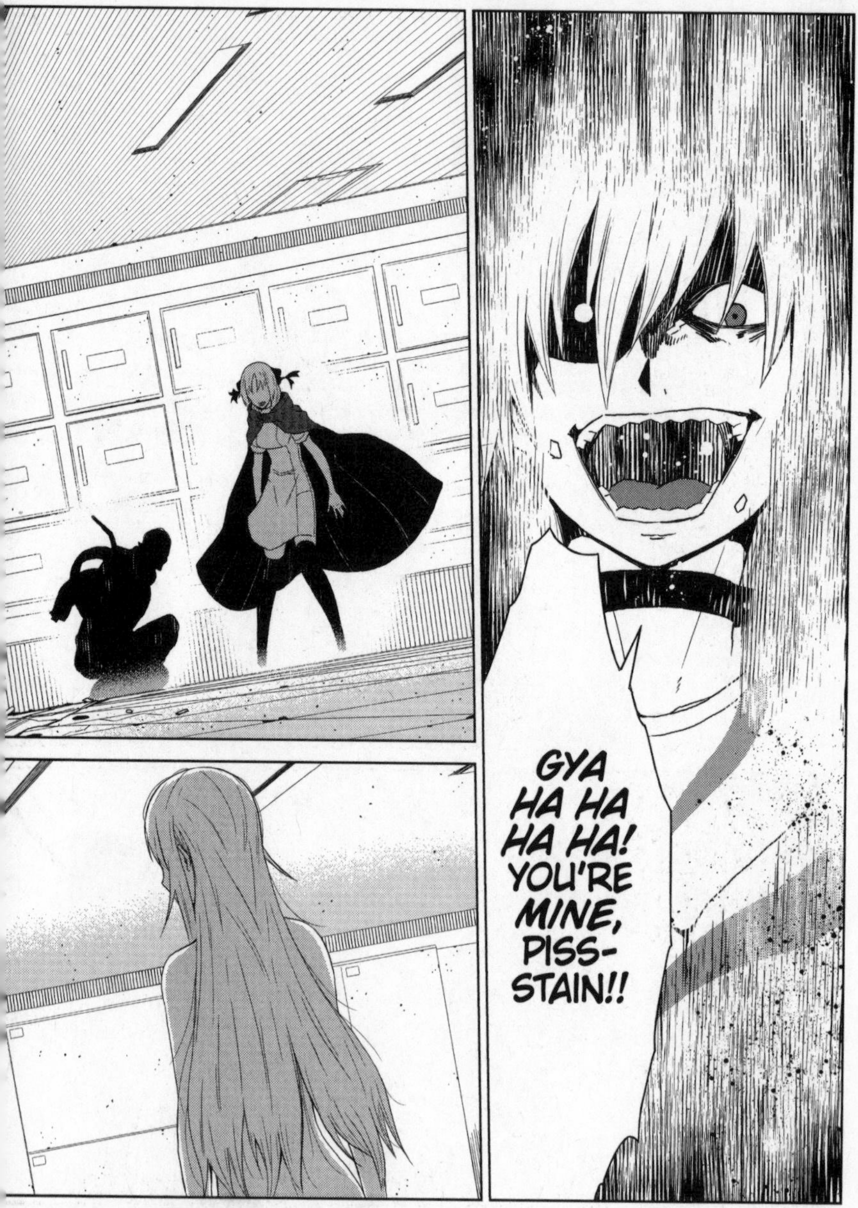
GYA HA HA HA HA! YOU'RE MINE, PISS-STAIN!!

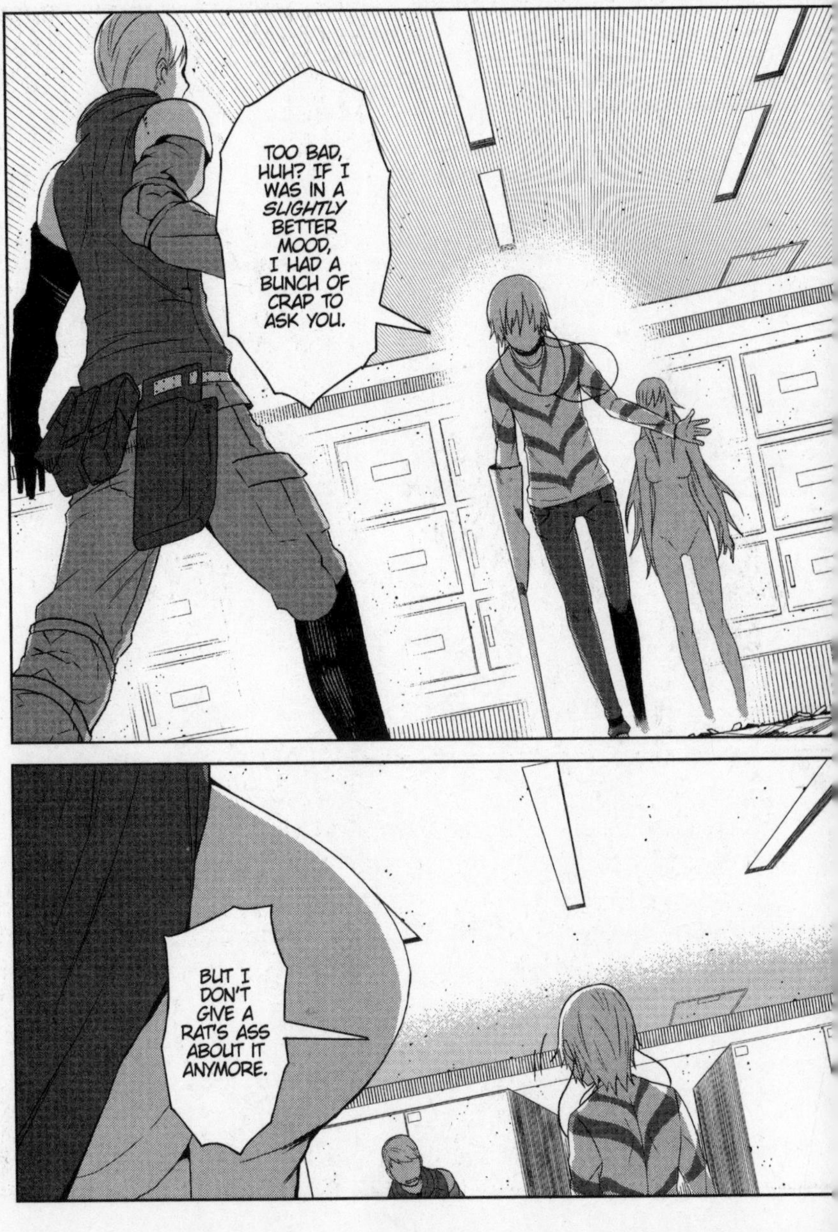
TOO BAD, HUH? IF I WAS IN A *SLIGHTLY* BETTER MOOD, I HAD A BUNCH OF CRAP TO ASK YOU.
BUT I DON'T GIVE A RAT'S ASS ABOUT IT ANYMORE.

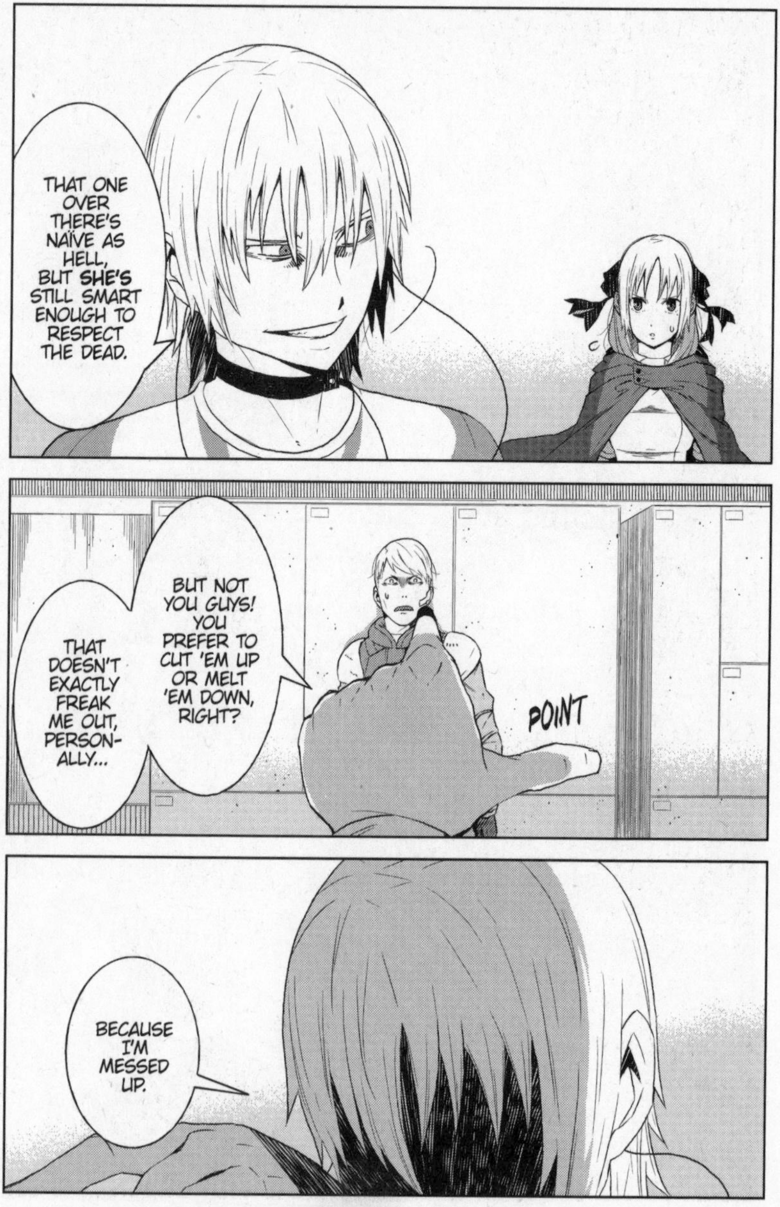
THAT ONE OVER THERE'S NAÏVE AS HELL, BUT SHE'S STILL SMART ENOUGH TO RESPECT THE DEAD.
BUT NOT YOU GUYS! YOU PREFER TO CUT 'EM UP OR MELT 'EM DOWN, RIGHT?
THAT DOESN'T EXACTLY FREAK ME OUT, PERSON-ALLY...
POINT
BECAUSE I'M MESSED UP.

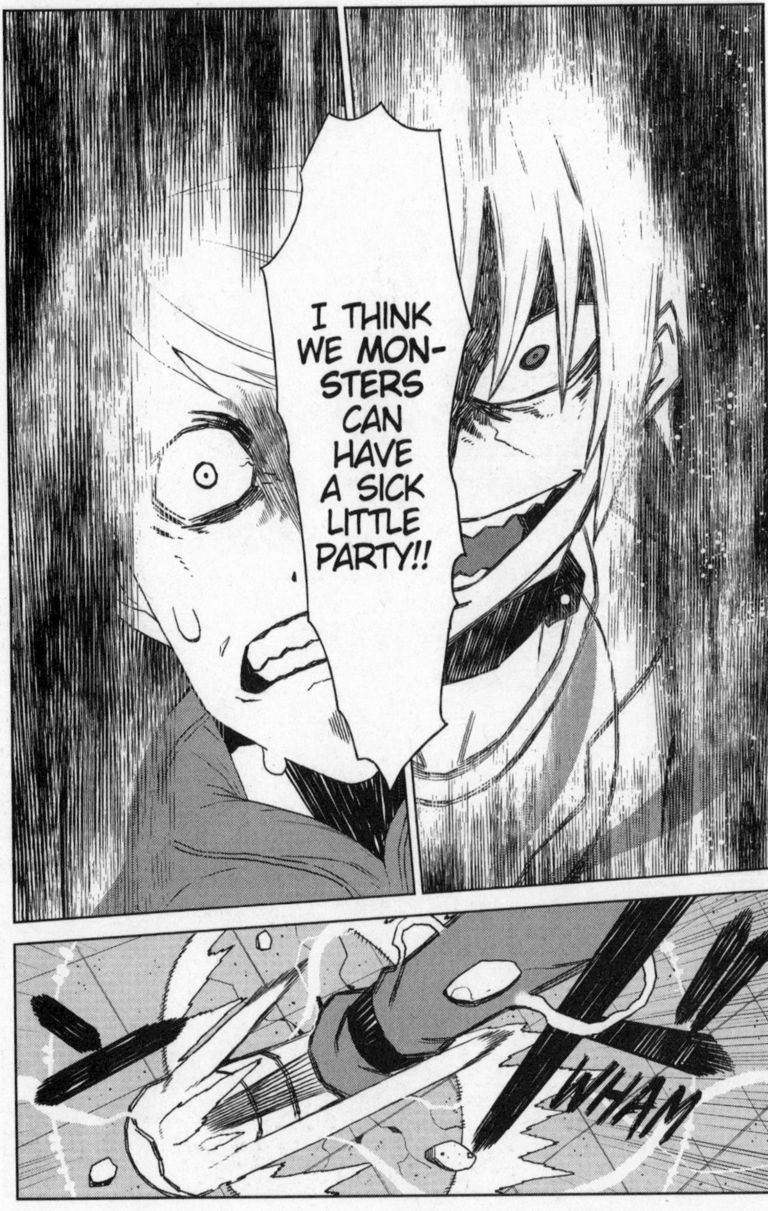
I THINK WE MON-STERS CAN HAVE A SICK LITTLE PARTY!!
WHAM

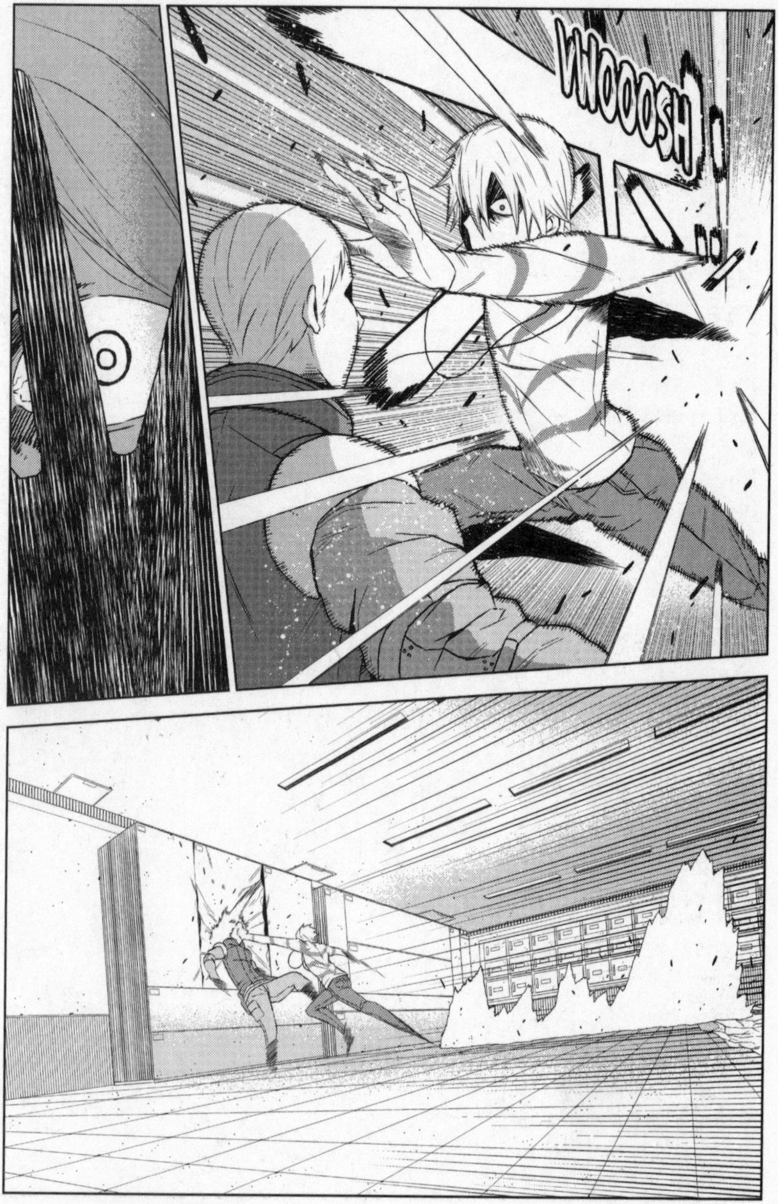
WOOOSH

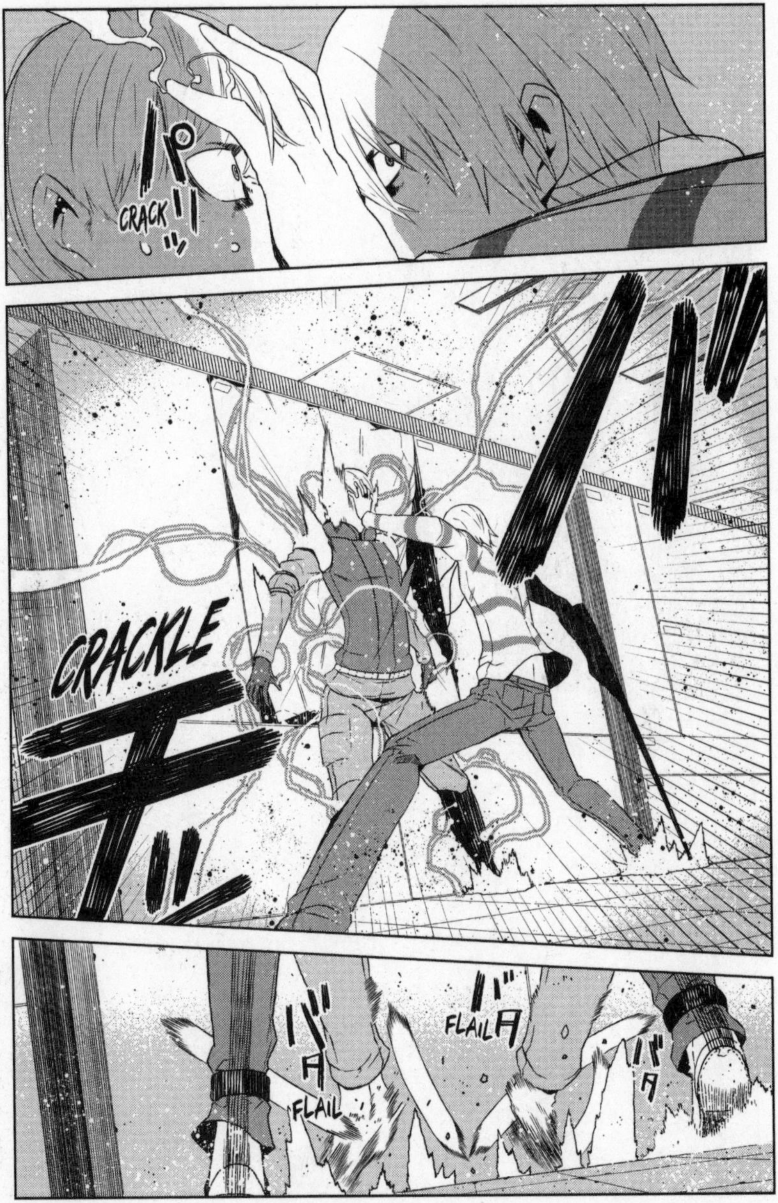
CRACK
CRACKLE
FLAIL
FLAIL

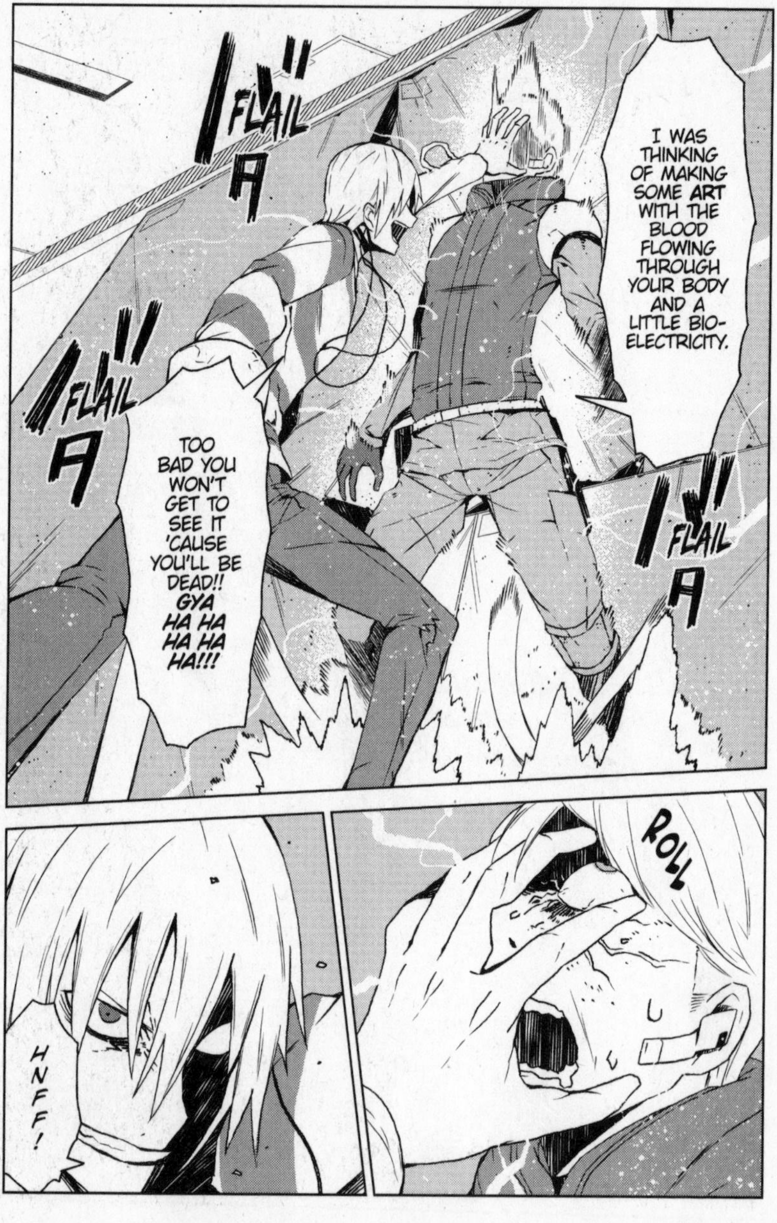

I WAS THINKING OF MAKING SOME ART WITH THE BLOOD FLOWING THROUGH YOUR BODY AND A LITTLE BIO-ELECTRICITY.
FLAIL
FLAIL
FLAIL
TOO BAD YOU WON'T GET TO SEE IT 'CAUSE YOU'LL BE DEAD!! GYA HA HA HA HA HA!!!
ROLL
HNFF!

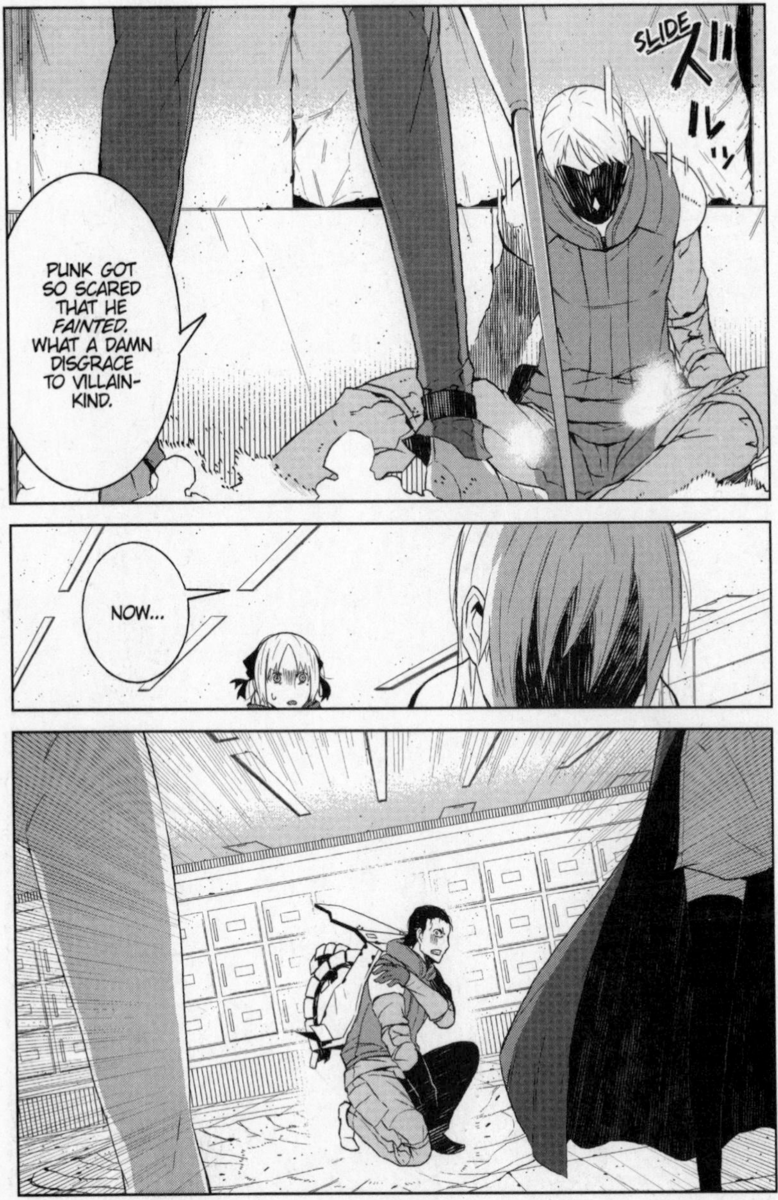
SLIDE
ズルッ
PUNK GOT SO SCARED THAT HE *FAINTED.* WHAT A DAMN DISGRACE TO VILLAIN-KIND.
NOW...

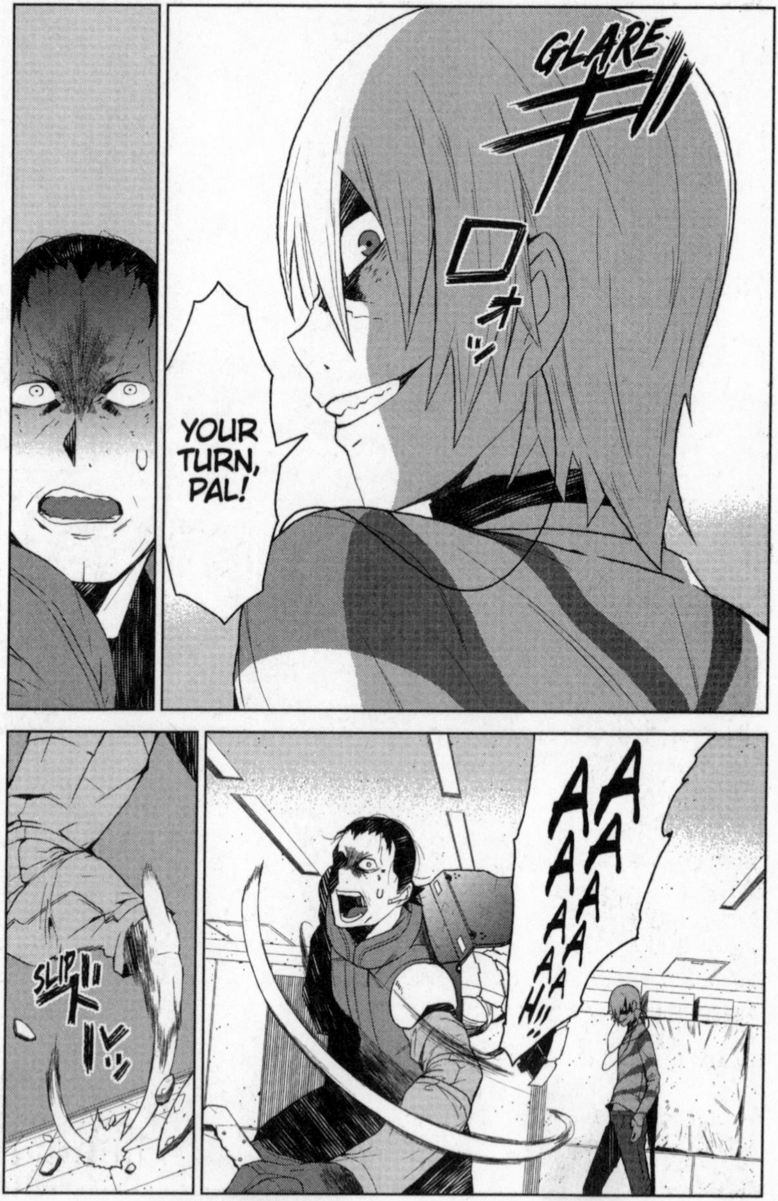
GLARE
ギロッ
YOUR TURN, PAL!
AAAAAAAAAAAAH!!!
SLIP
ドルッ

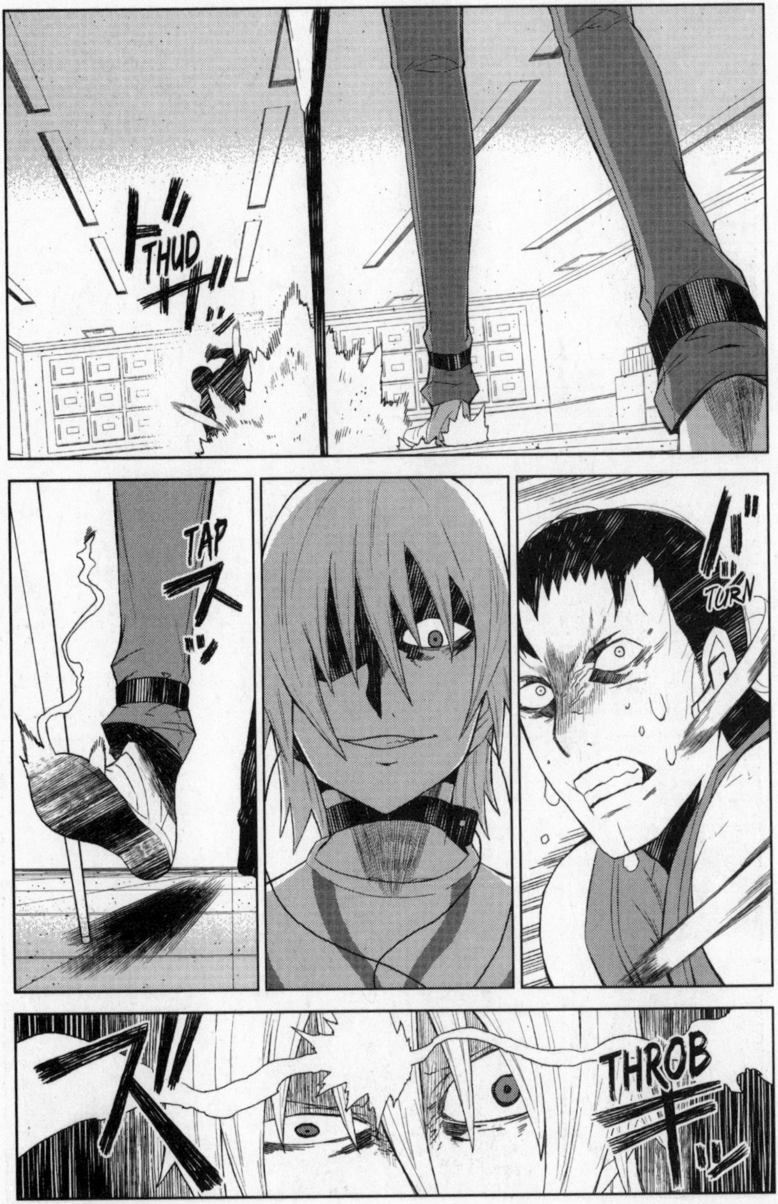
THUD
TAP
TURN
THROB

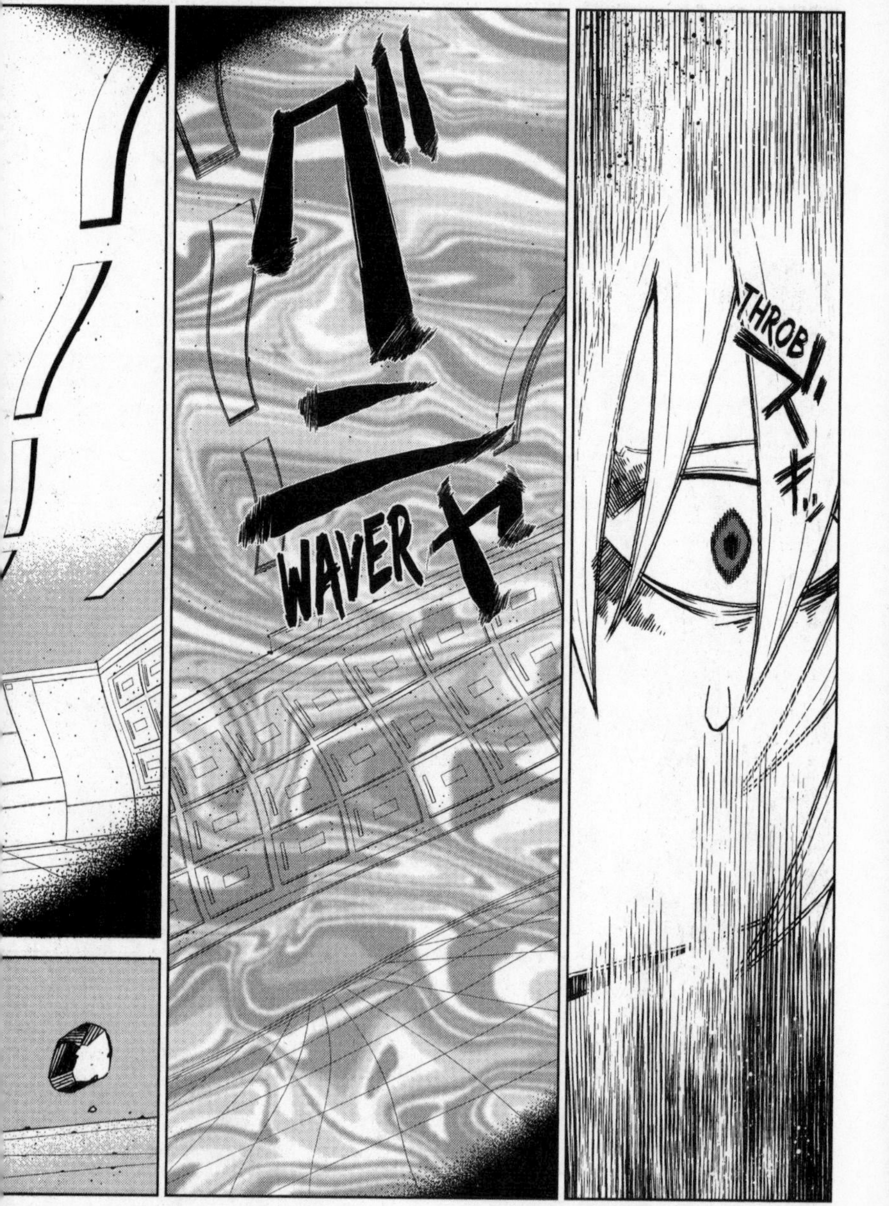
THROB
WAVER

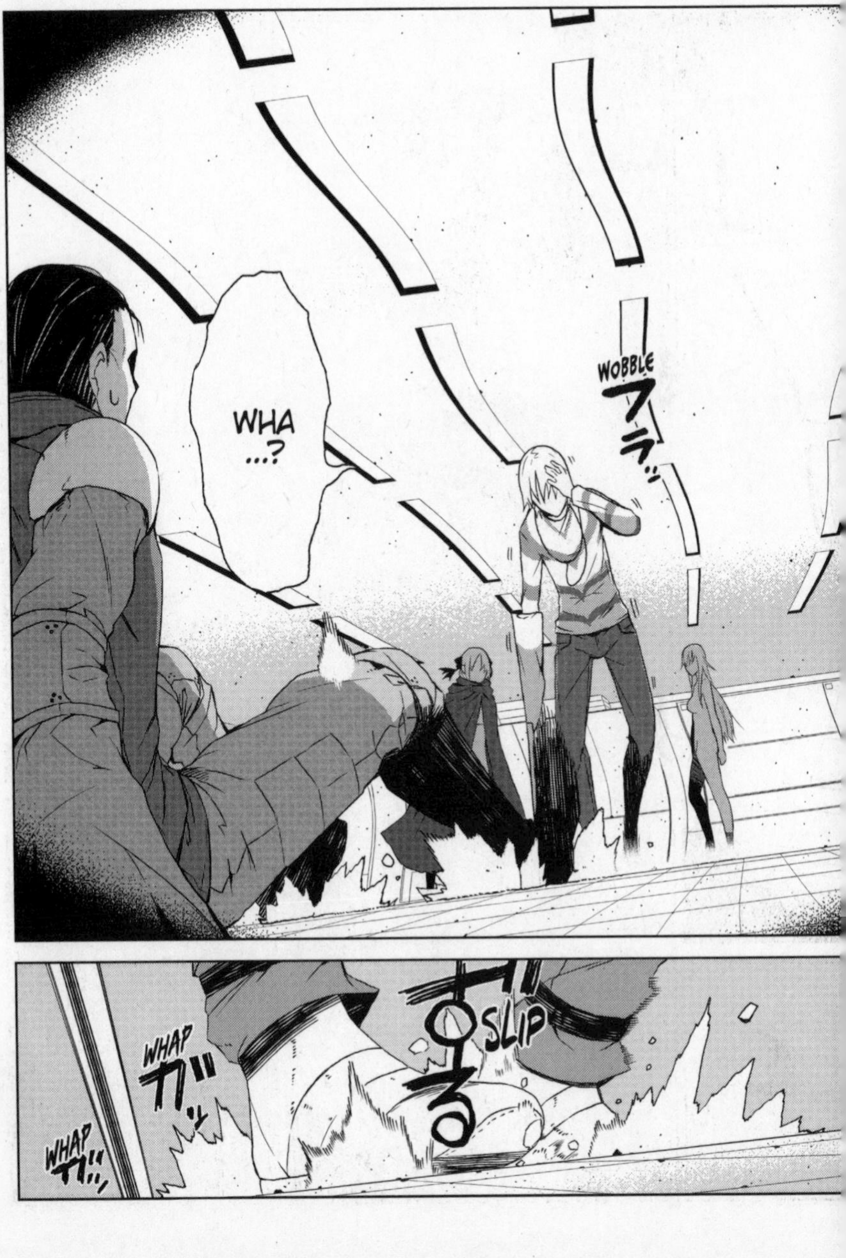
WOBBLE
フラ
WHA ...?
SLIP
する
WHAP
ガッ
WHAP

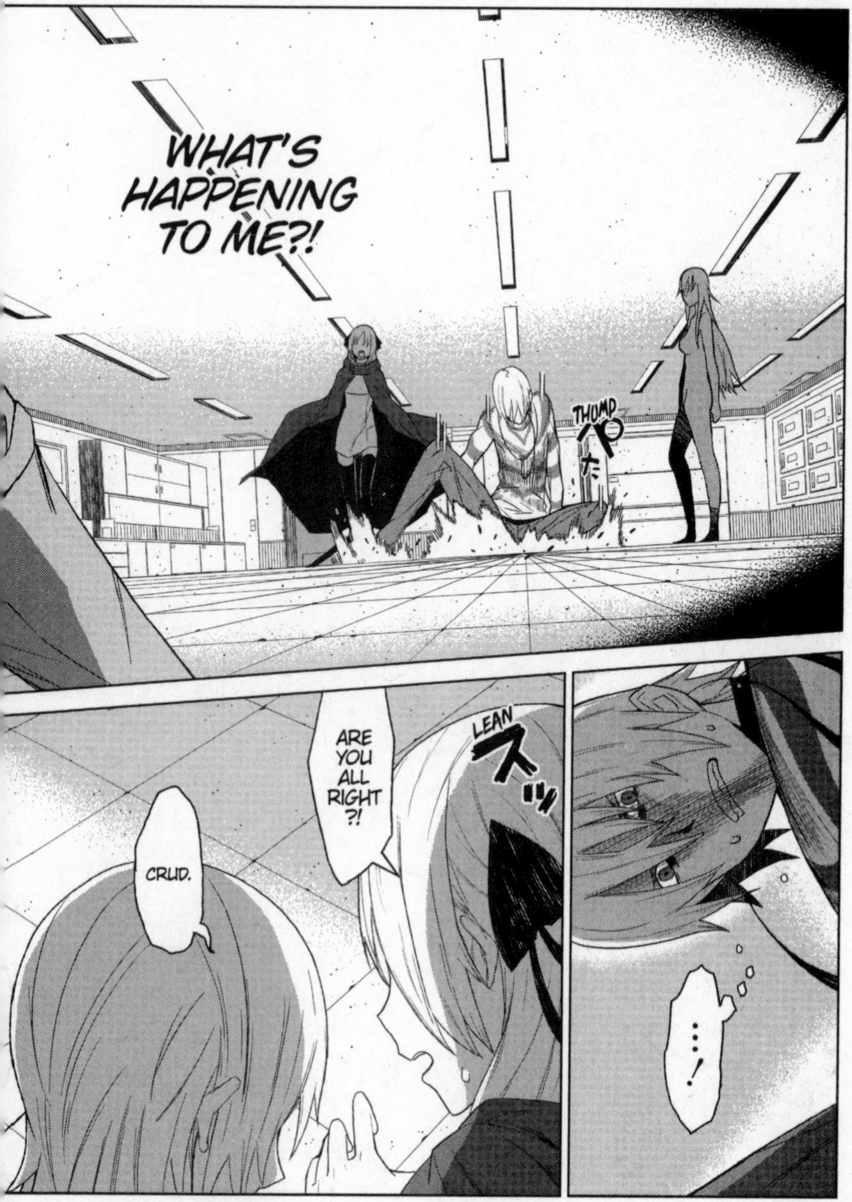
WHAT'S HAPPENING TO ME?!
THUMP
ARE YOU ALL RIGHT?!
LEAN
CRUD.
...!

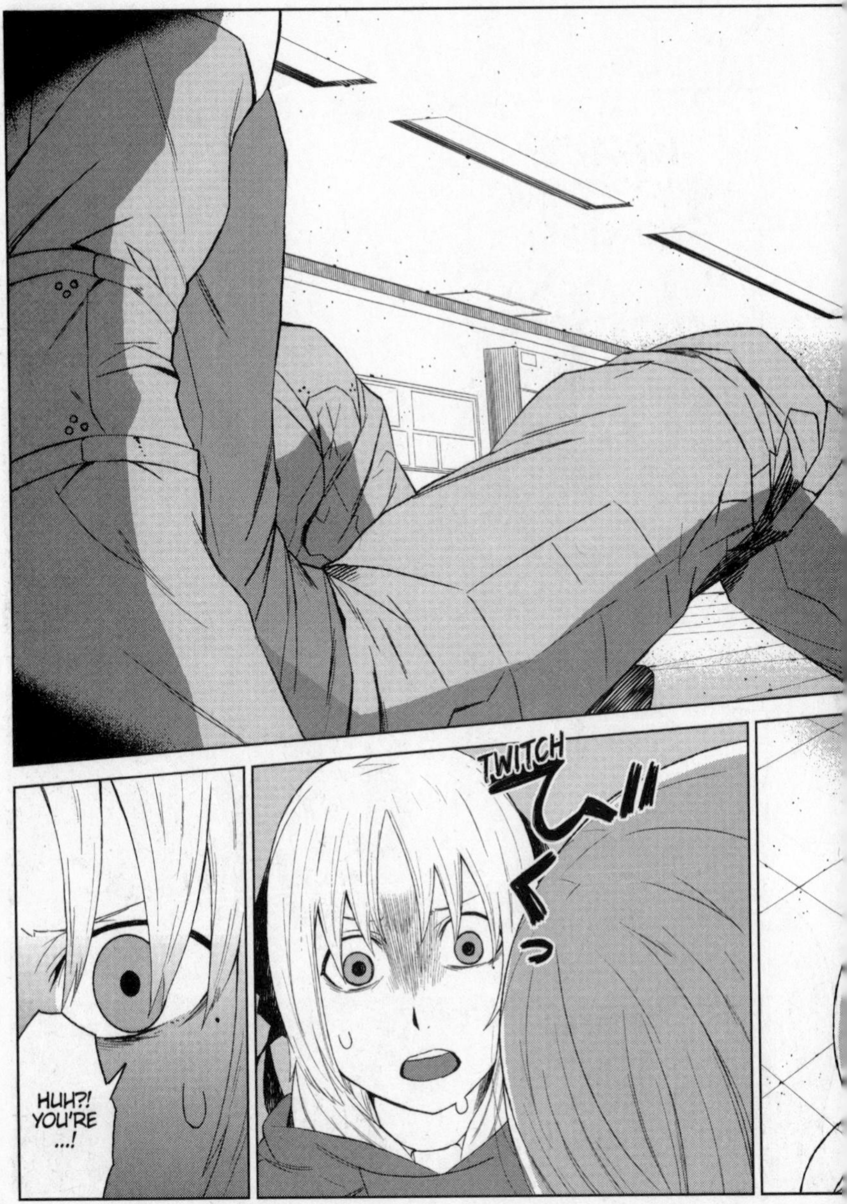
TWITCH
HUH?! YOU'RE ...!

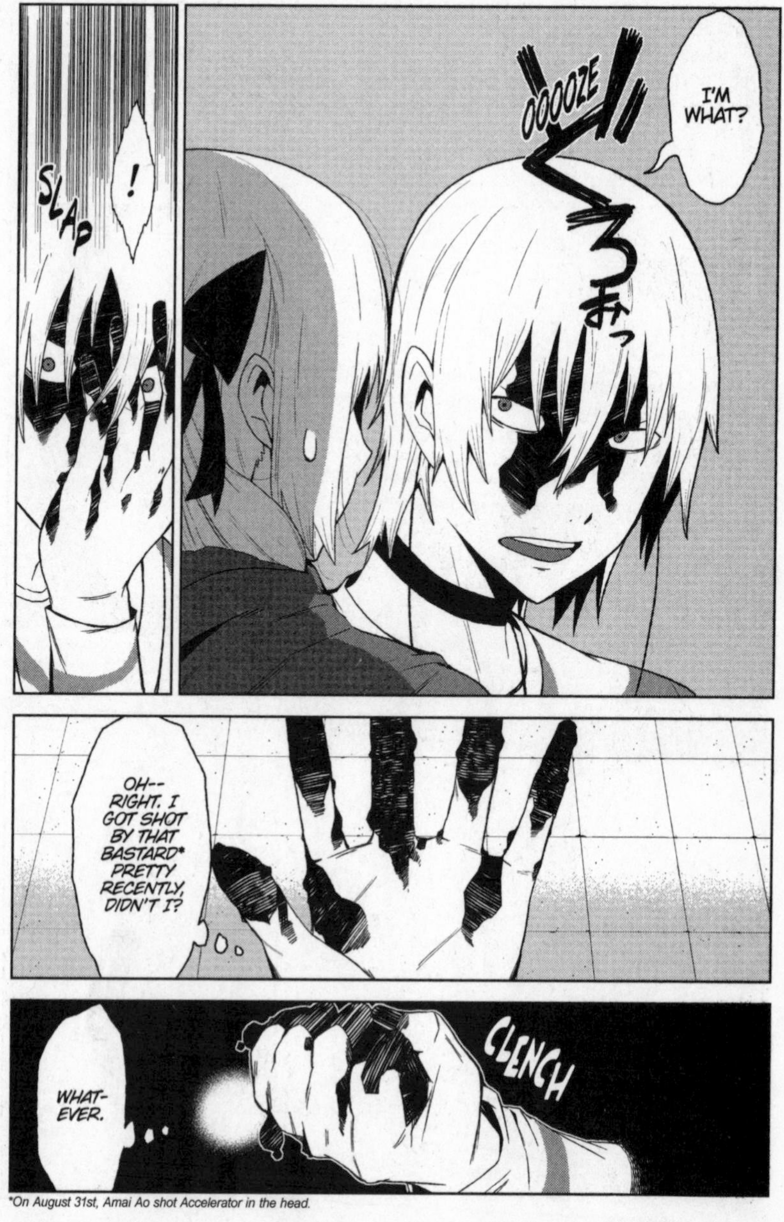
I'M WHAT?
OOOOZE
SLAP
!
OH-- RIGHT. I GOT SHOT BY THAT BASTARD* PRETTY RECENTLY, DIDN'T I?
CLENCH
WHAT-EVER.

*On August 31st, Amai Ao shot Accelerator in the head.

BANG

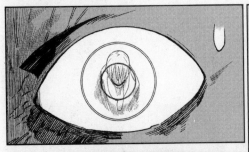

THAT HAS NOTHING TO DO WITH THIS!

WOBBLE

HA... HA HA!

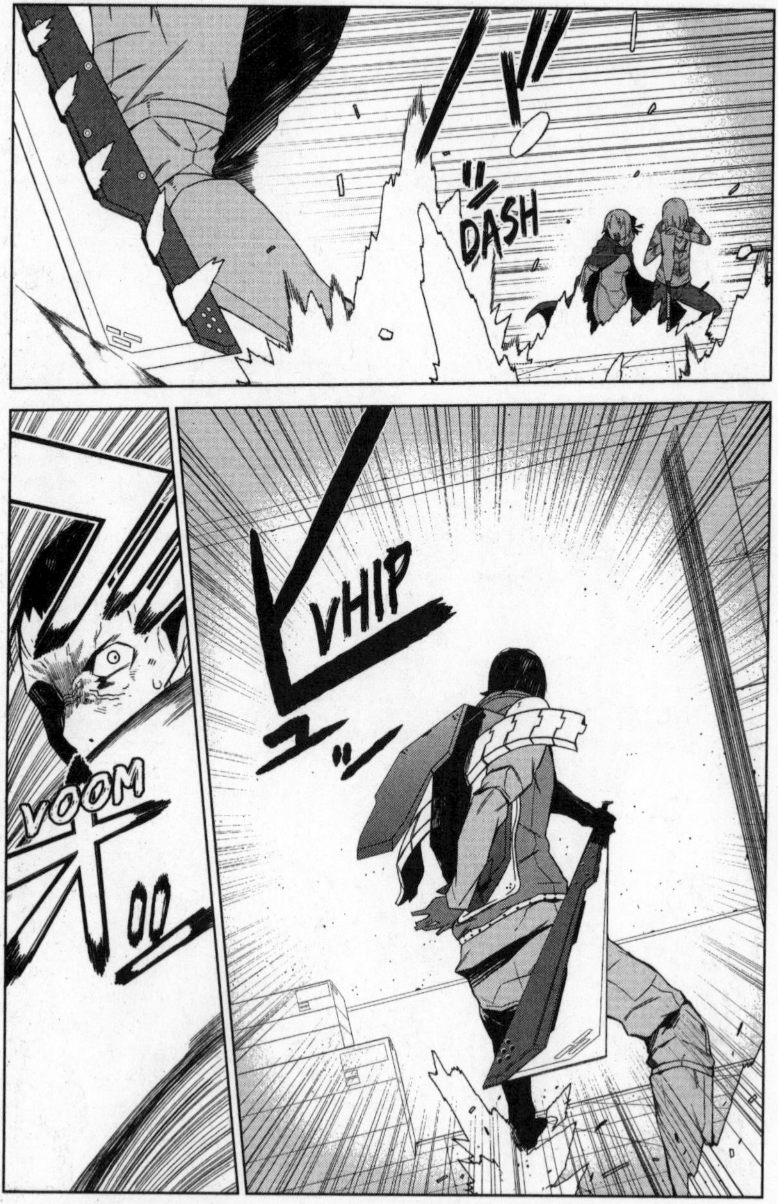
DASH
VHIP
VOOM

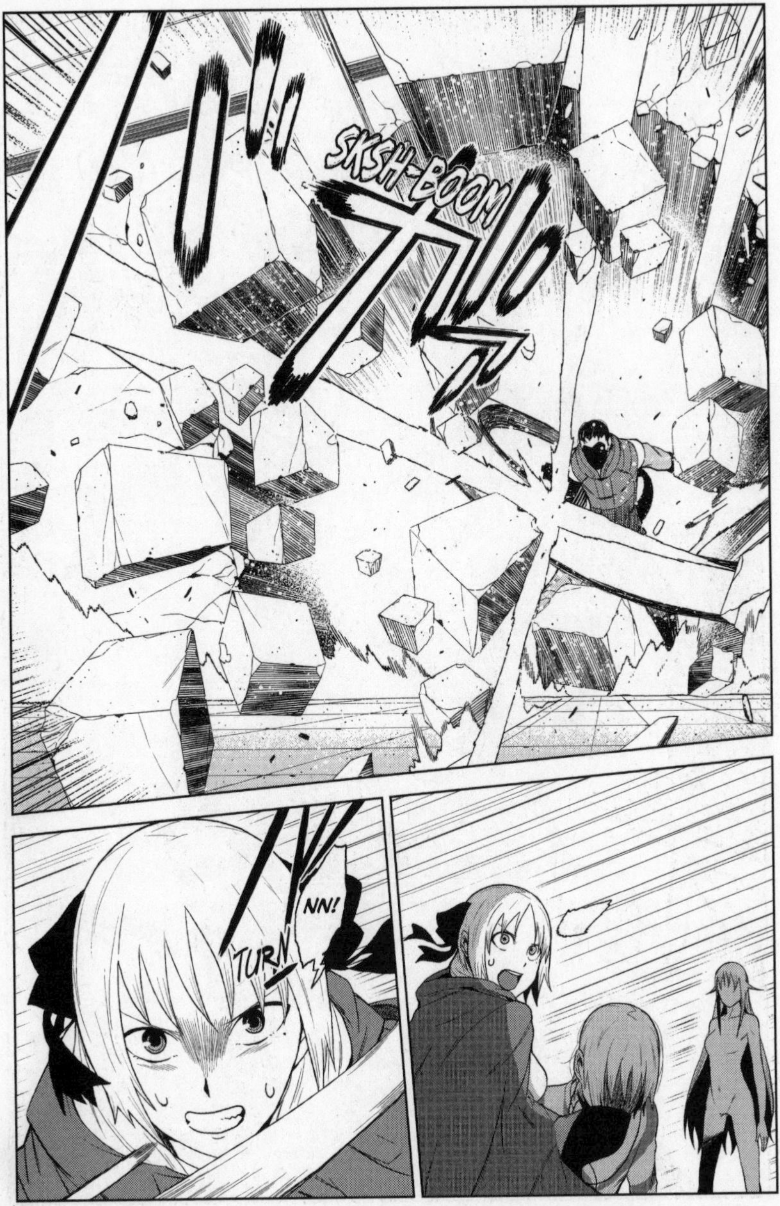

SKSH-BOOM
NN!
TURN

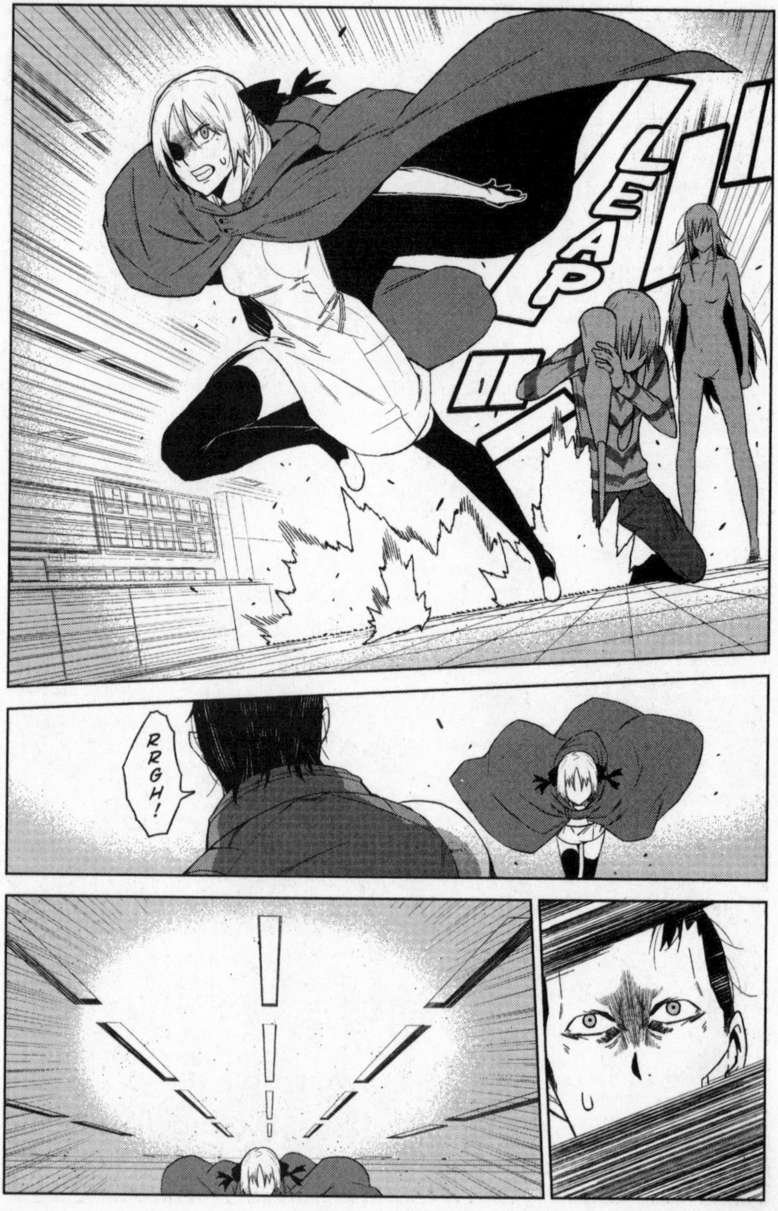
LEAP
RRGH!
!

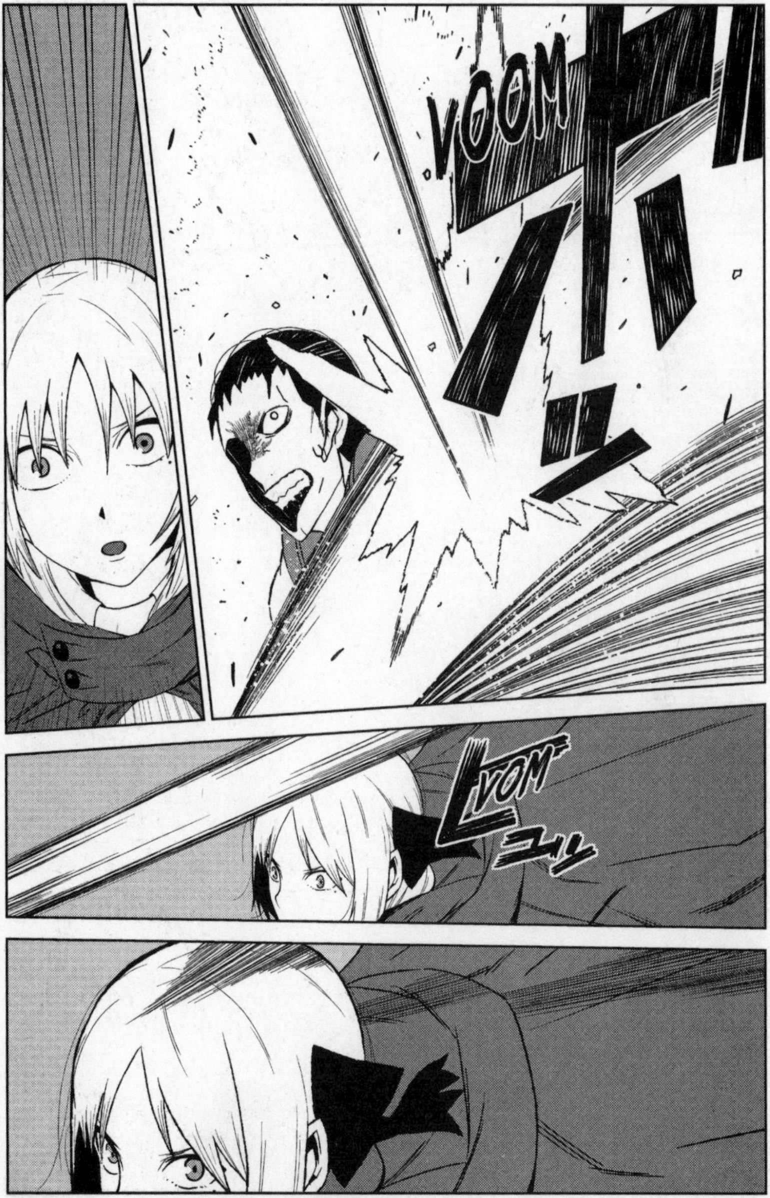
VOOM
VOM

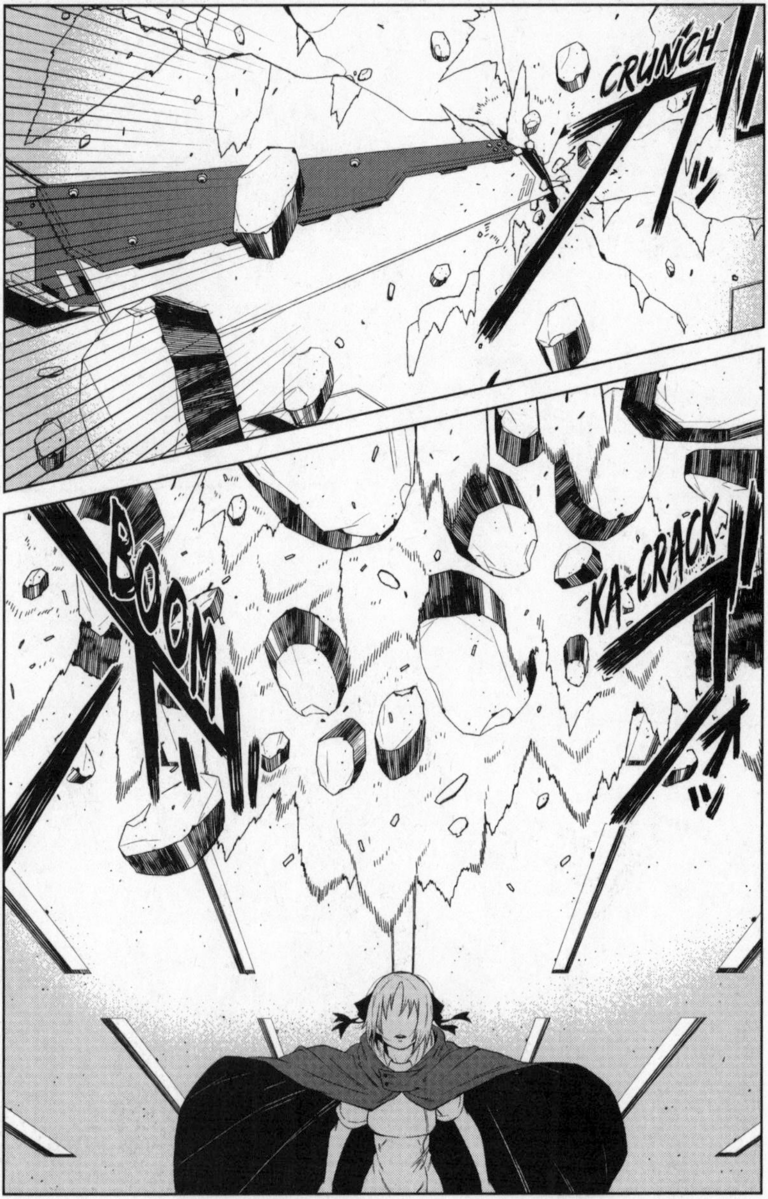
CRUNCH
KA-CRACK
BOOM

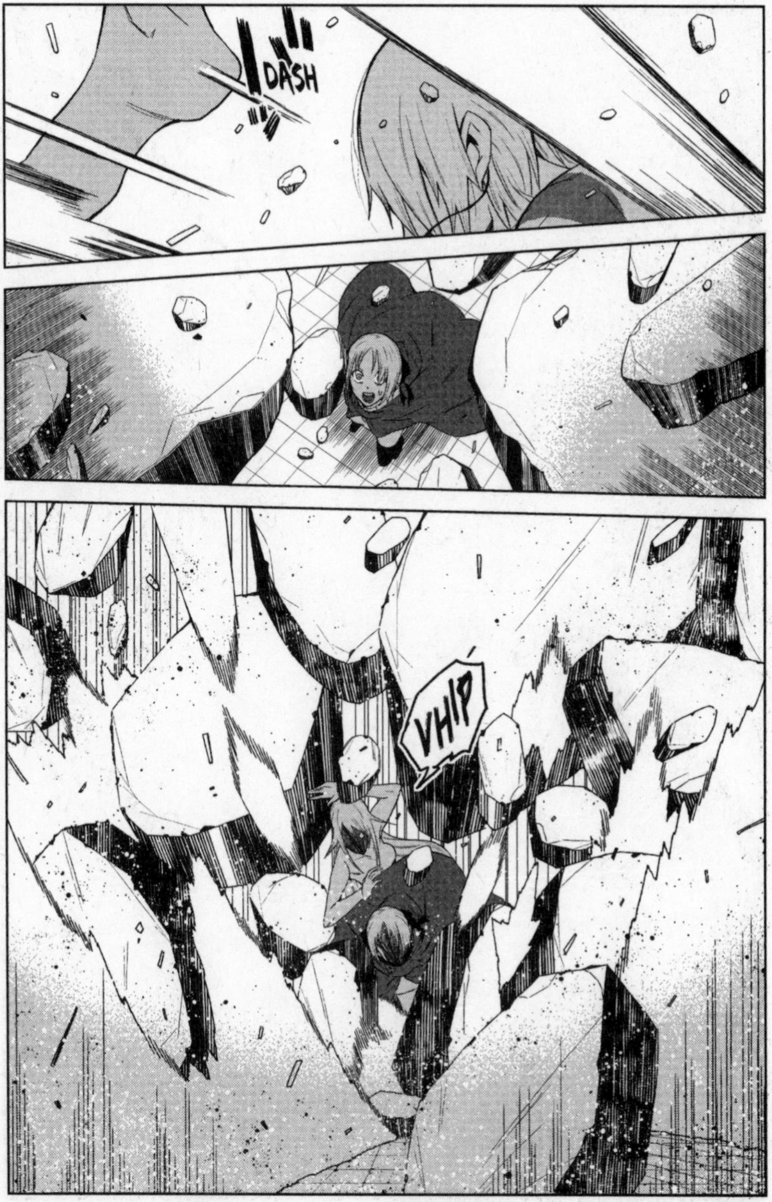
DASH
VHIP

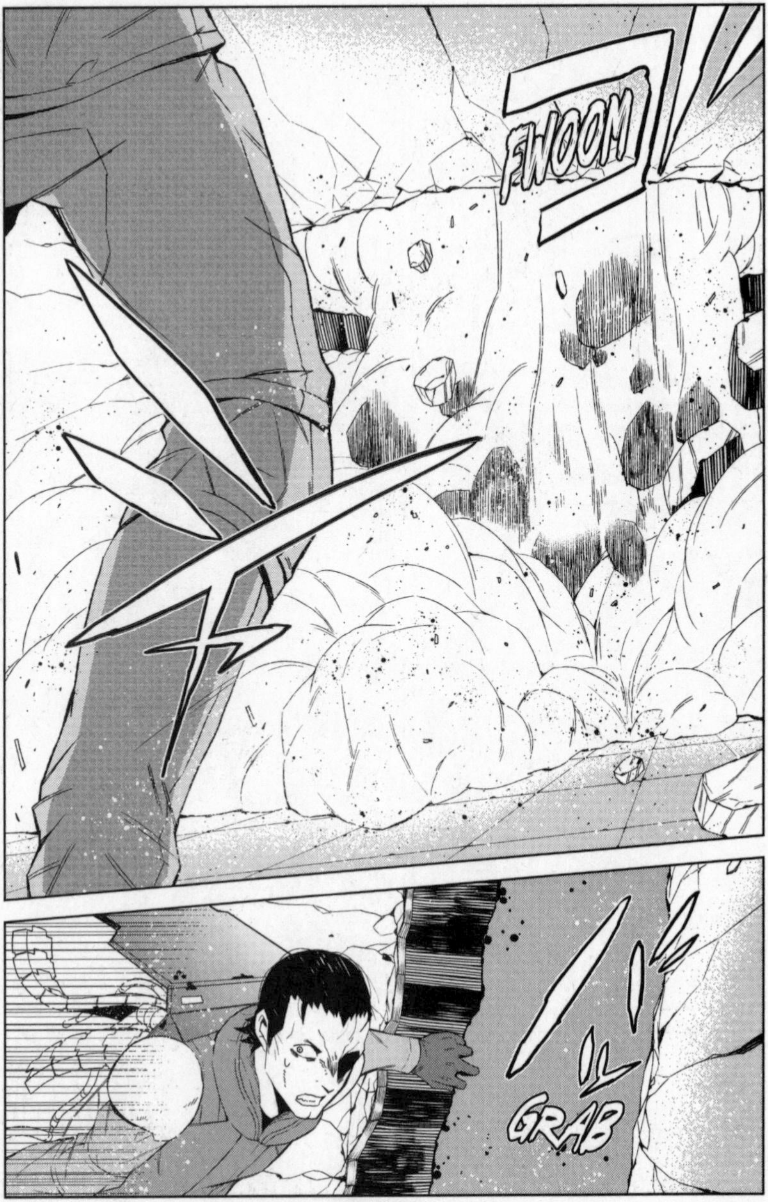
FWOOM
GRAB

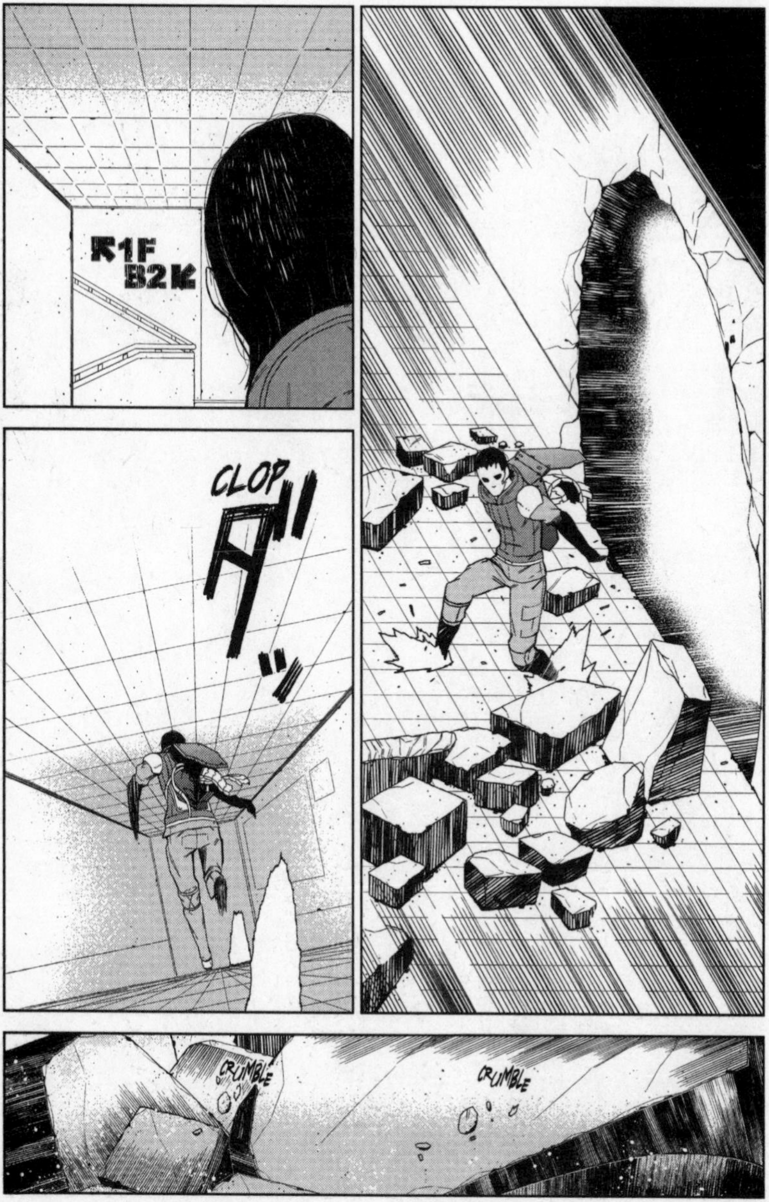

1F
B2
CLOP
CRUMBLE
CRUMBLE

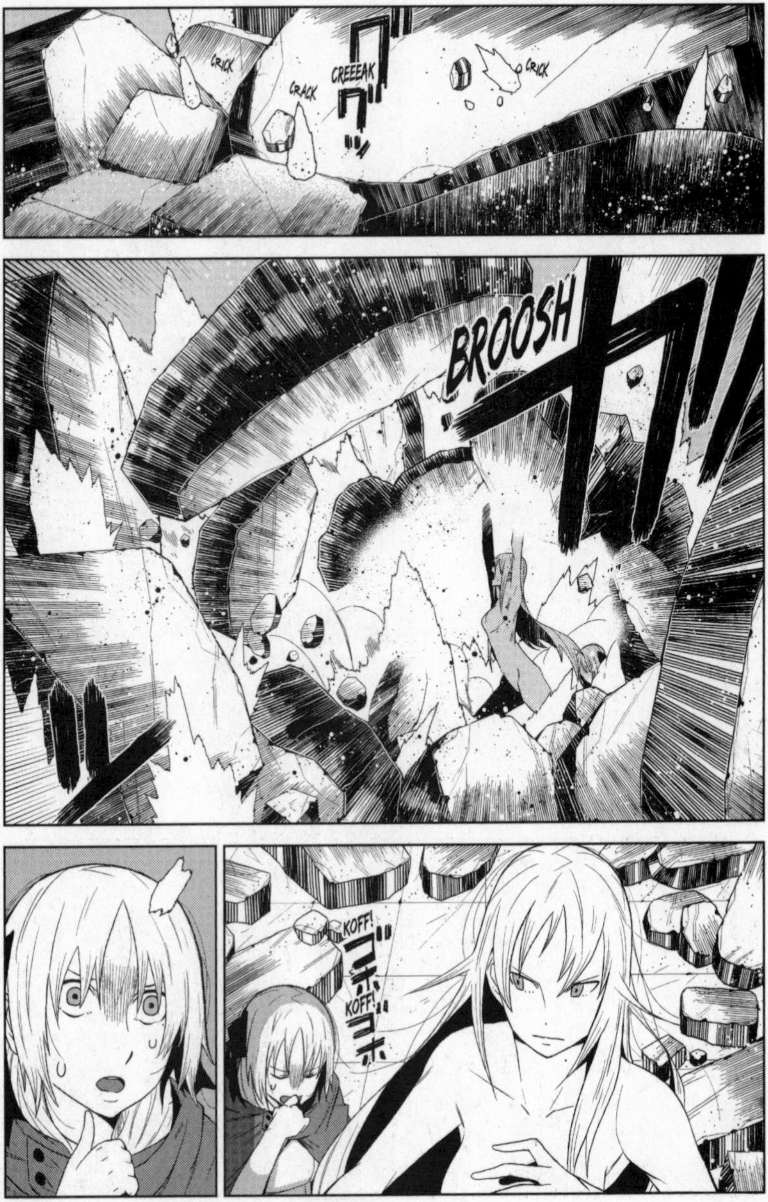
CRICK
CREEEAK
CRACK
CRICK
BROOSH
KOFF!
KOFF!

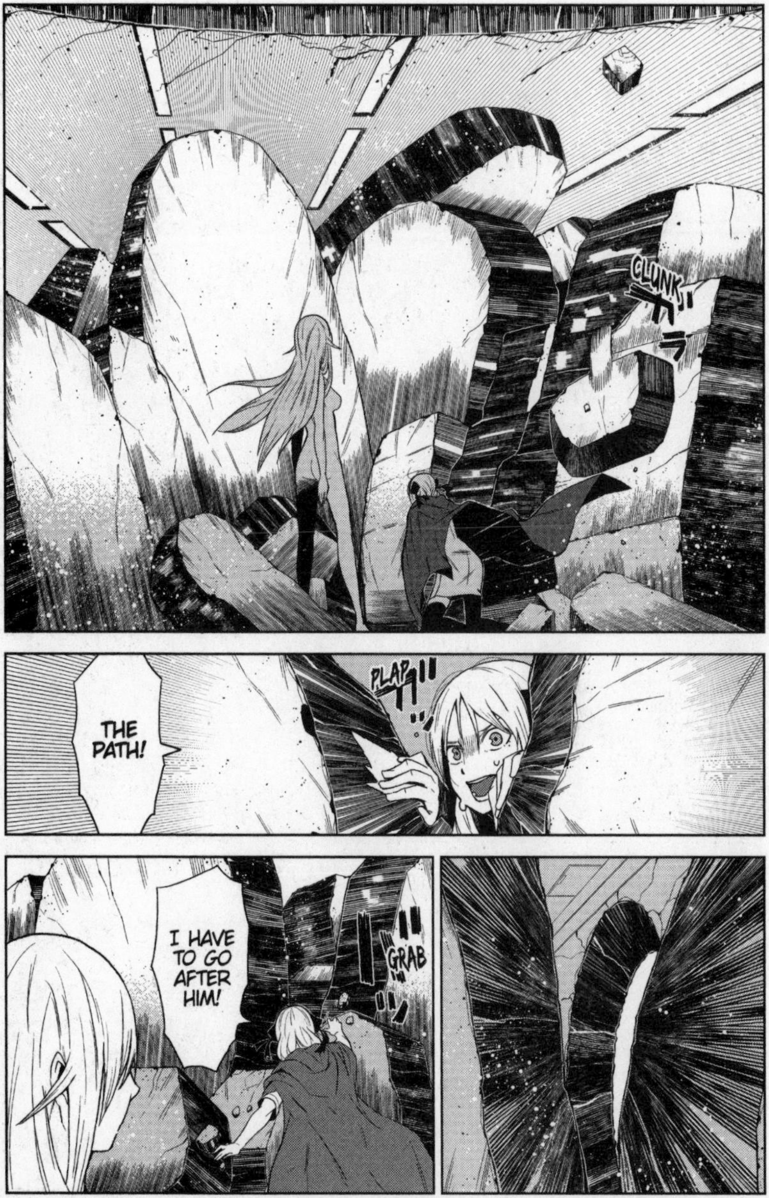
CLUNK
PLAP
THE PATH!
GRAB
I HAVE TO GO AFTER HIM!

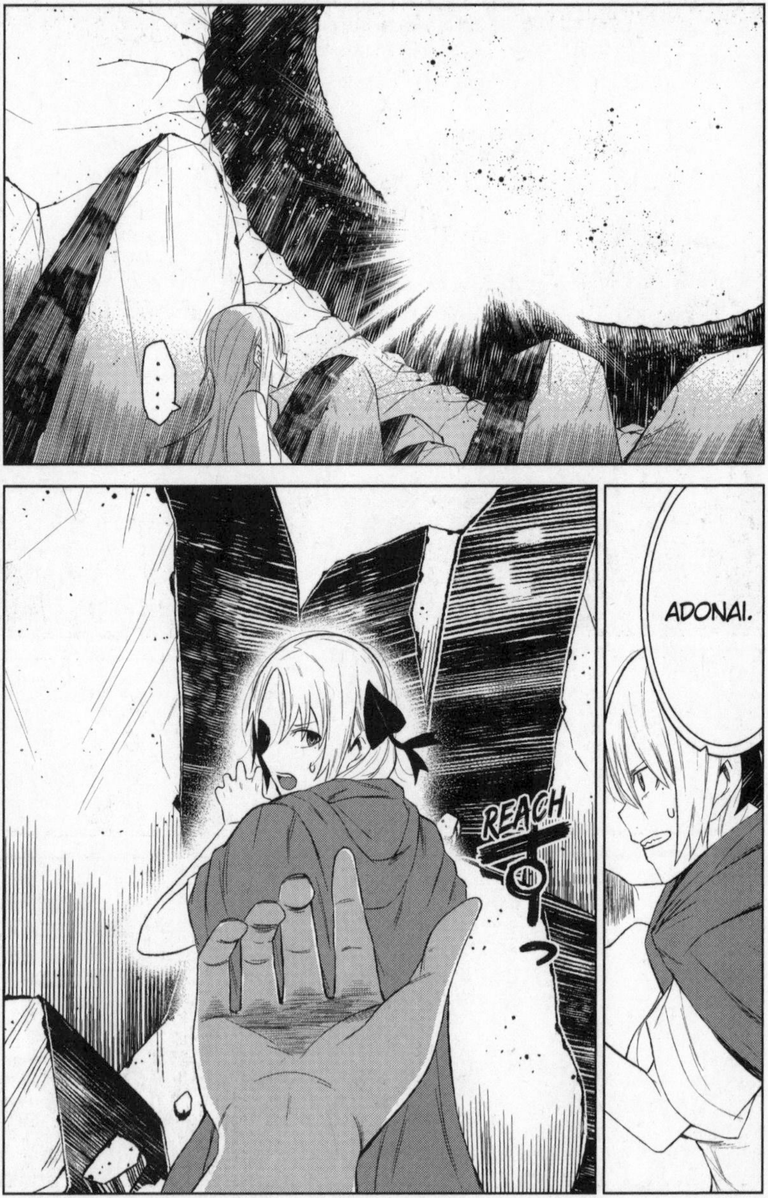
...
ADONAI.
REACH
すっ

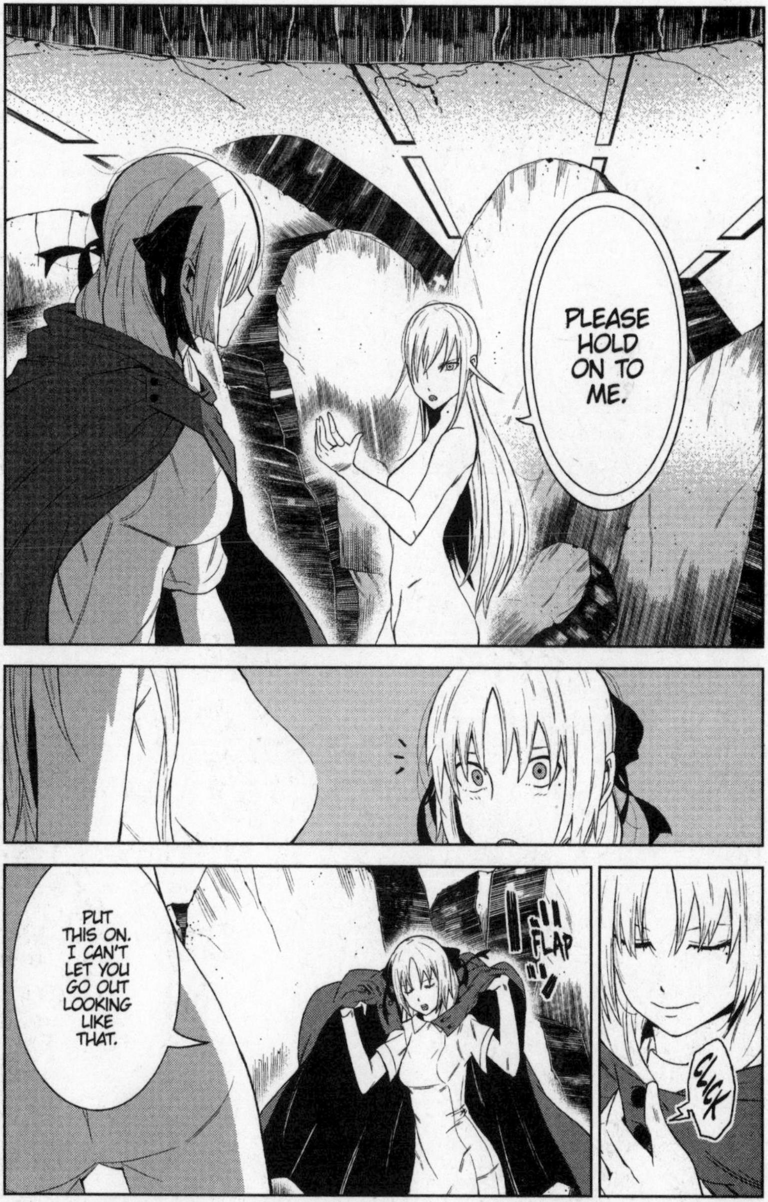
PLEASE HOLD ON TO ME.
PUT THIS ON. I CAN'T LET YOU GO OUT LOOKING LIKE THAT.
FLAP
CLICK

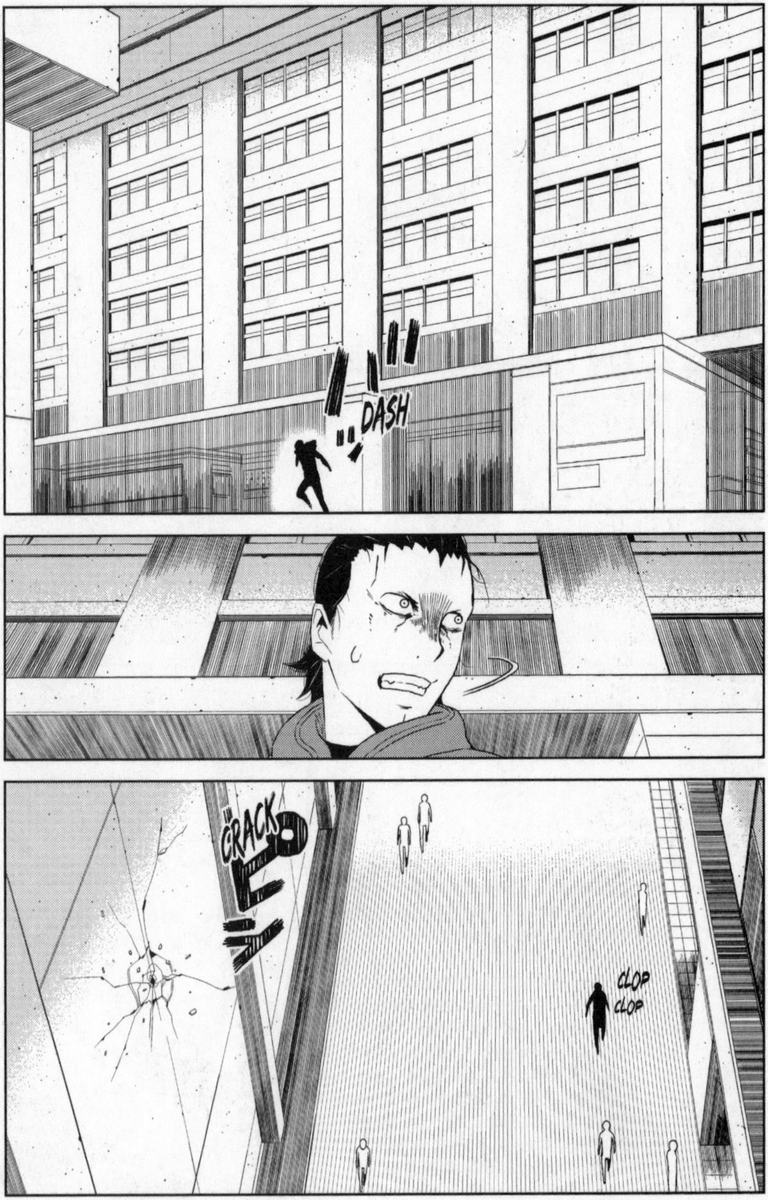
DASH
CRACK
CLOP
CLOP

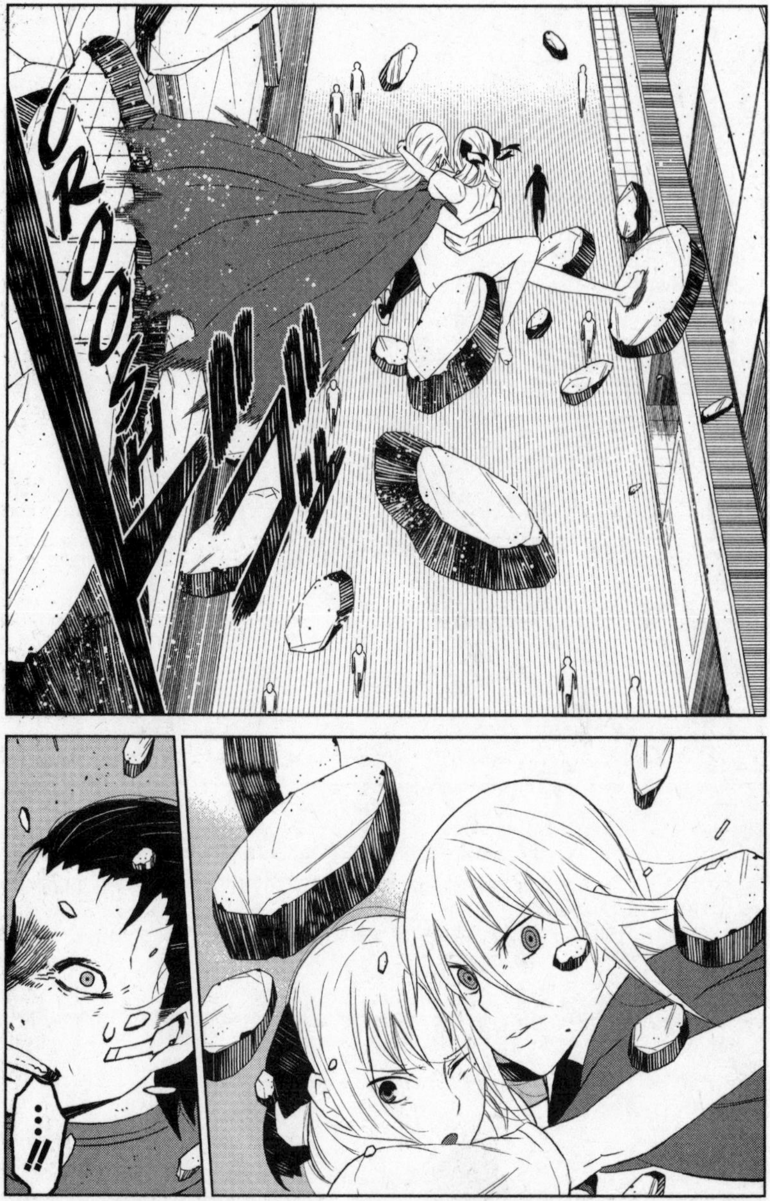
VROOSH
...!!

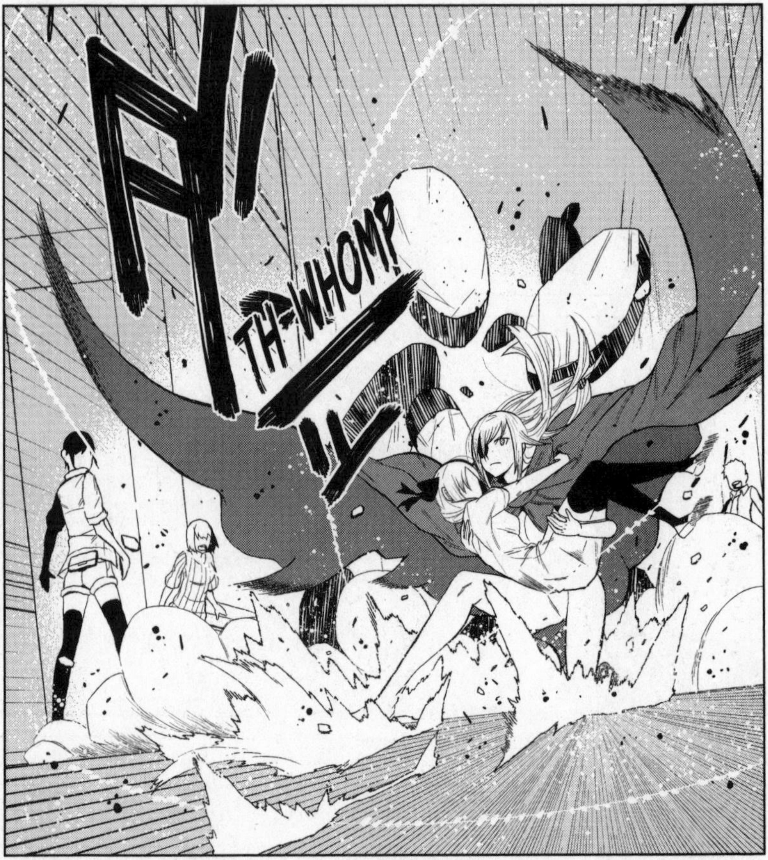
TH-WHOMP!
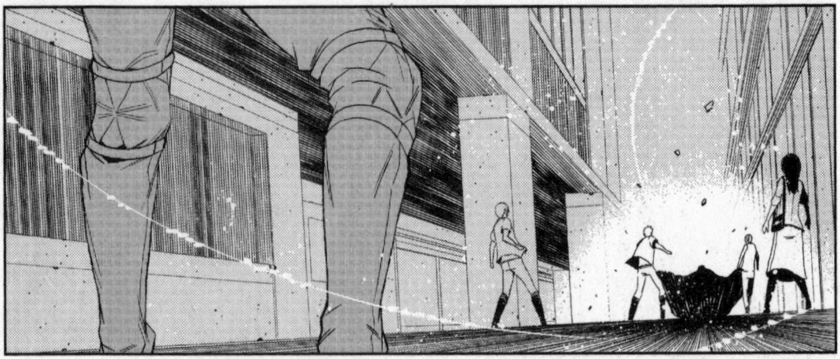

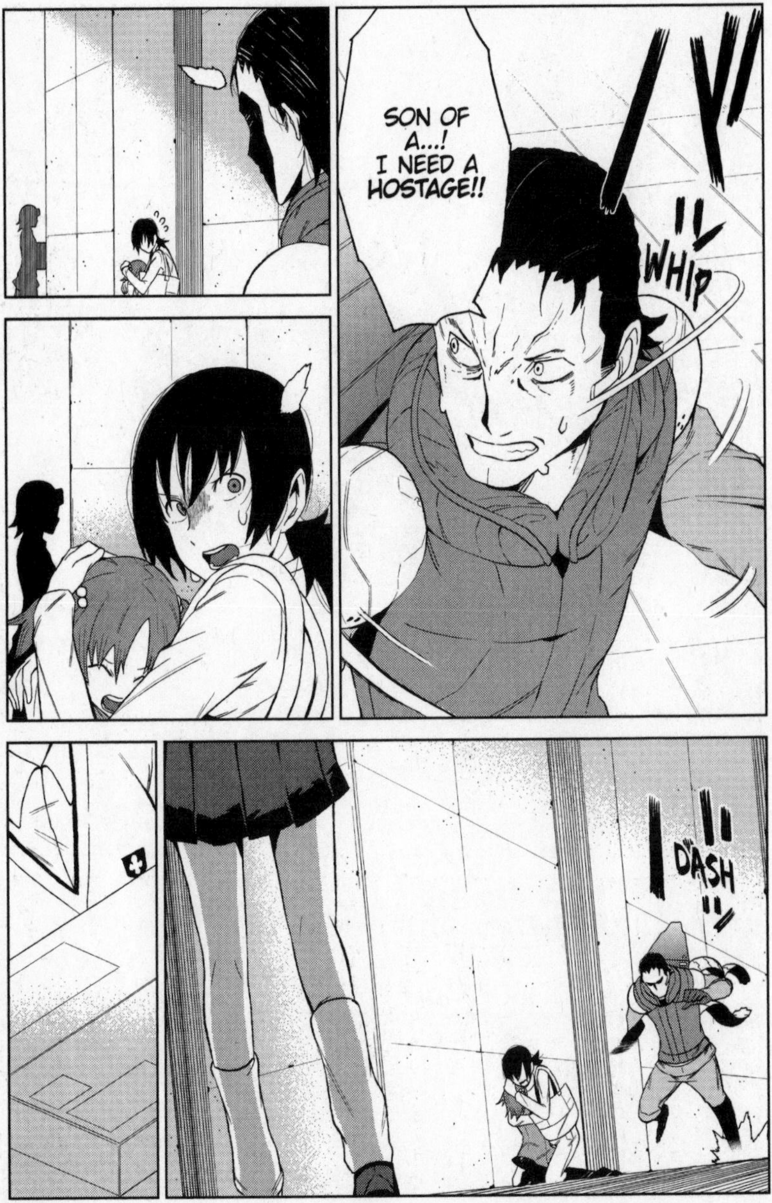
SON OF A...! I NEED A HOSTAGE!!
WHIP
DASH

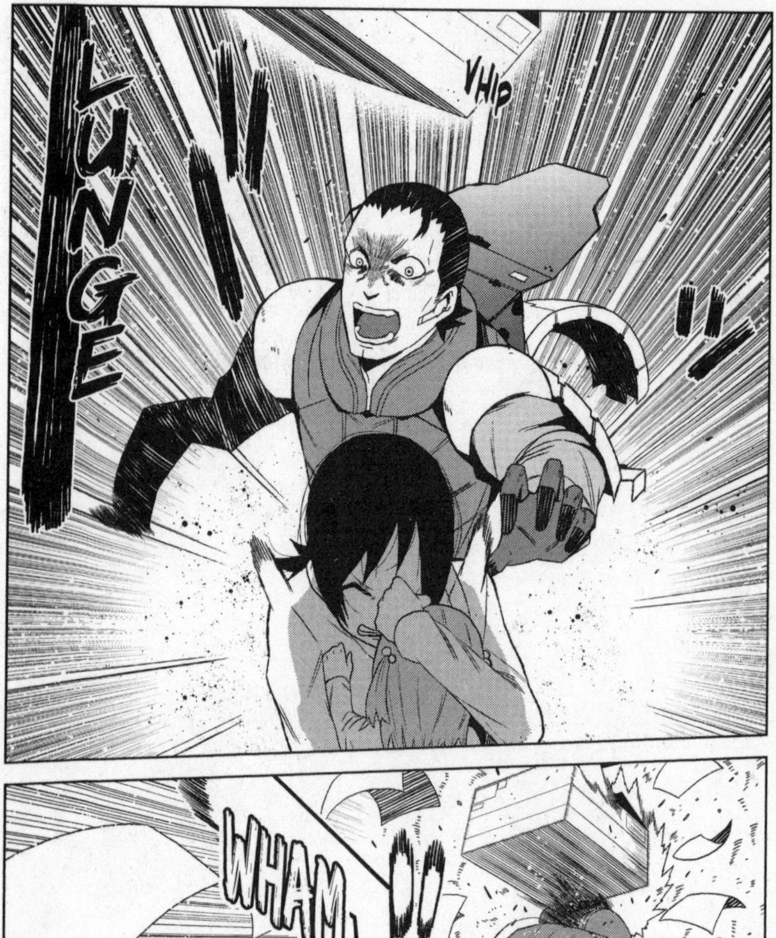
VHIP
LUNGE

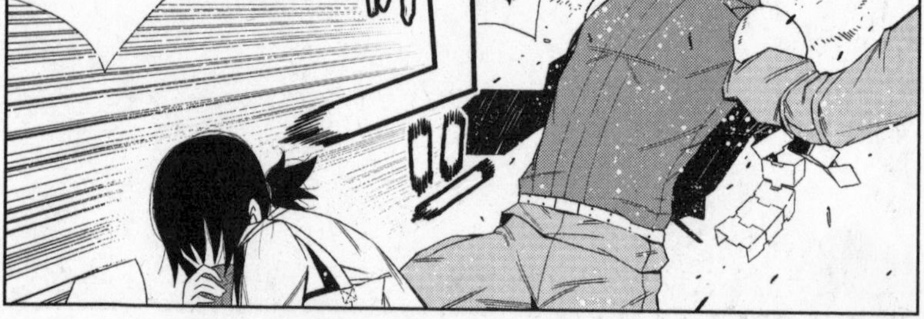
WHAM

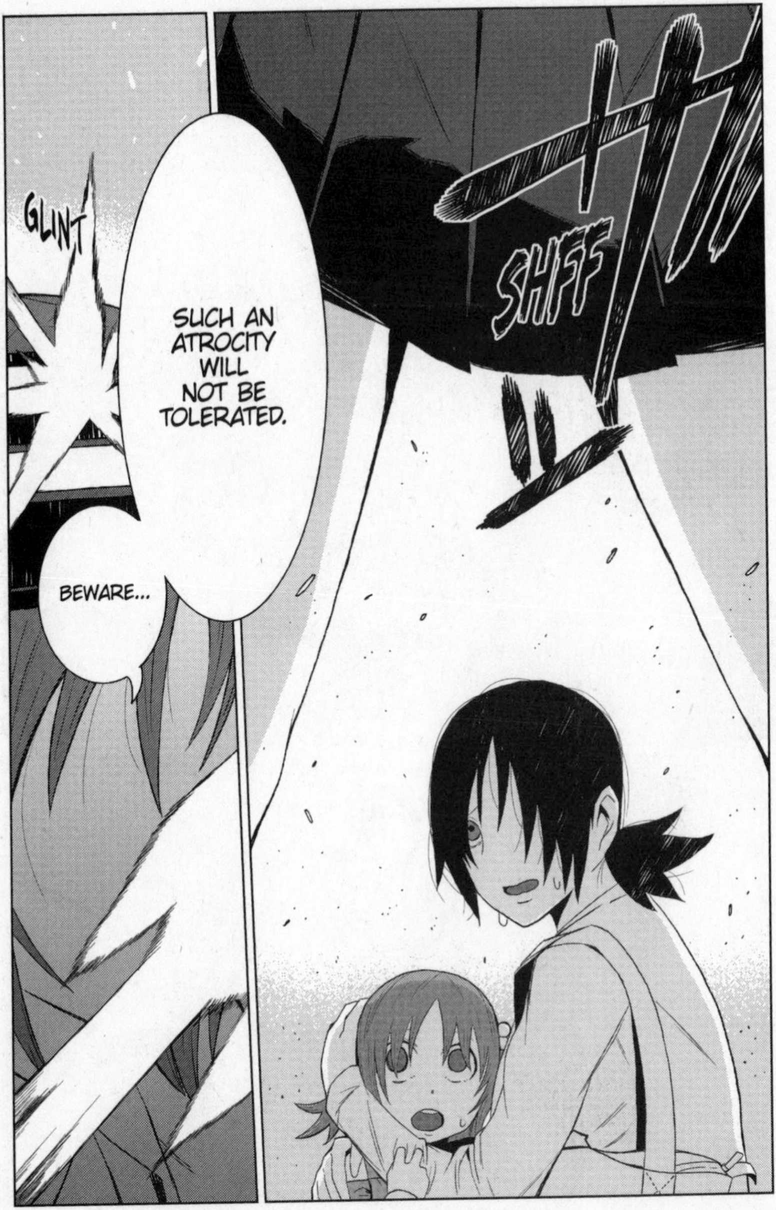
SHFF
SUCH AN ATROCITY WILL NOT BE TOLERATED.
BEWARE...
GLINT

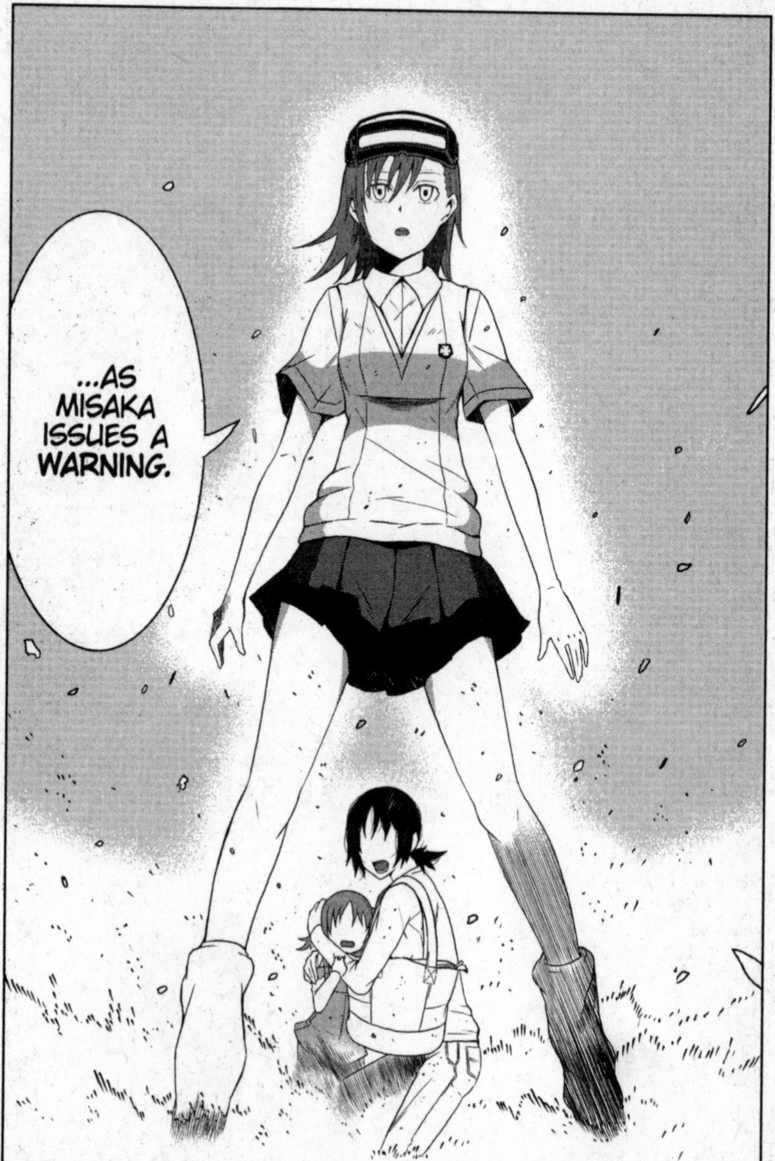
...AS MISAKA ISSUES A WARNING.

a certain SCIENTIFIC ACCELERATOR

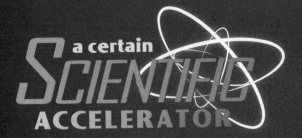

とある科学の一方通行

とある魔術の禁書目録外伝

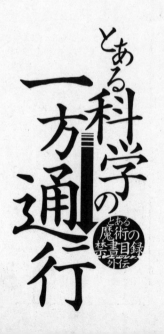

CHAPTER 6

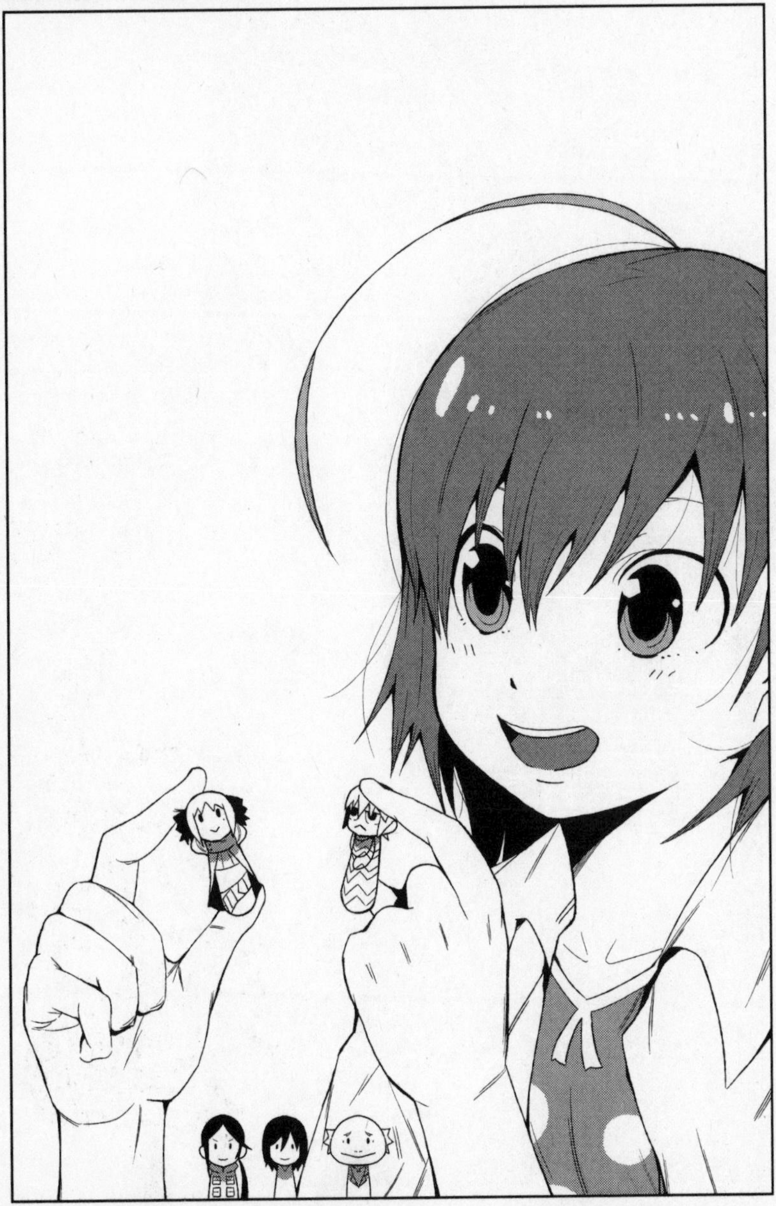

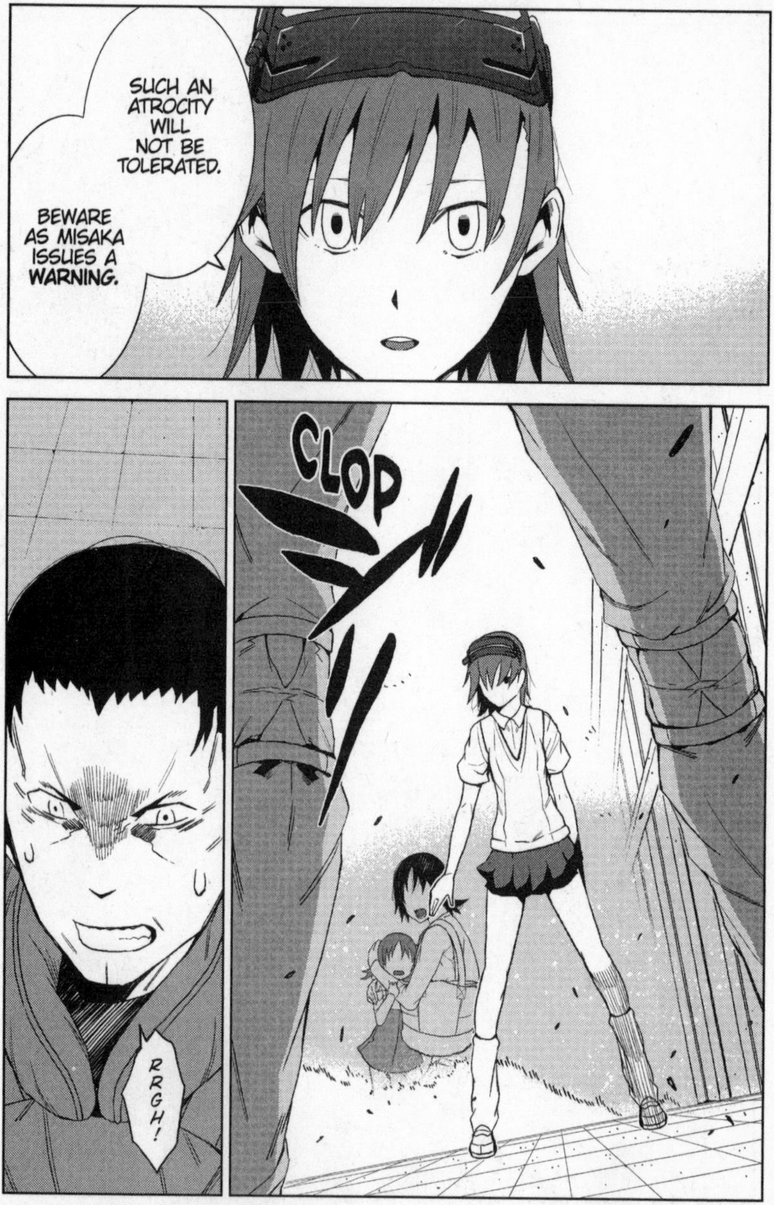
SUCH AN ATROCITY WILL NOT BE TOLERATED.
BEWARE AS MISAKA ISSUES A WARNING.
CLOP
RRGH!

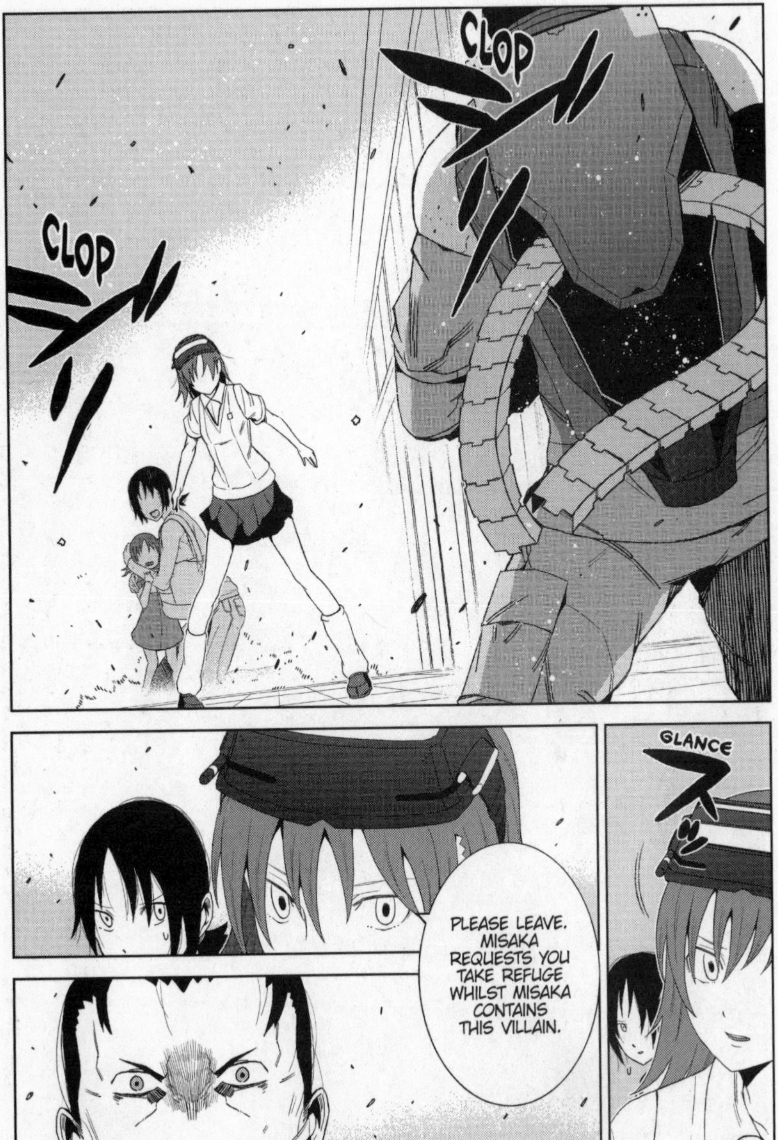
CLOP
CLOP
GLANCE
PLEASE LEAVE. MISAKA REQUESTS YOU TAKE REFUGE WHILST MISAKA CONTAINS THIS VILLAIN.

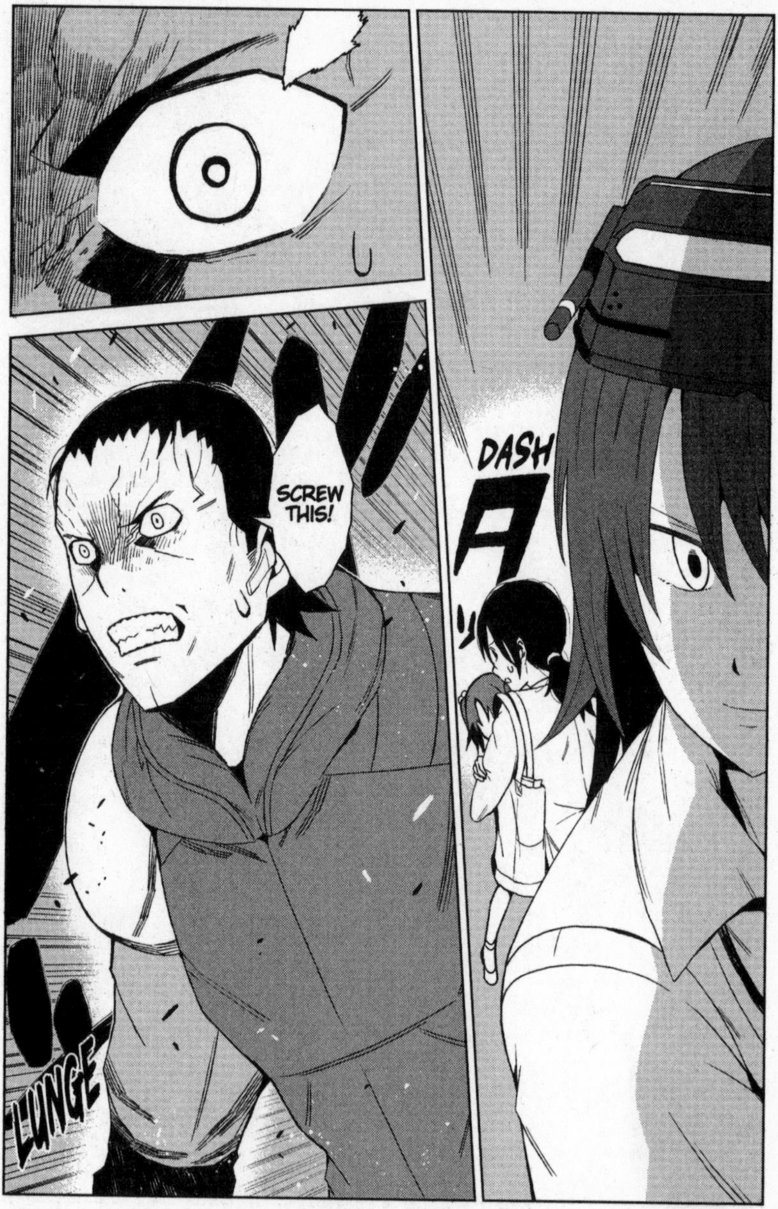
DASH
SCREW THIS!
LUNGE

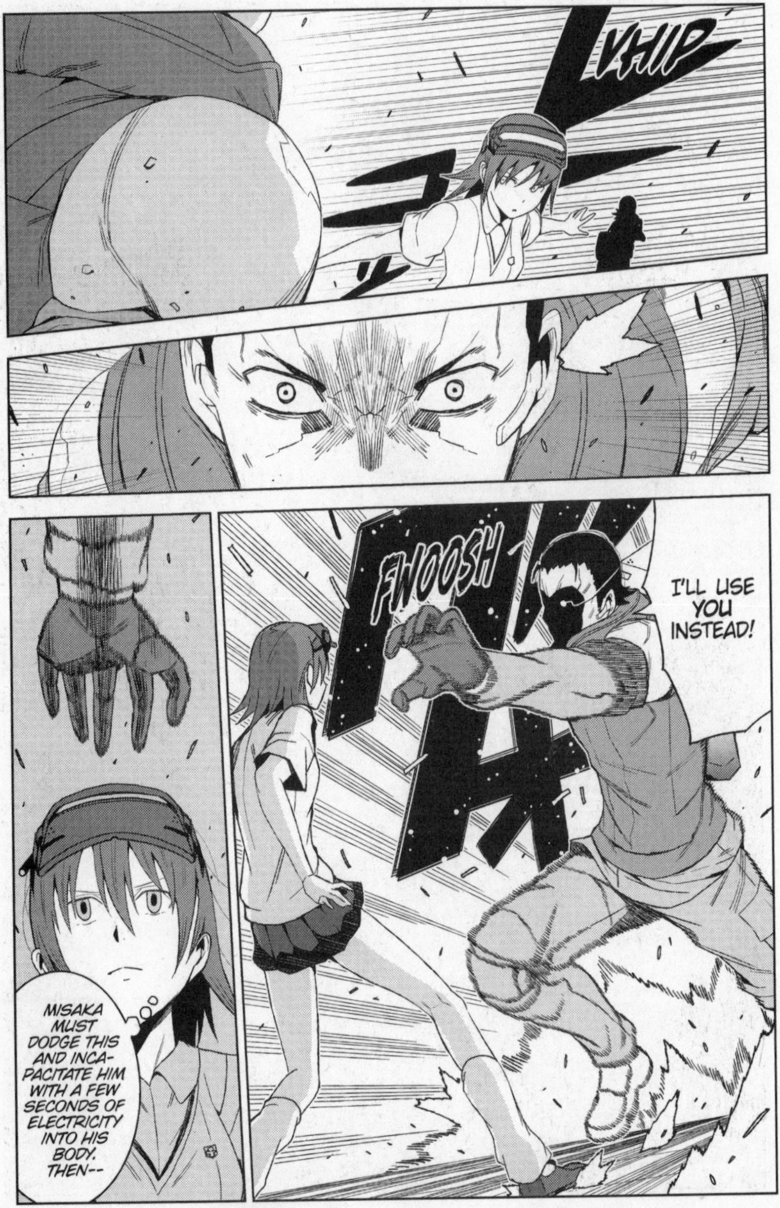
WHIP
FWOOSH
I'LL USE YOU INSTEAD!
MISAKA MUST DODGE THIS AND INCA-PACITATE HIM WITH A FEW SECONDS OF ELECTRICITY INTO HIS BODY. THEN--

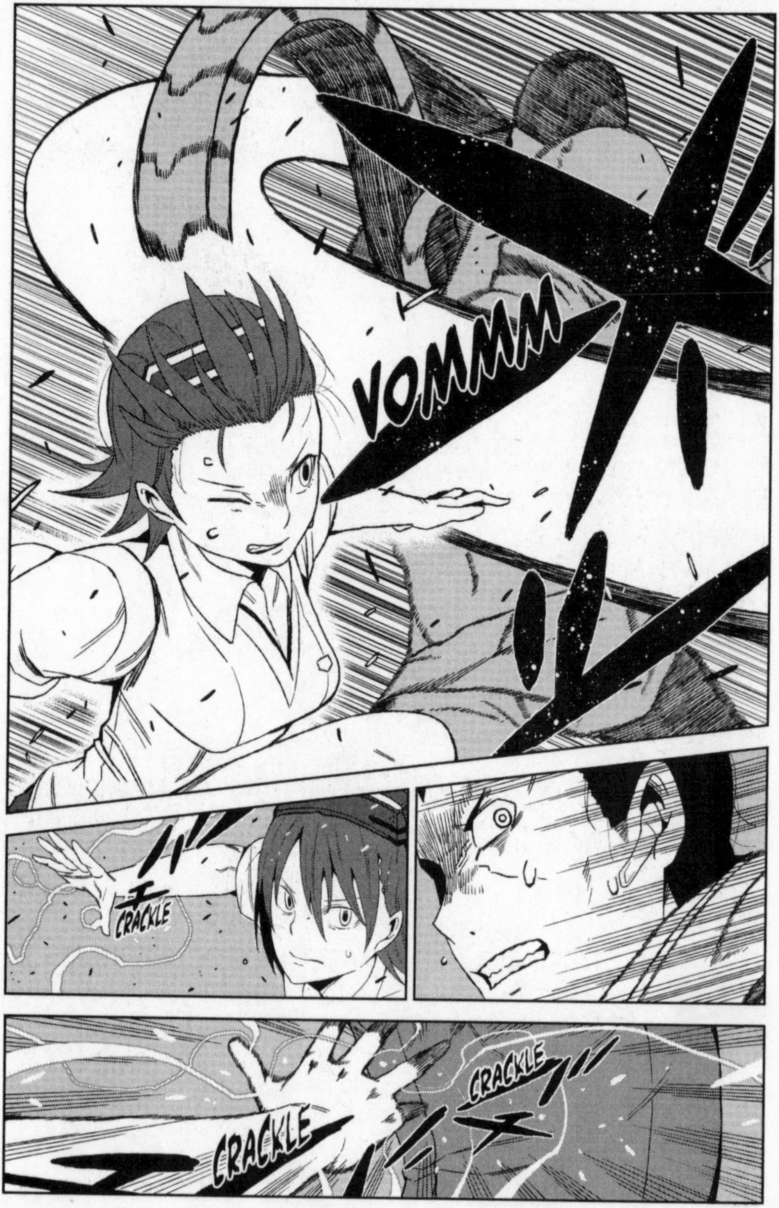
VOMMM
CRACKLE
CRACKLE
CRACKLE

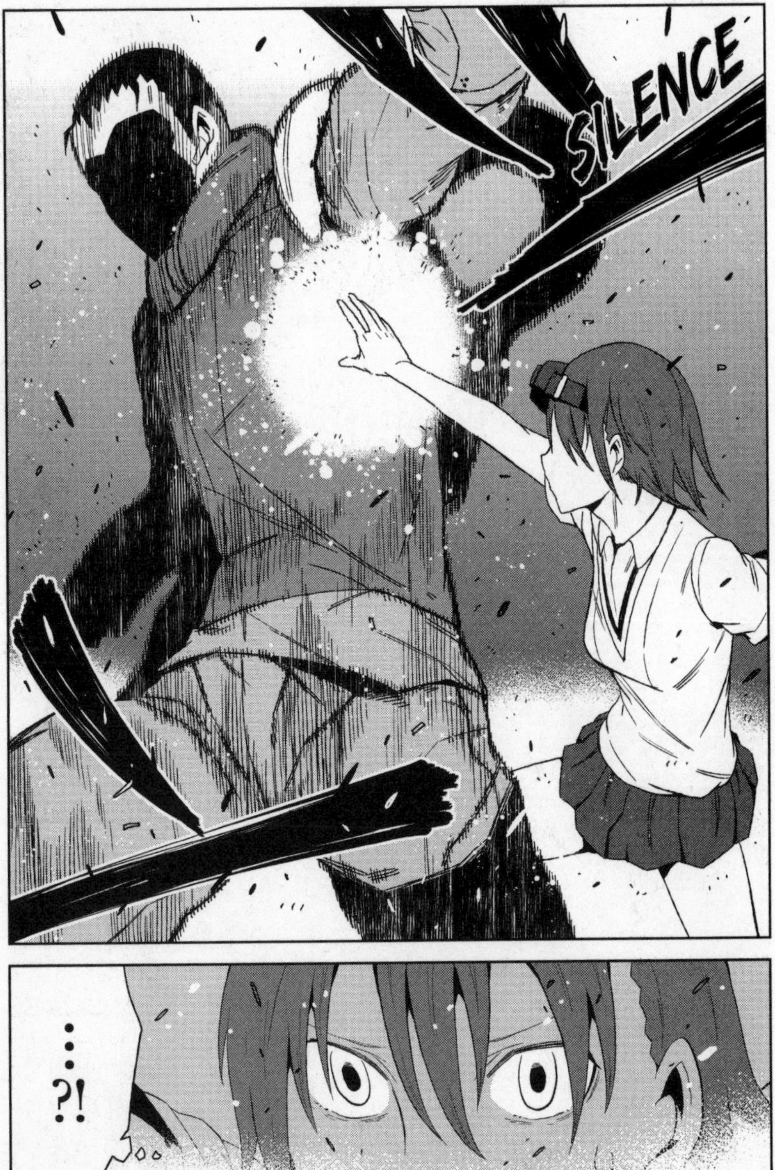
SILENCE
...
?!

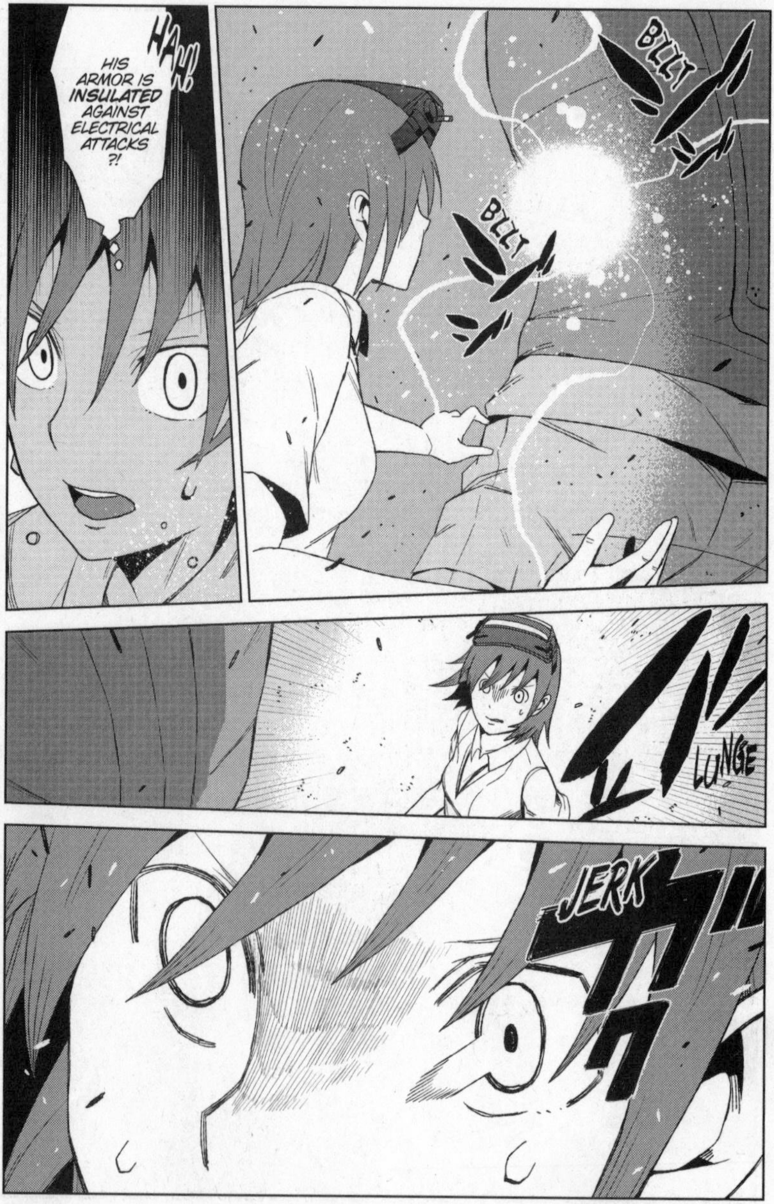
HAH!
HIS ARMOR IS INSULATED AGAINST ELECTRICAL ATTACKS ?!
BLLLT
BLLLT
LUNGE
JERK

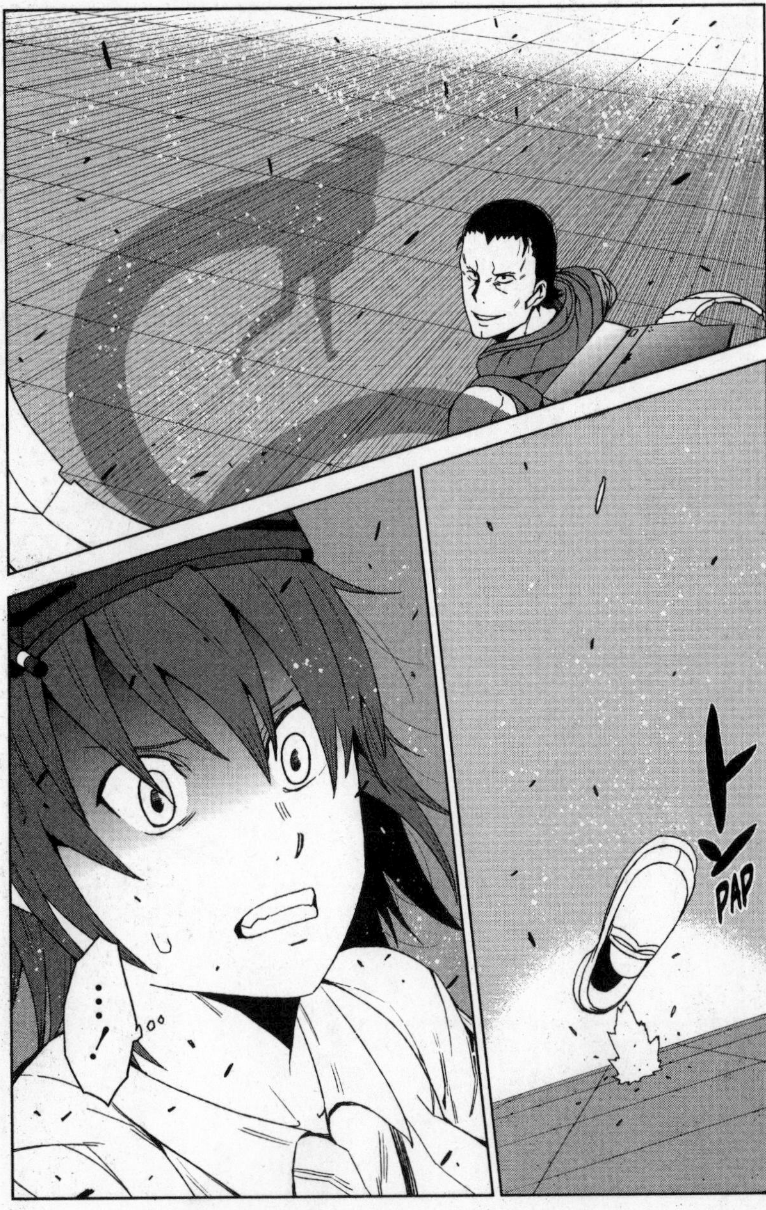
...!
PAP

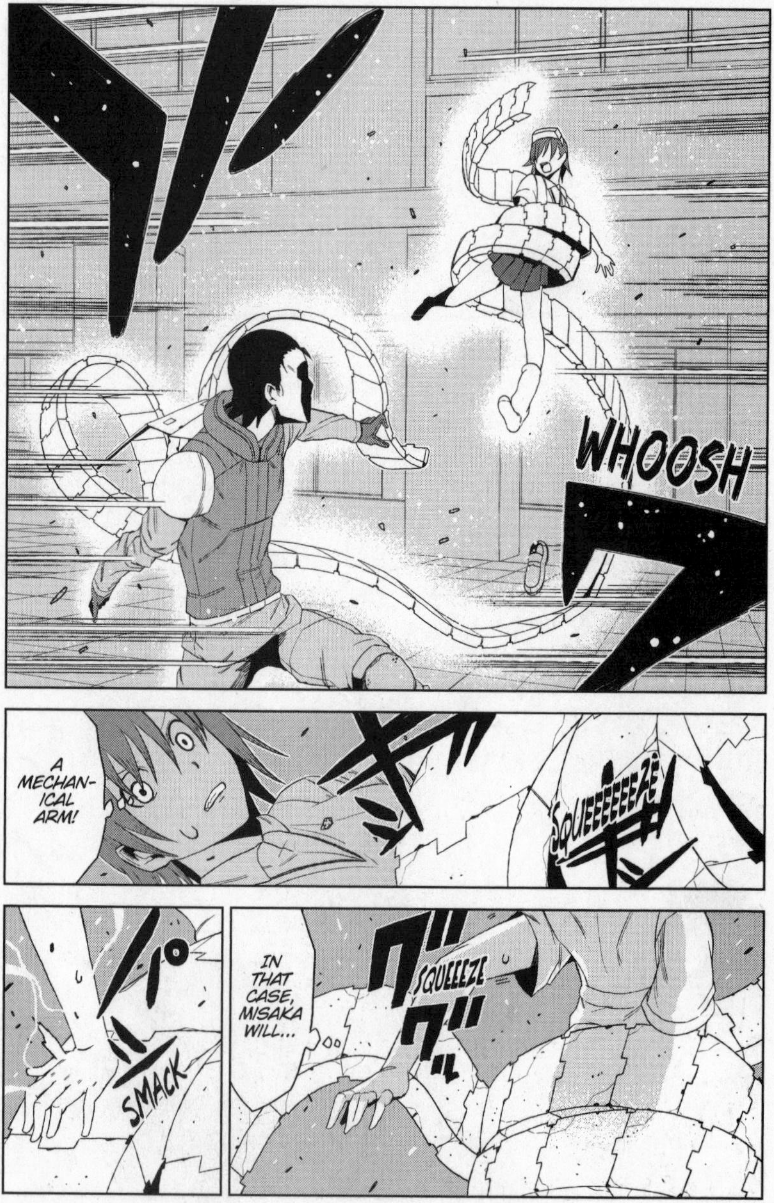
WHOOSH
SQUEEEEEEEZE
A MECHANICAL ARM!
IN THAT CASE, MISAKA WILL...
SQUEEEZE
SMACK

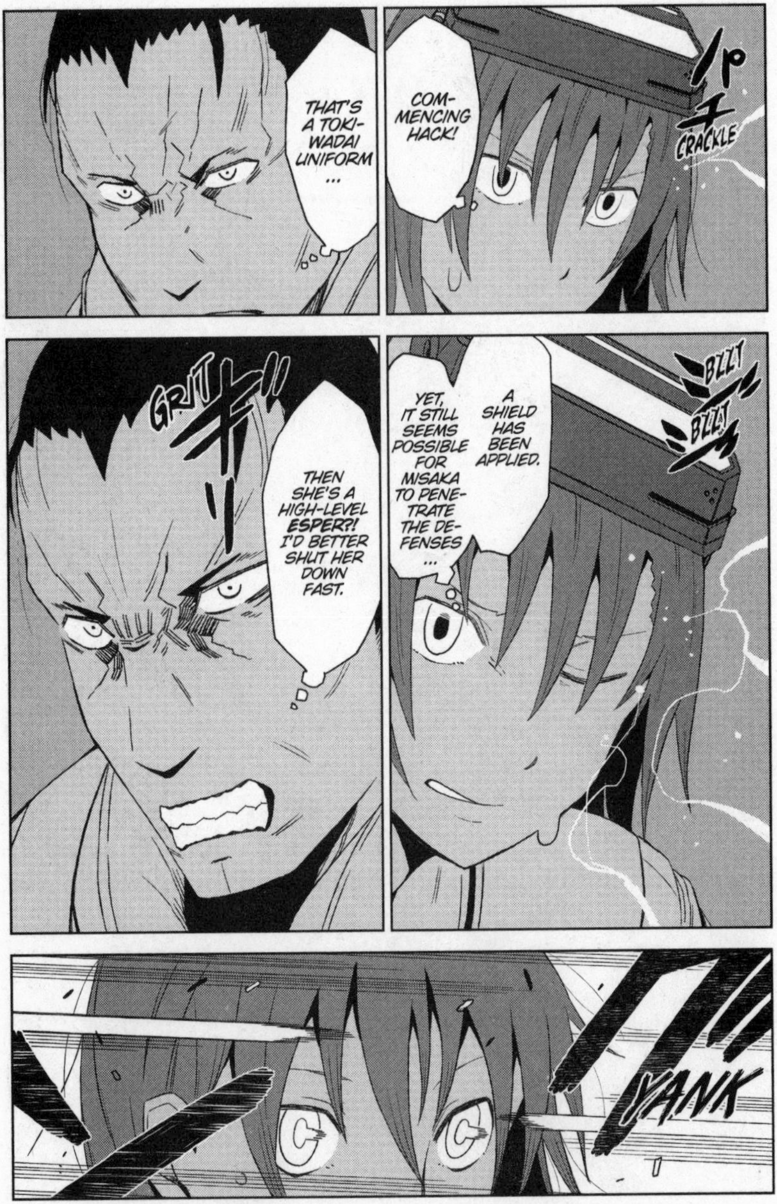
COMMENCING HACK!
CRACKLE
THAT'S A TOKIWADAI UNIFORM...
A SHIELD HAS BEEN APPLIED.
YET, IT STILL SEEMS POSSIBLE FOR MISAKA TO PENETRATE THE DEFENSES...
BZZT
BZZT
GRIT
THEN SHE'S A HIGH-LEVEL ESPER?! I'D BETTER SHUT HER DOWN FAST.
YANK

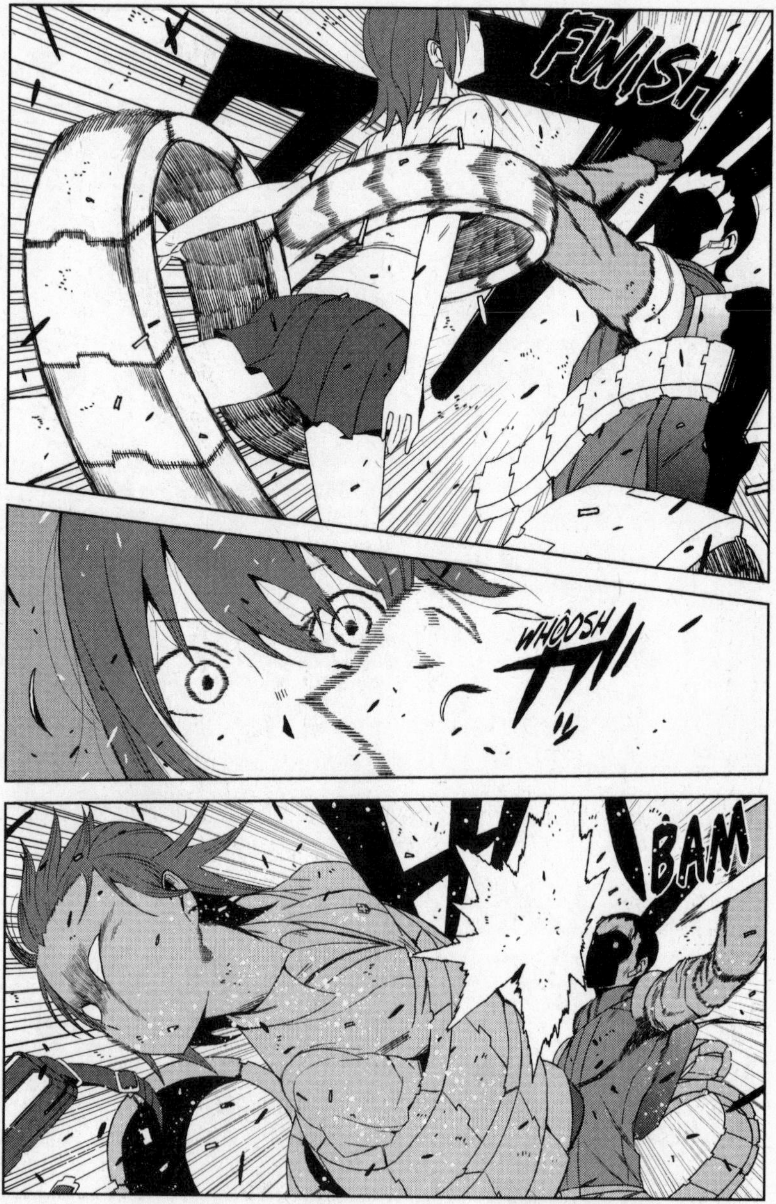
FWISH
WHOOSH
BAM

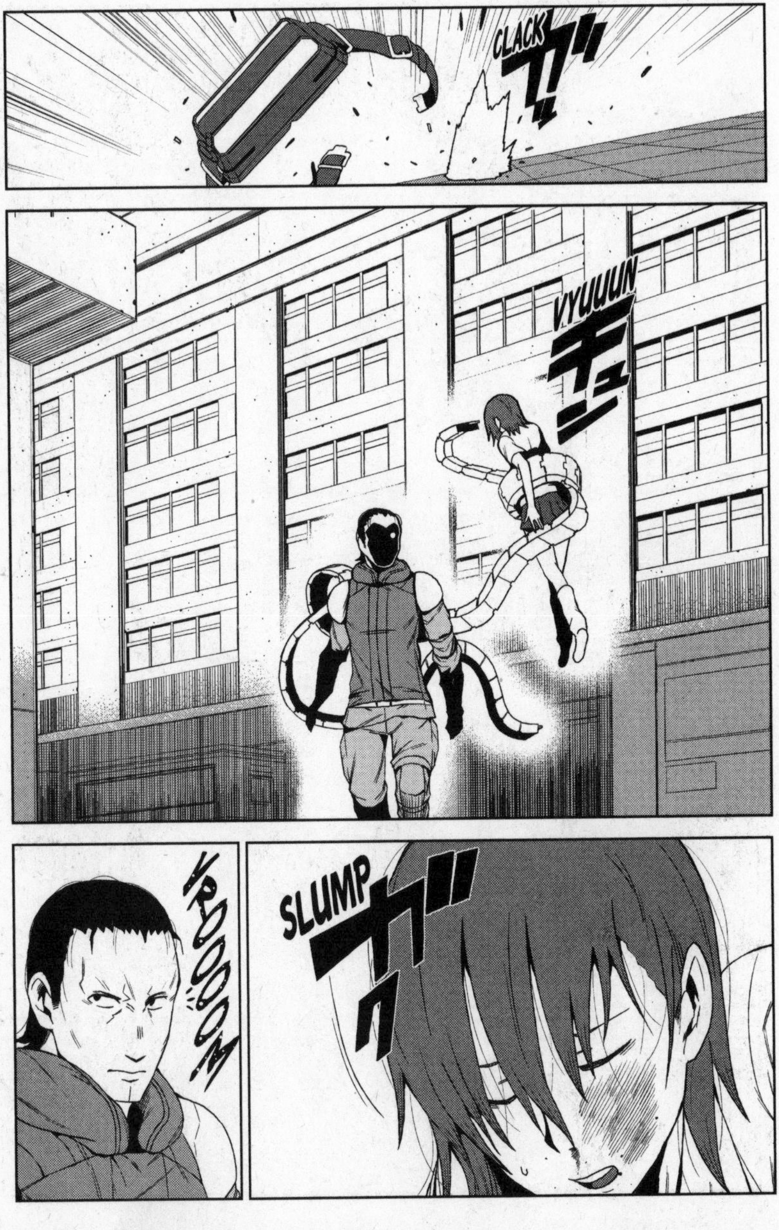
CLACK
VYUUUN
SLUMP
VROOOOM

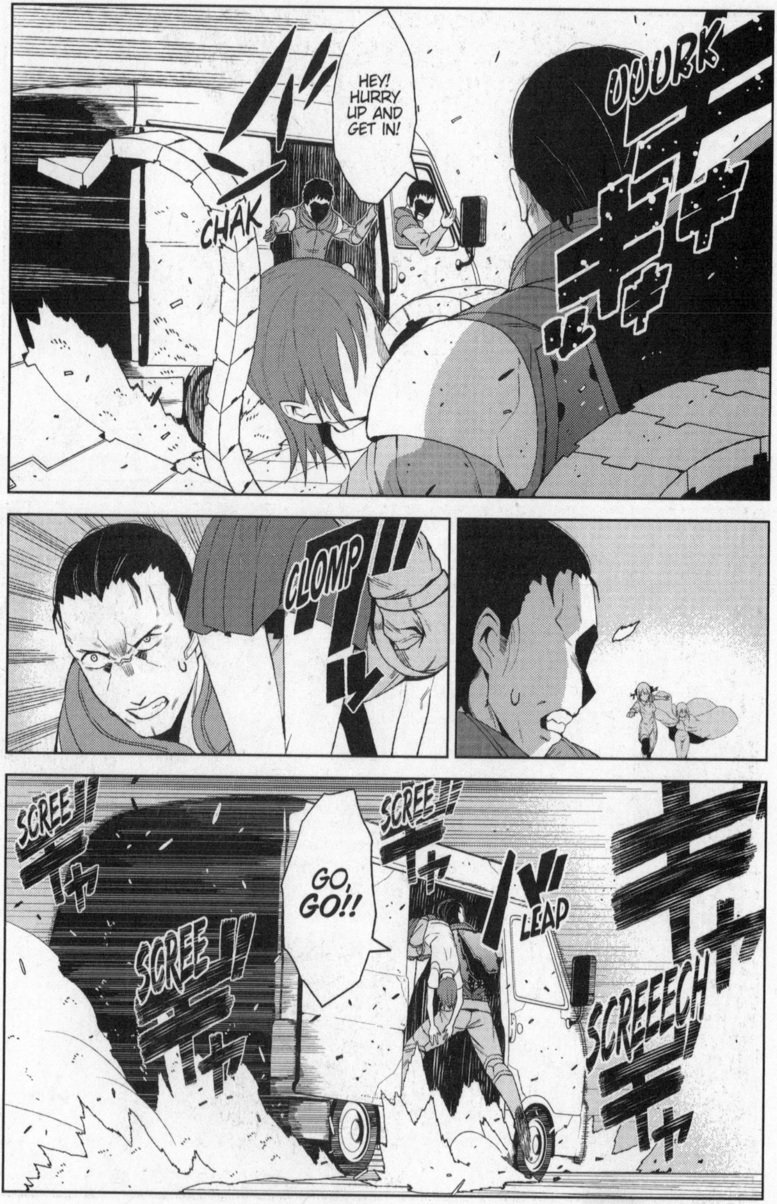

UUURK
HEY! HURRY UP AND GET IN!
CHAK
CLOMP
SCREEECH
LEAP
SCREE
GO, GO!!
SCREE
SCREE

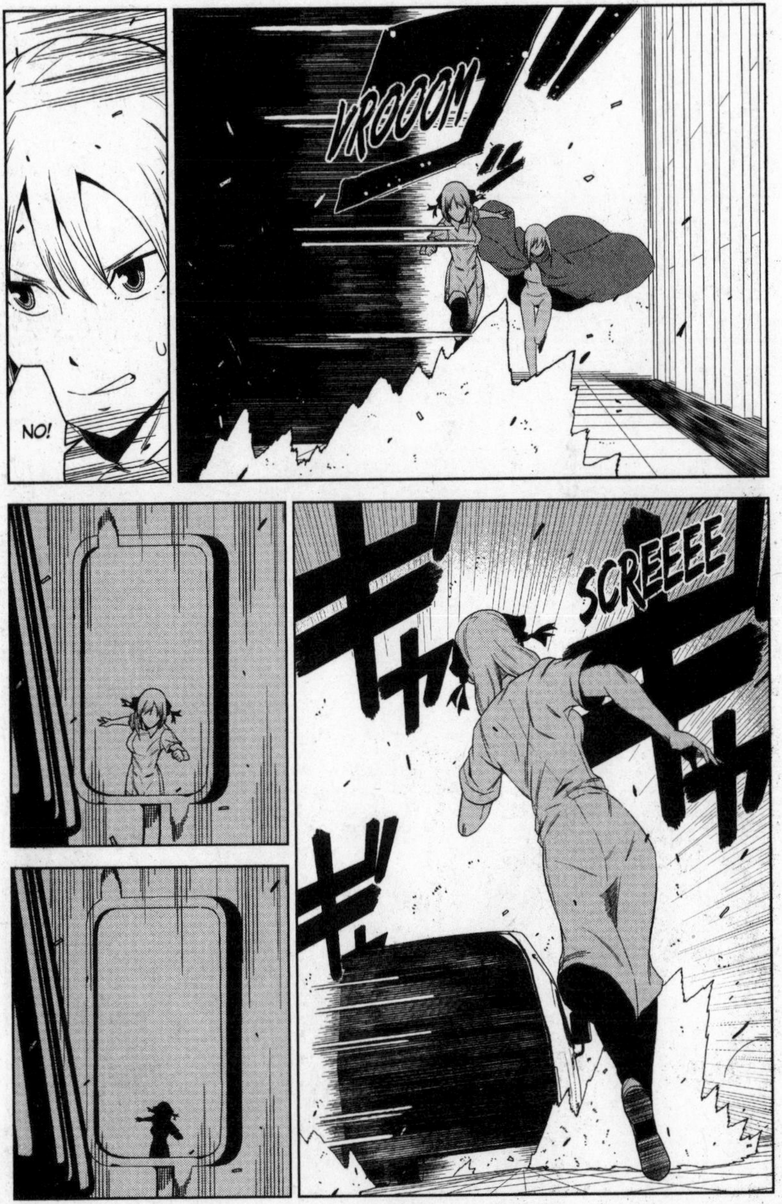
VROOOM
NO!
SCREEEE

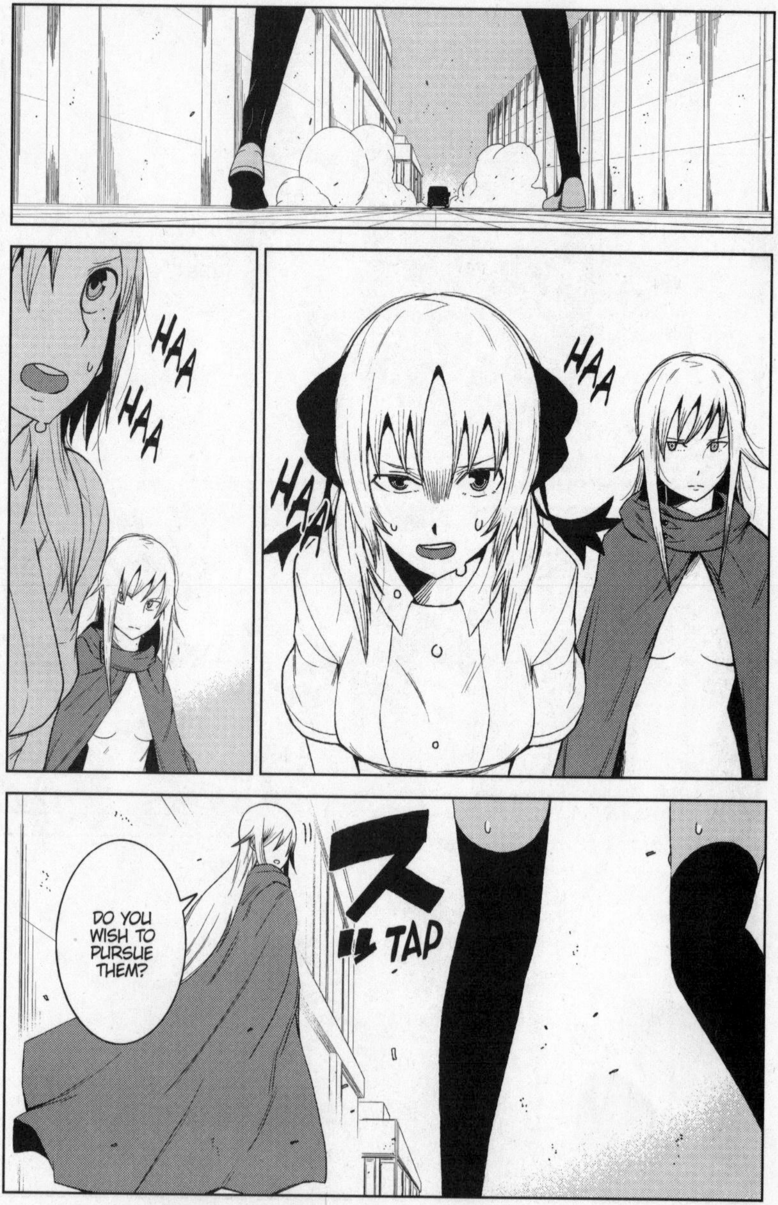
HAA
HAA
HAA
HAA
ス
TAP
DO YOU WISH TO PURSUE THEM?

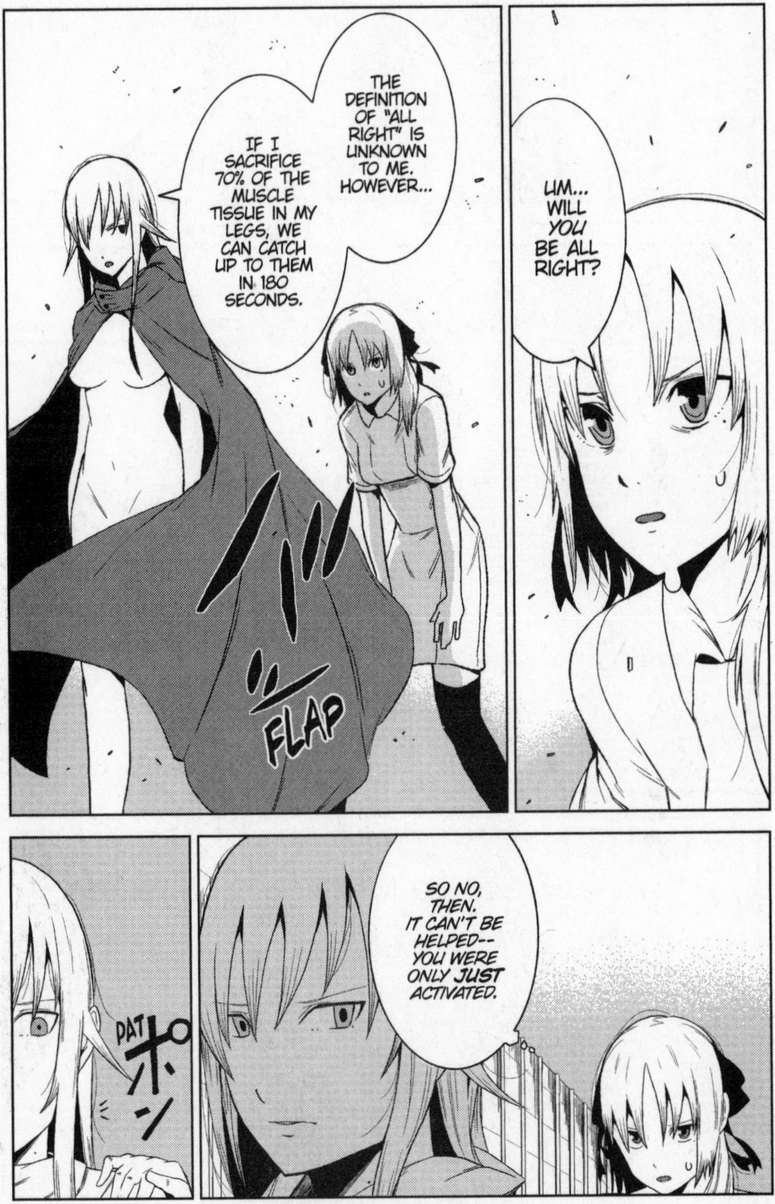
UM... WILL YOU BE ALL RIGHT?
THE DEFINITION OF "ALL RIGHT" IS UNKNOWN TO ME. HOWEVER...
IF I SACRIFICE 70% OF THE MUSCLE TISSUE IN MY LEGS, WE CAN CATCH UP TO THEM IN 180 SECONDS.
FLAP
SO NO, THEN. IT CAN'T BE HELPED-- YOU WERE ONLY JUST ACTIVATED.
PAT

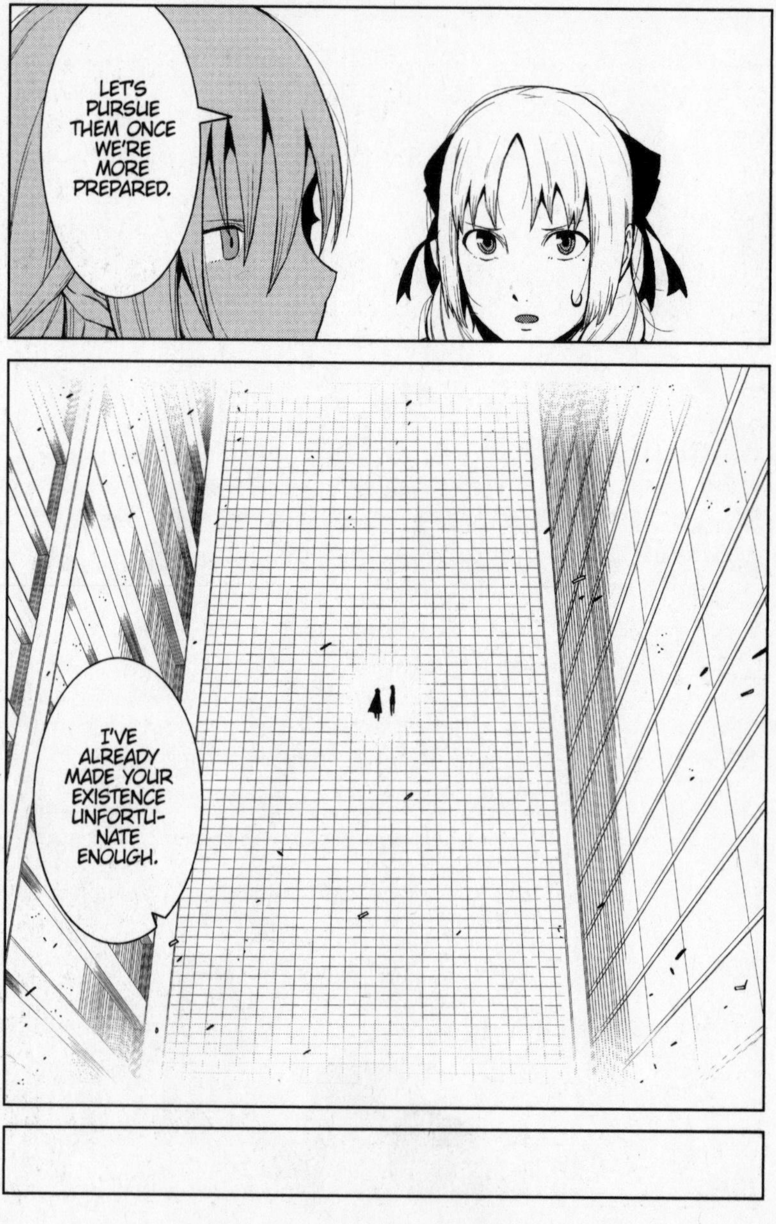
LET'S PURSUE THEM ONCE WE'RE MORE PREPARED.
I'VE ALREADY MADE YOUR EXISTENCE UNFORTU-NATE ENOUGH.

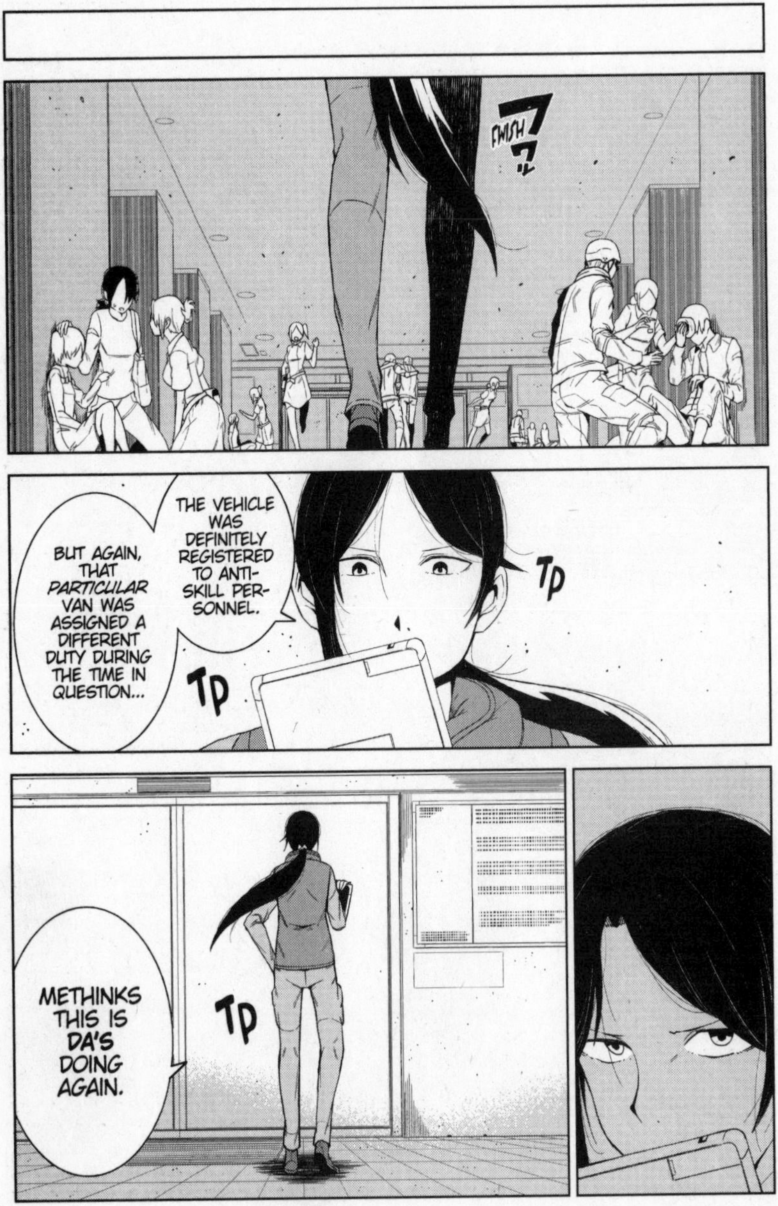
FWISH
THE VEHICLE WAS DEFINITELY REGISTERED TO ANTI-SKILL PER-SONNEL.
BUT AGAIN, THAT *PARTICULAR* VAN WAS ASSIGNED A DIFFERENT DUTY DURING THE TIME IN QUESTION...
Tp
Tp
Tp
METHINKS THIS IS **DA'S** DOING AGAIN.

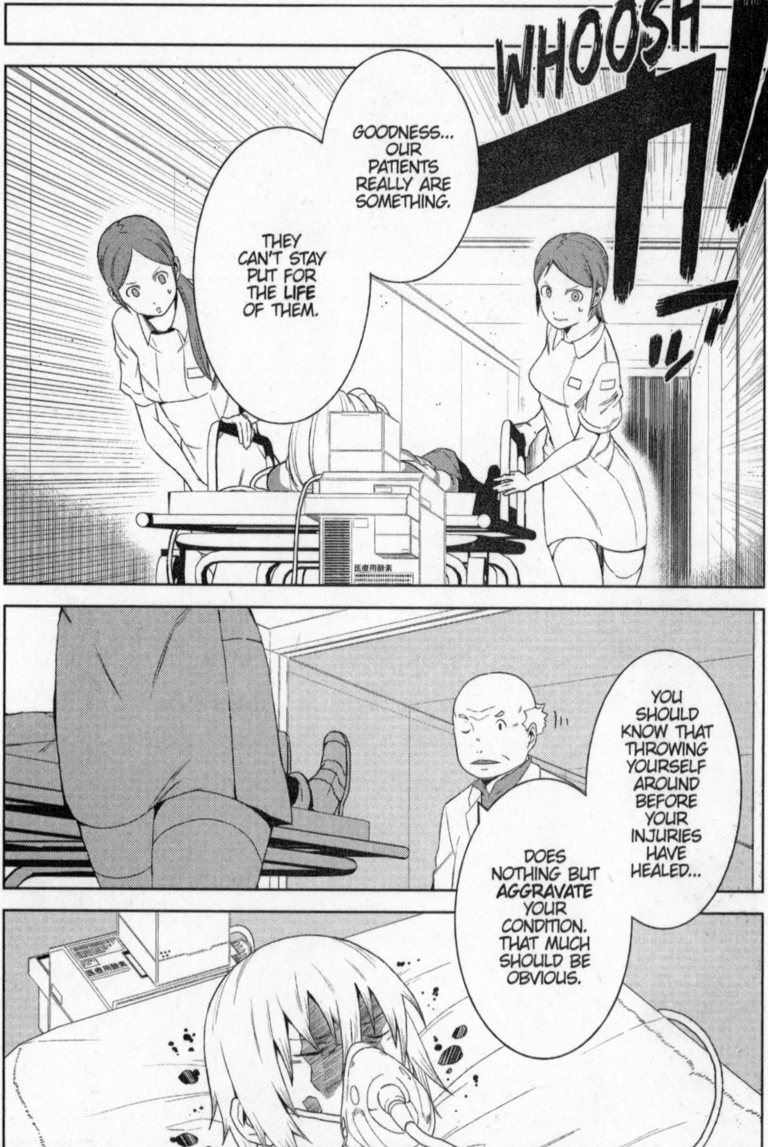
WHOOSH
GOODNESS... OUR PATIENTS REALLY ARE SOMETHING.
THEY CAN'T STAY PUT FOR THE LIFE OF THEM.
医療用酸素
YOU SHOULD KNOW THAT THROWING YOURSELF AROUND BEFORE YOUR INJURIES HAVE HEALED...
DOES NOTHING BUT AGGRAVATE YOUR CONDITION. THAT MUCH SHOULD BE OBVIOUS.

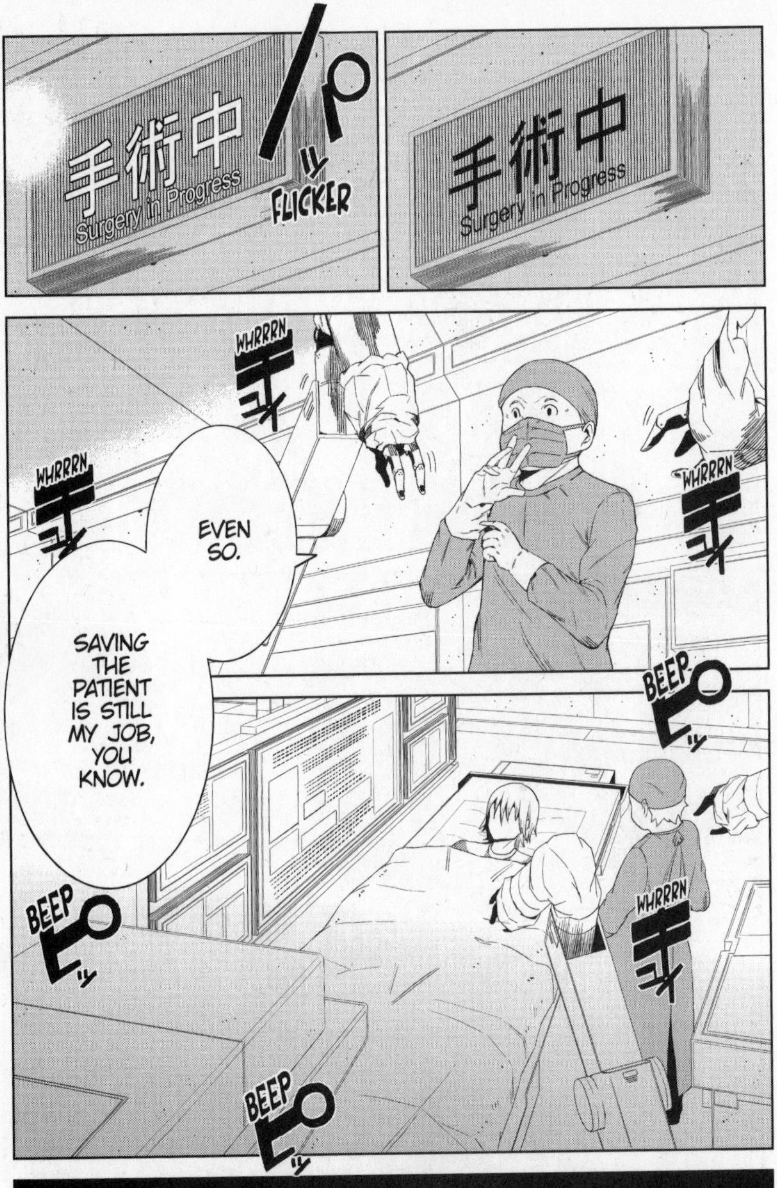
手術中
Surgery in Progress
手術中
Surgery in Progress
FLICKER
WHRRRN
WHRRRN
WHRRRN
EVEN SO.
SAVING THE PATIENT IS STILL MY JOB, YOU KNOW.
BEEP
WHRRRN
BEEP
BEEP

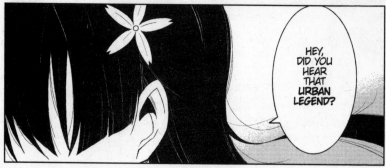

HEY, DID YOU HEAR THAT URBAN LEGEND?

NOT MORE URBAN LEGENDS, PLEASE~!

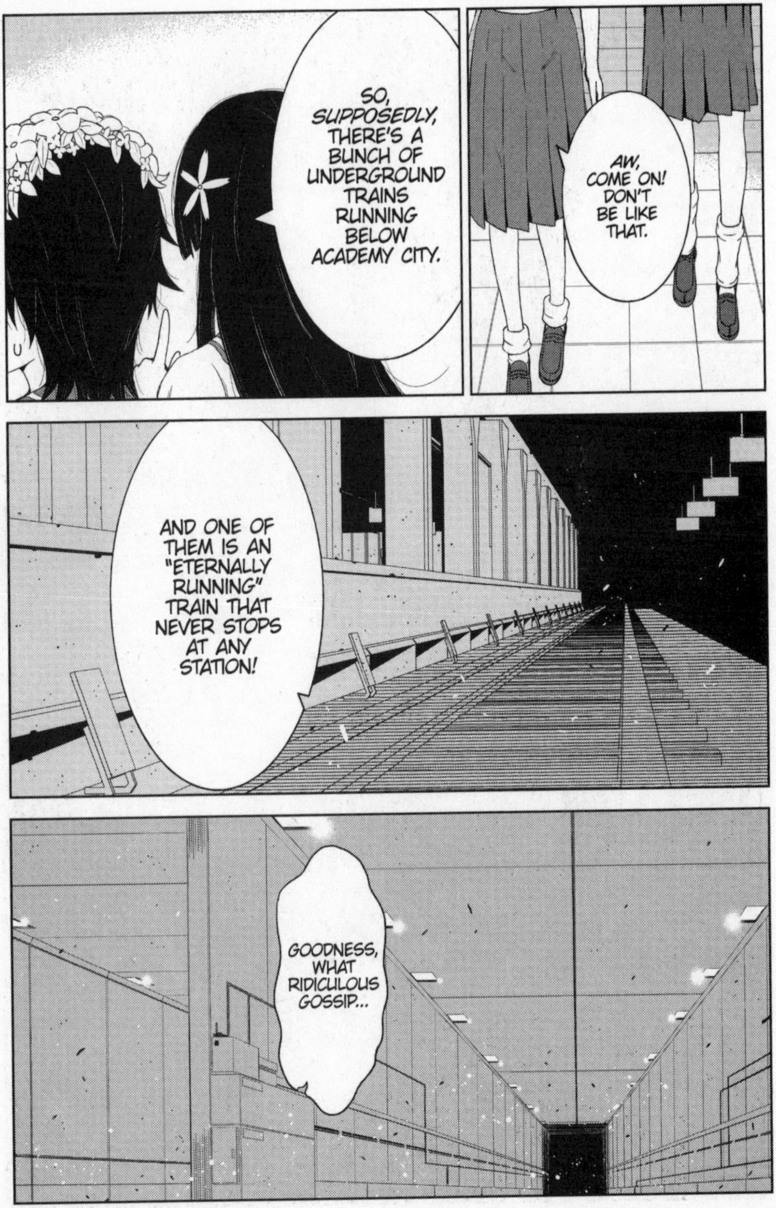
AW, COME ON! DON'T BE LIKE THAT.
SO, SUPPOSEDLY, THERE'S A BUNCH OF UNDERGROUND TRAINS RUNNING BELOW ACADEMY CITY.
AND ONE OF THEM IS AN "ETERNALLY RUNNING" TRAIN THAT NEVER STOPS AT ANY STATION!
GOODNESS, WHAT RIDICULOUS GOSSIP...

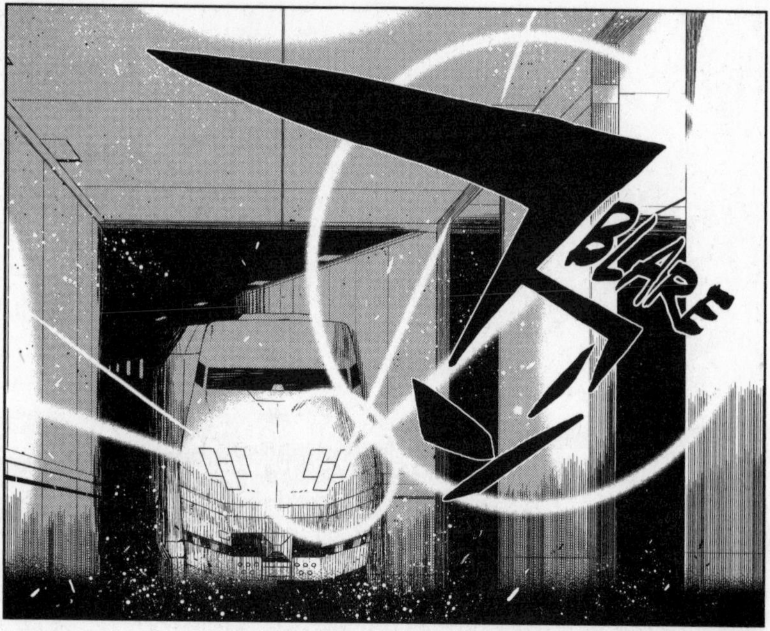
BLARE

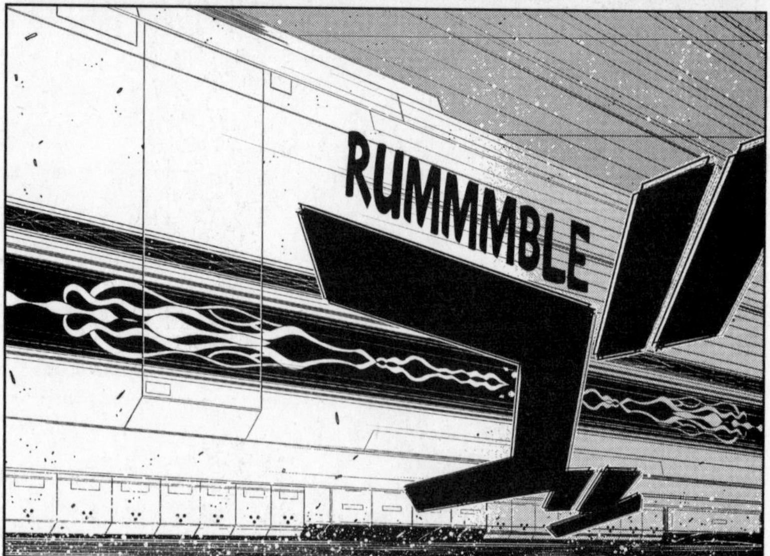
RUMMMBLE

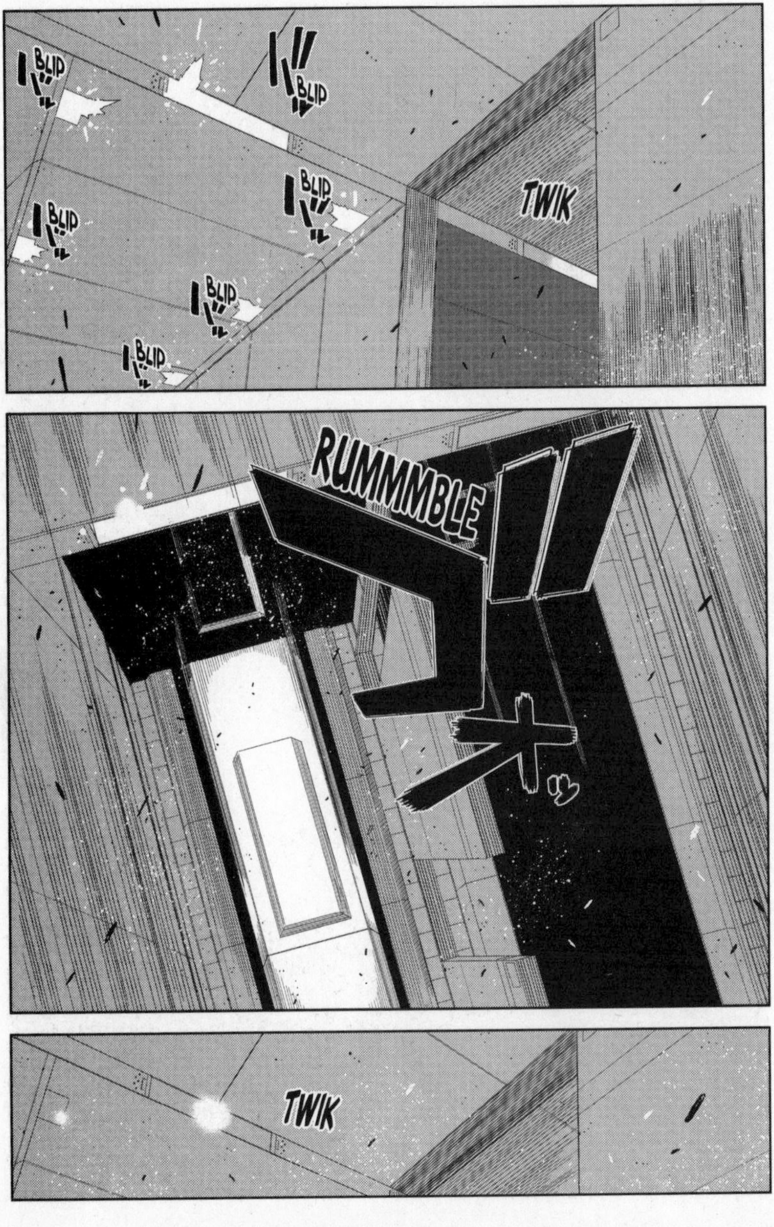
TWIK
BLIP
BLIP
BLIP
BLIP
BLIP
BLIP
RUMMMBLE
TWIK

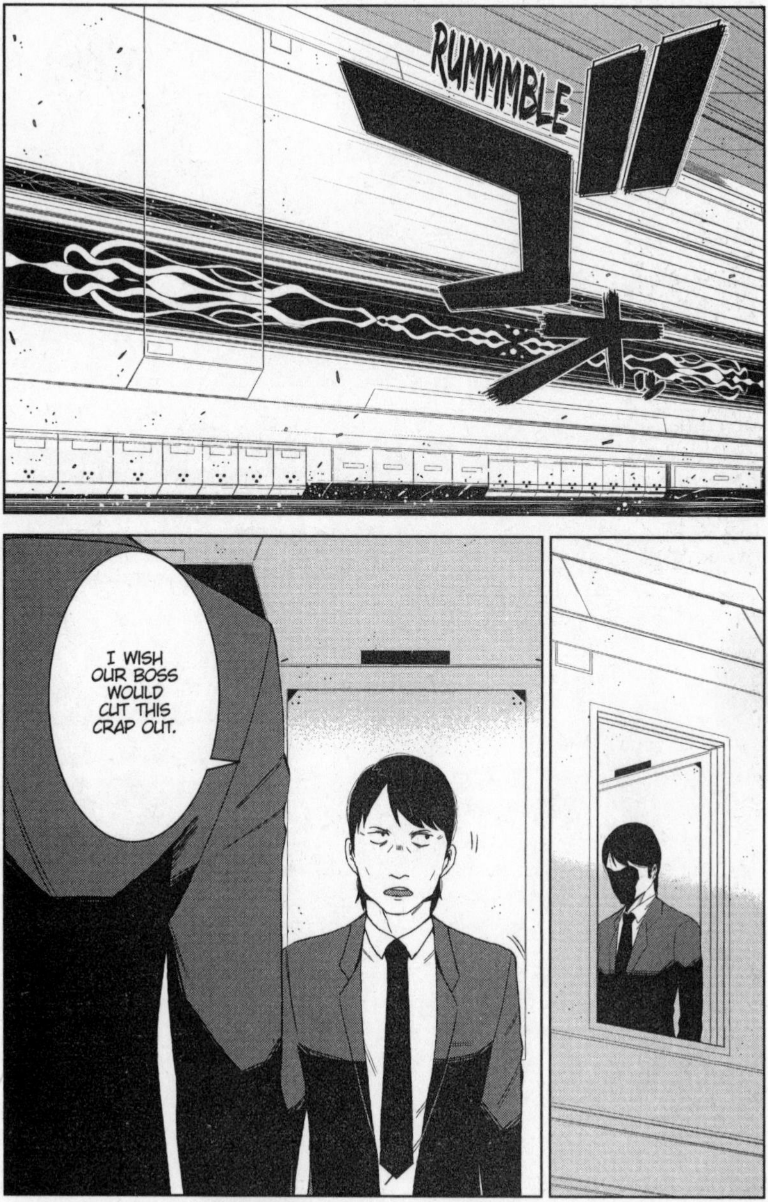
RUMMMBLE
I WISH OUR BOSS WOULD CUT THIS CRAP OUT.

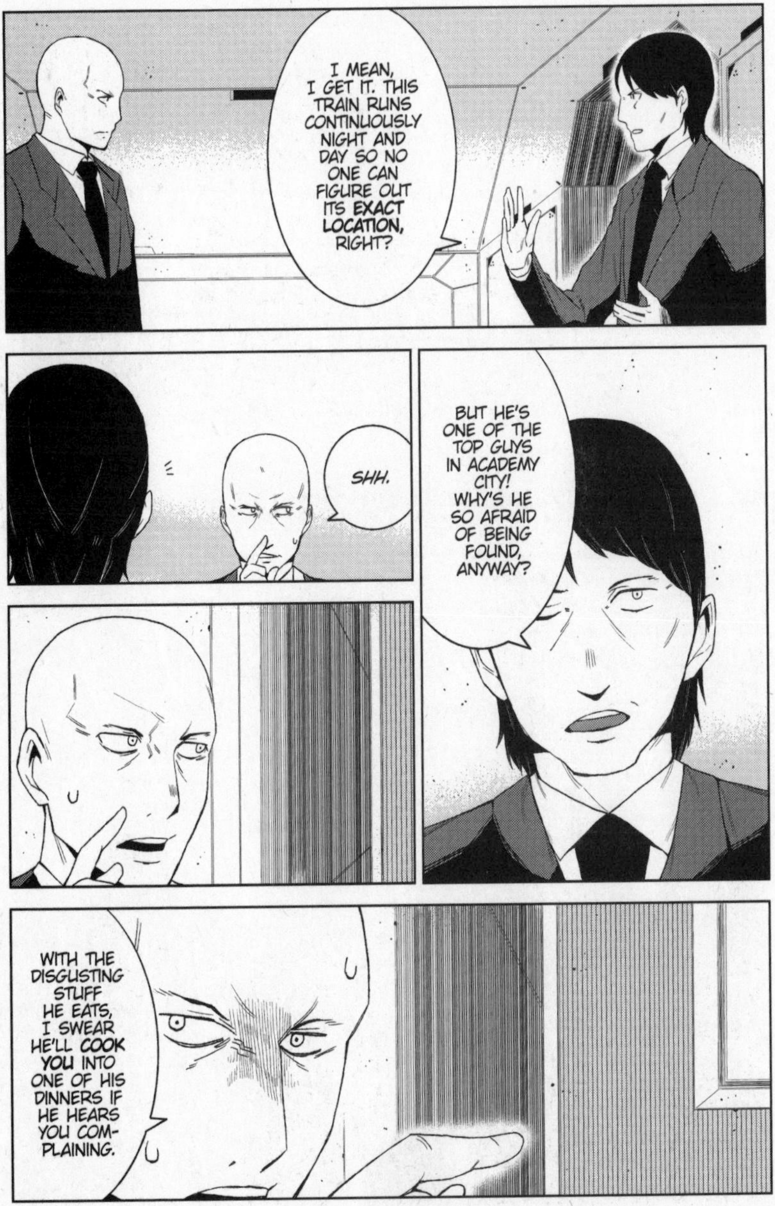
I MEAN, I GET IT. THIS TRAIN RUNS CONTINUOUSLY NIGHT AND DAY SO NO ONE CAN FIGURE OUT ITS EXACT LOCATION, RIGHT?
BUT HE'S ONE OF THE TOP GUYS IN ACADEMY CITY! WHY'S HE SO AFRAID OF BEING FOUND, ANYWAY?
SHH.
WITH THE DISGUSTING STUFF HE EATS, I SWEAR HE'LL COOK YOU INTO ONE OF HIS DINNERS IF HE HEARS YOU COMPLAINING.

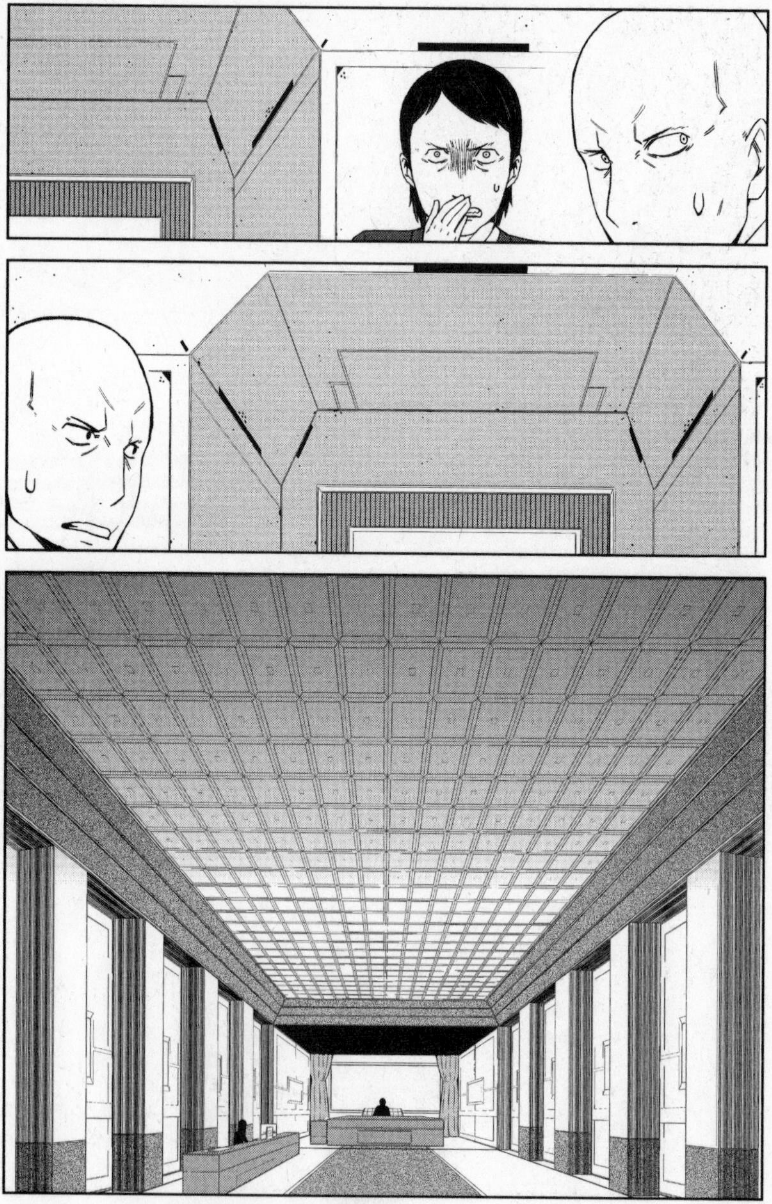

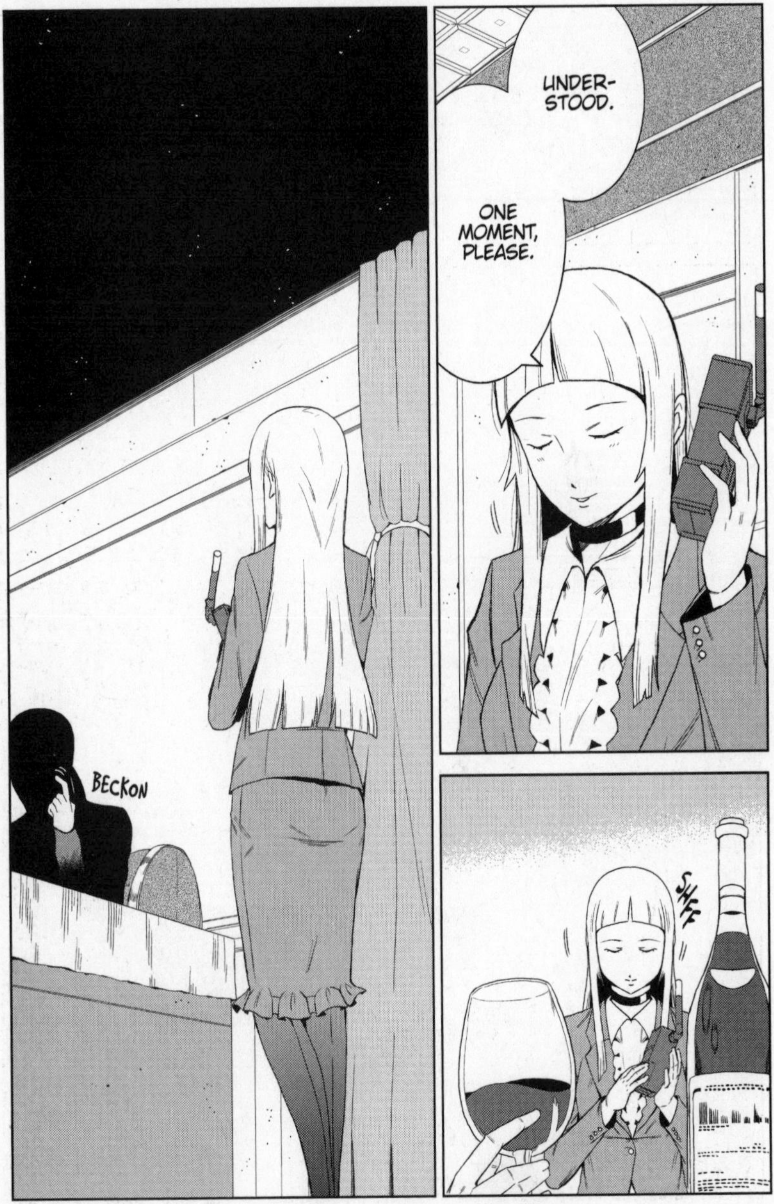
UNDER-
STOOD.
ONE
MOMENT,
PLEASE.
SHFF
BECKON

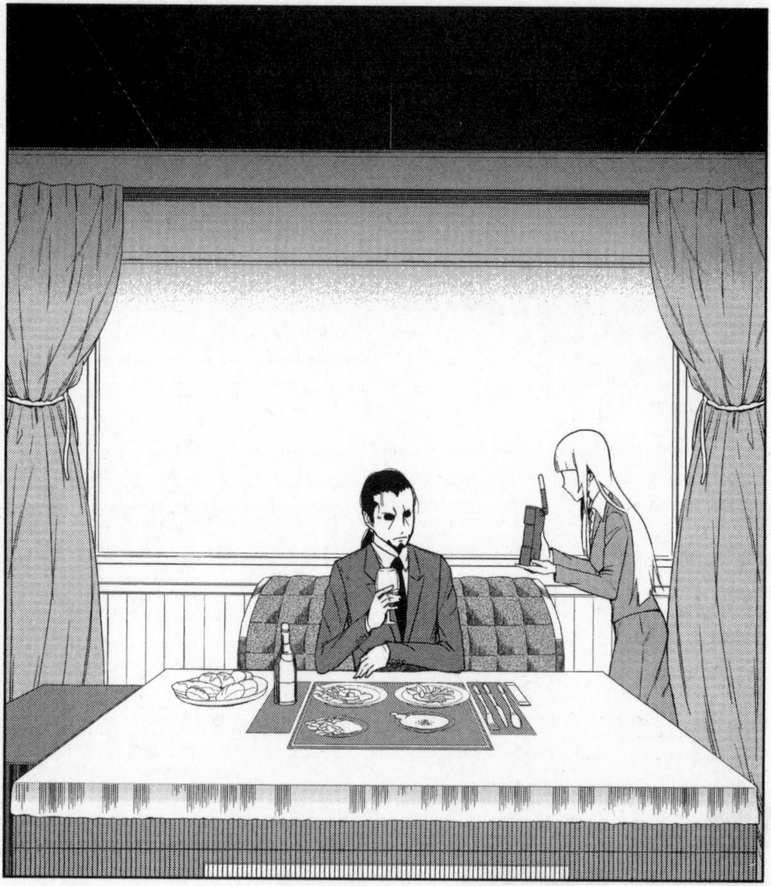
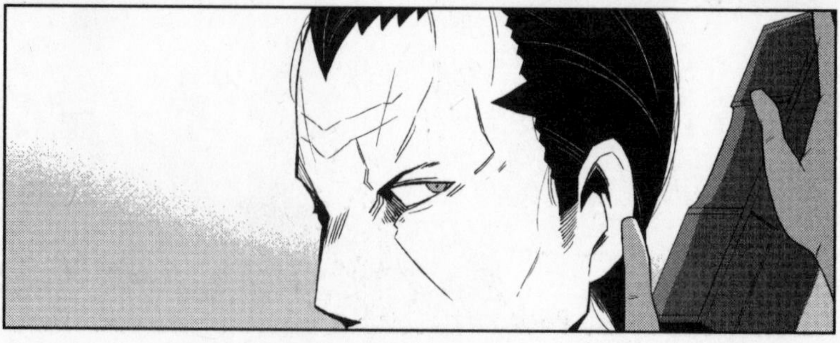

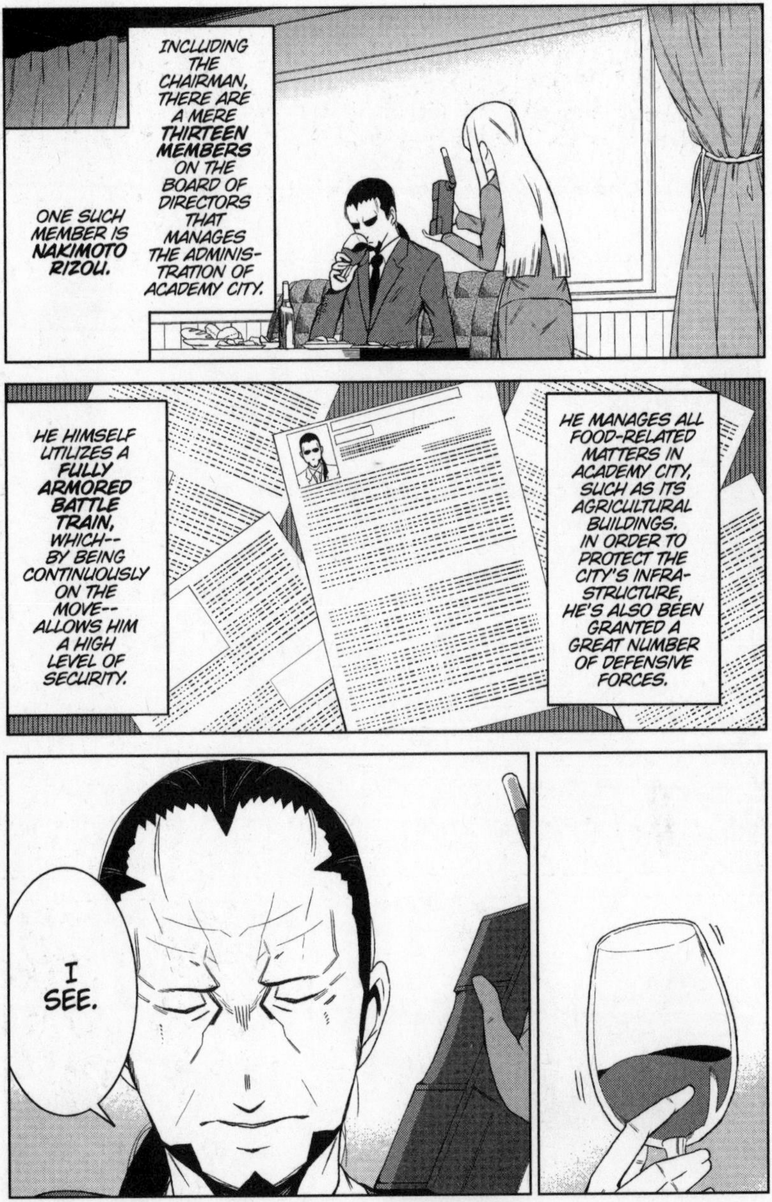
INCLUDING THE CHAIRMAN, THERE ARE A MERE THIRTEEN MEMBERS ON THE BOARD OF DIRECTORS THAT MANAGES THE ADMINISTRATION OF ACADEMY CITY.
ONE SUCH MEMBER IS NAKIMOTO RIZOU.
HE MANAGES ALL FOOD-RELATED MATTERS IN ACADEMY CITY, SUCH AS ITS AGRICULTURAL BUILDINGS. IN ORDER TO PROTECT THE CITY'S INFRASTRUCTURE, HE'S ALSO BEEN GRANTED A GREAT NUMBER OF DEFENSIVE FORCES.
HE HIMSELF UTILIZES A FULLY ARMORED BATTLE TRAIN, WHICH--BY BEING CONTINUOUSLY ON THE MOVE--ALLOWS HIM A HIGH LEVEL OF SECURITY.
I SEE.

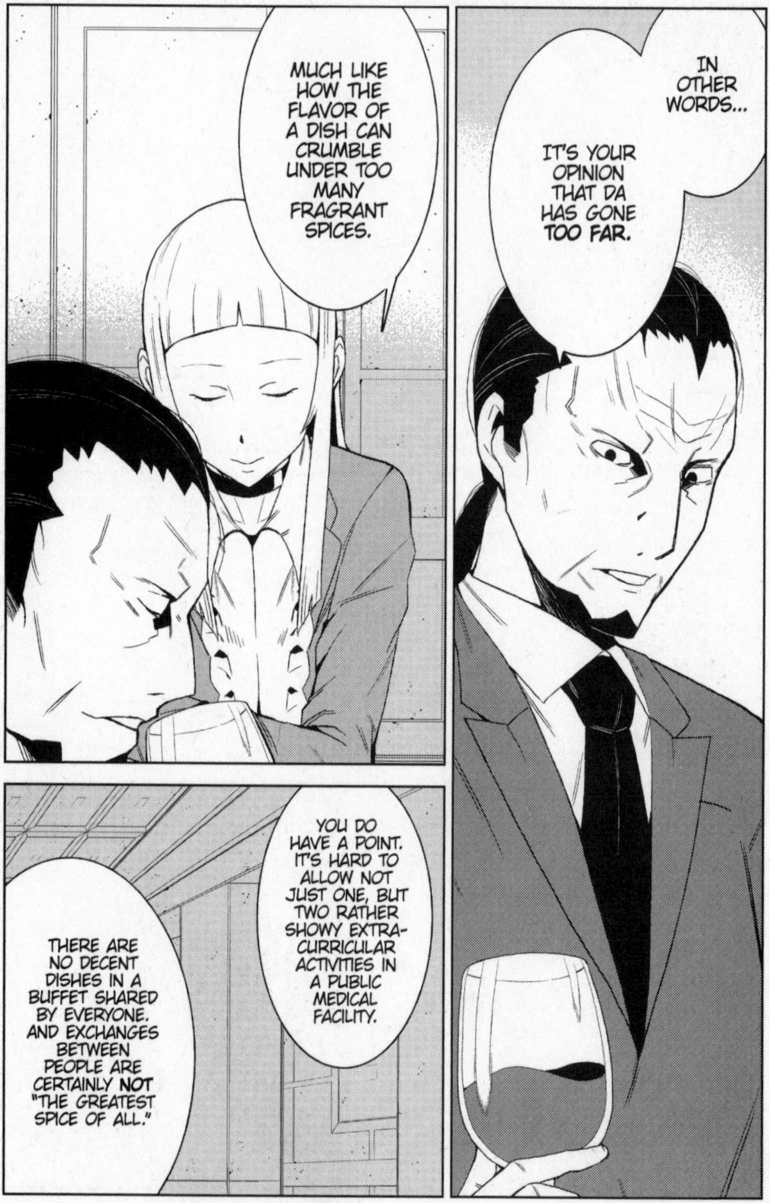
IN OTHER WORDS...
IT'S YOUR OPINION THAT DA HAS GONE TOO FAR.
MUCH LIKE HOW THE FLAVOR OF A DISH CAN CRUMBLE UNDER TOO MANY FRAGRANT SPICES.
YOU DO HAVE A POINT. IT'S HARD TO ALLOW NOT JUST ONE, BUT TWO RATHER SHOWY EXTRA-CURRICULAR ACTIVITIES IN A PUBLIC MEDICAL FACILITY.
THERE ARE NO DECENT DISHES IN A BUFFET SHARED BY EVERYONE. AND EXCHANGES BETWEEN PEOPLE ARE CERTAINLY NOT "THE GREATEST SPICE OF ALL."

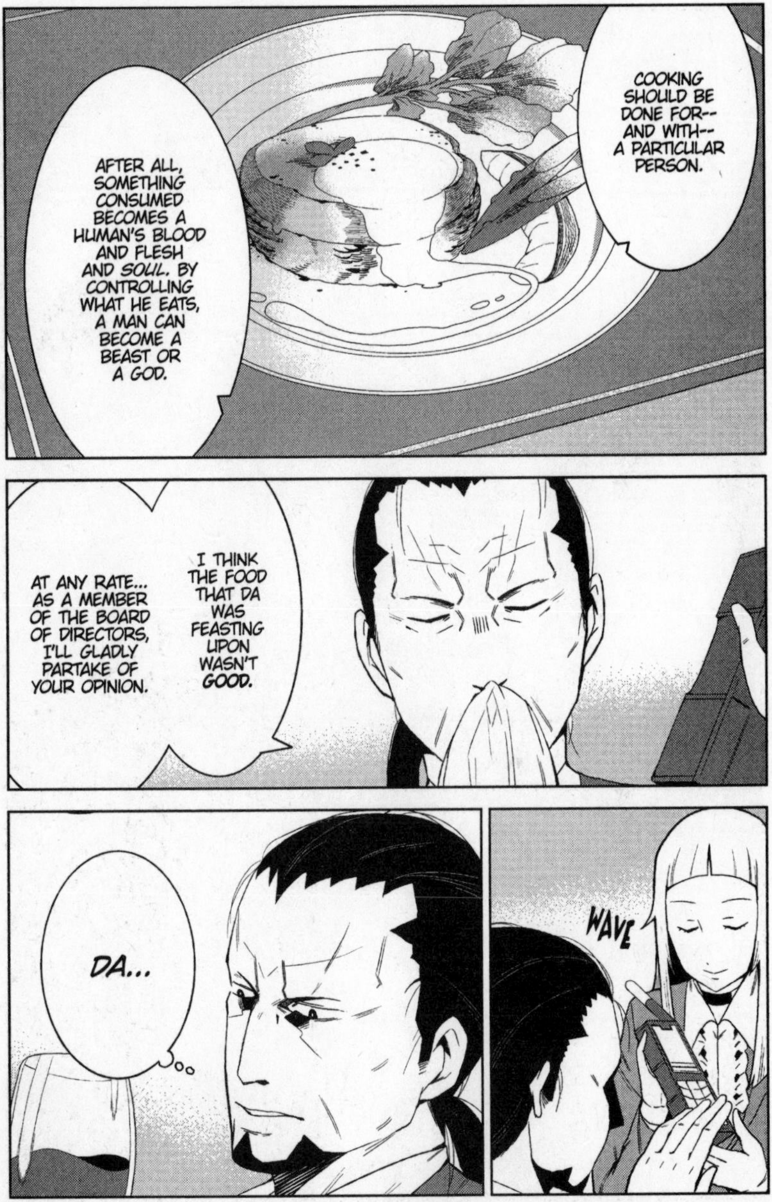
COOKING SHOULD BE DONE FOR-- AND WITH-- A PARTICULAR PERSON.
AFTER ALL, SOMETHING CONSUMED BECOMES A HUMAN'S BLOOD AND FLESH AND *SOUL*. BY CONTROLLING WHAT HE EATS, A MAN CAN BECOME A BEAST OR A GOD.
I THINK THE FOOD THAT DA WAS FEASTING UPON WASN'T GOOD.
AT ANY RATE... AS A MEMBER OF THE BOARD OF DIRECTORS, I'LL GLADLY PARTAKE OF YOUR OPINION.
WAVE
DA...

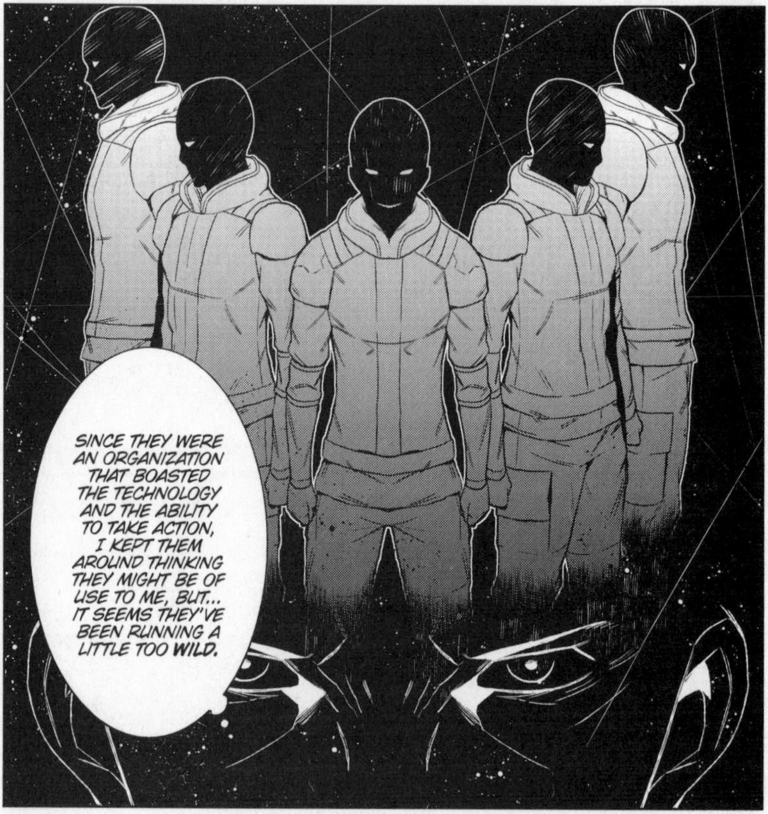
SINCE THEY WERE AN ORGANIZATION THAT BOASTED THE TECHNOLOGY AND THE ABILITY TO TAKE ACTION, I KEPT THEM AROUND THINKING THEY MIGHT BE OF USE TO ME, BUT... IT SEEMS THEY'VE BEEN RUNNING A LITTLE TOO WILD.

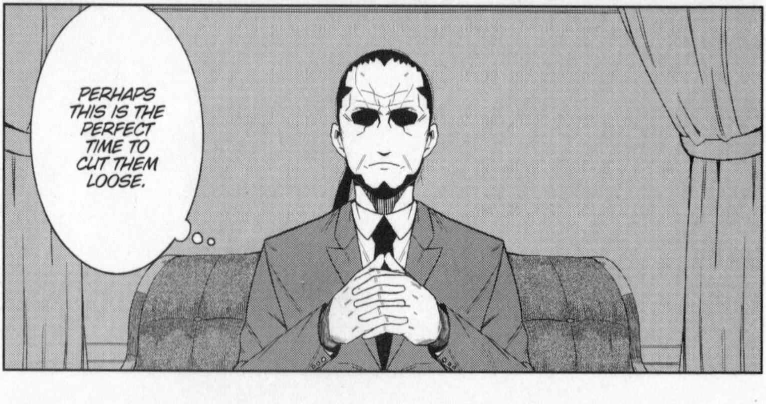
PERHAPS THIS IS THE PERFECT TIME TO CUT THEM LOOSE.

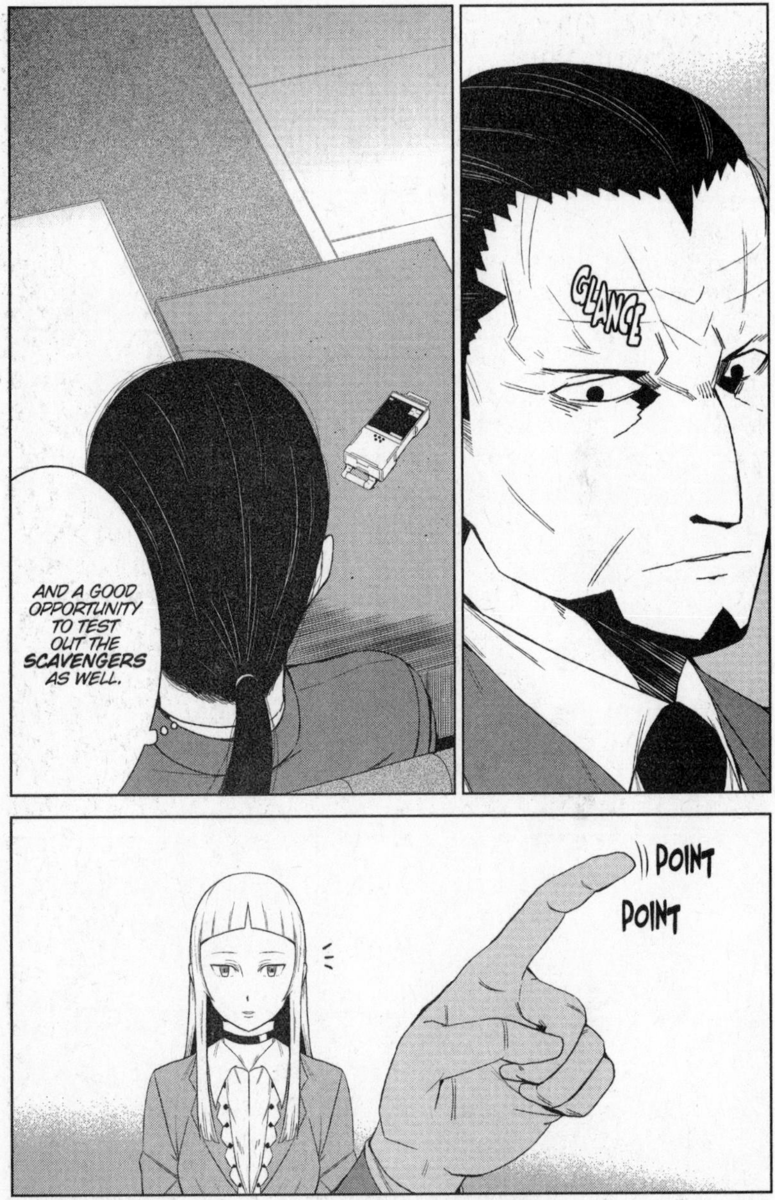
GLANCE
AND A GOOD OPPORTUNITY TO TEST OUT THE SCAVENGERS AS WELL.
POINT
POINT

*A doctor of food medicine, i.e. a nutritionist.

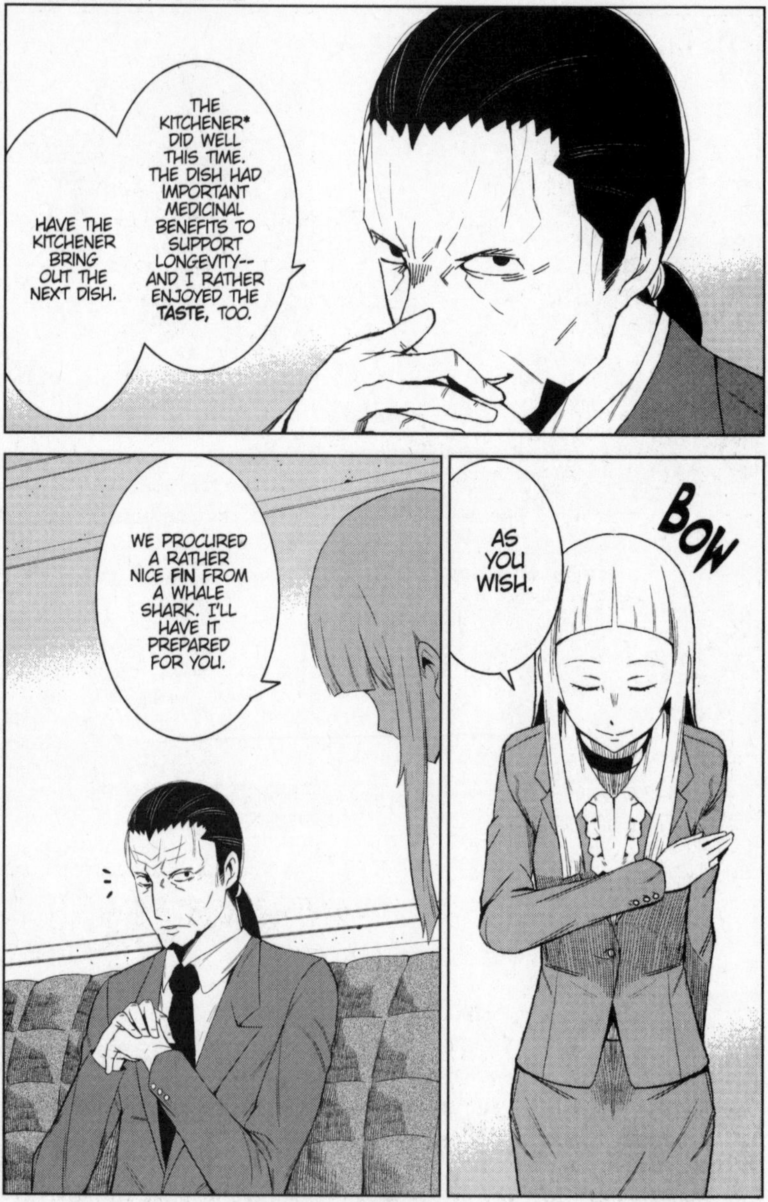
THE KITCHENER* DID WELL THIS TIME. THE DISH HAD IMPORTANT MEDICINAL BENEFITS TO SUPPORT LONGEVITY-- AND I RATHER ENJOYED THE TASTE, TOO.
HAVE THE KITCHENER BRING OUT THE NEXT DISH.
AS YOU WISH.
BOW
WE PROCURED A RATHER NICE FIN FROM A WHALE SHARK. I'LL HAVE IT PREPARED FOR YOU.

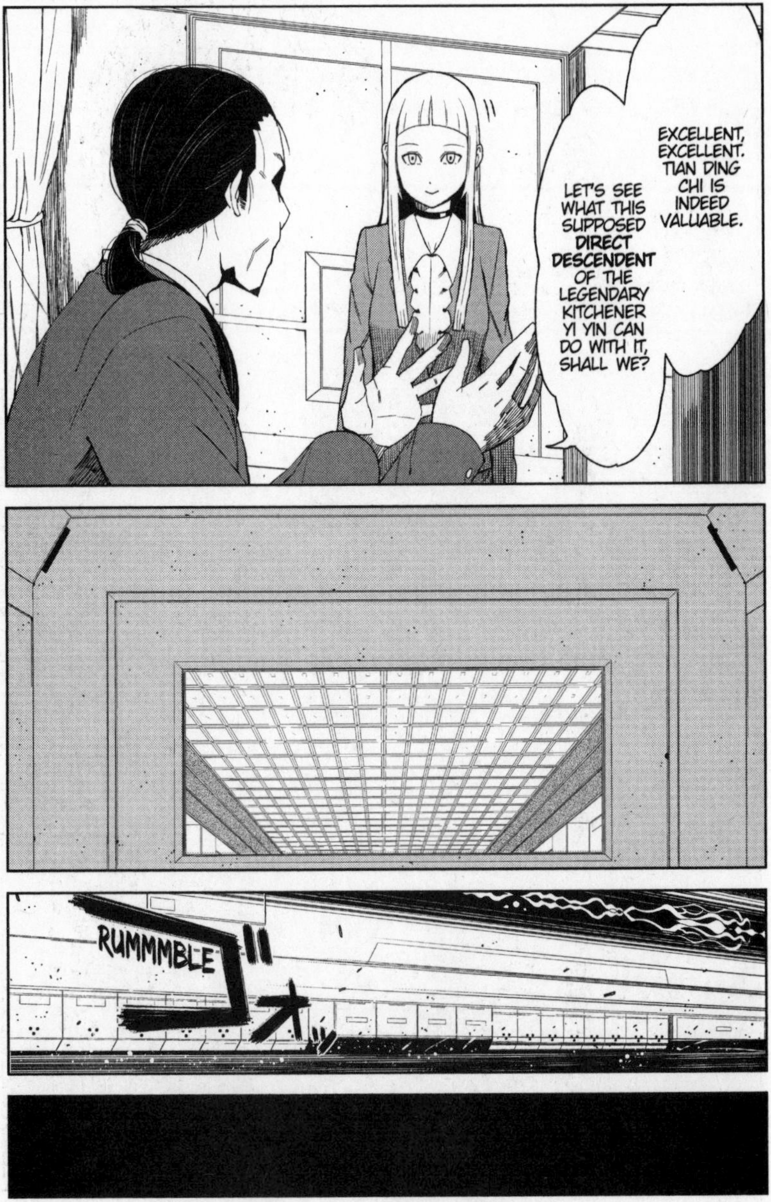
EXCELLENT, EXCELLENT. TIAN DING CHI IS INDEED VALUABLE.
LET'S SEE WHAT THIS SUPPOSED DIRECT DESCENDENT OF THE LEGENDARY KITCHENER YI YIN CAN DO WITH IT, SHALL WE?
RUMMMBLE

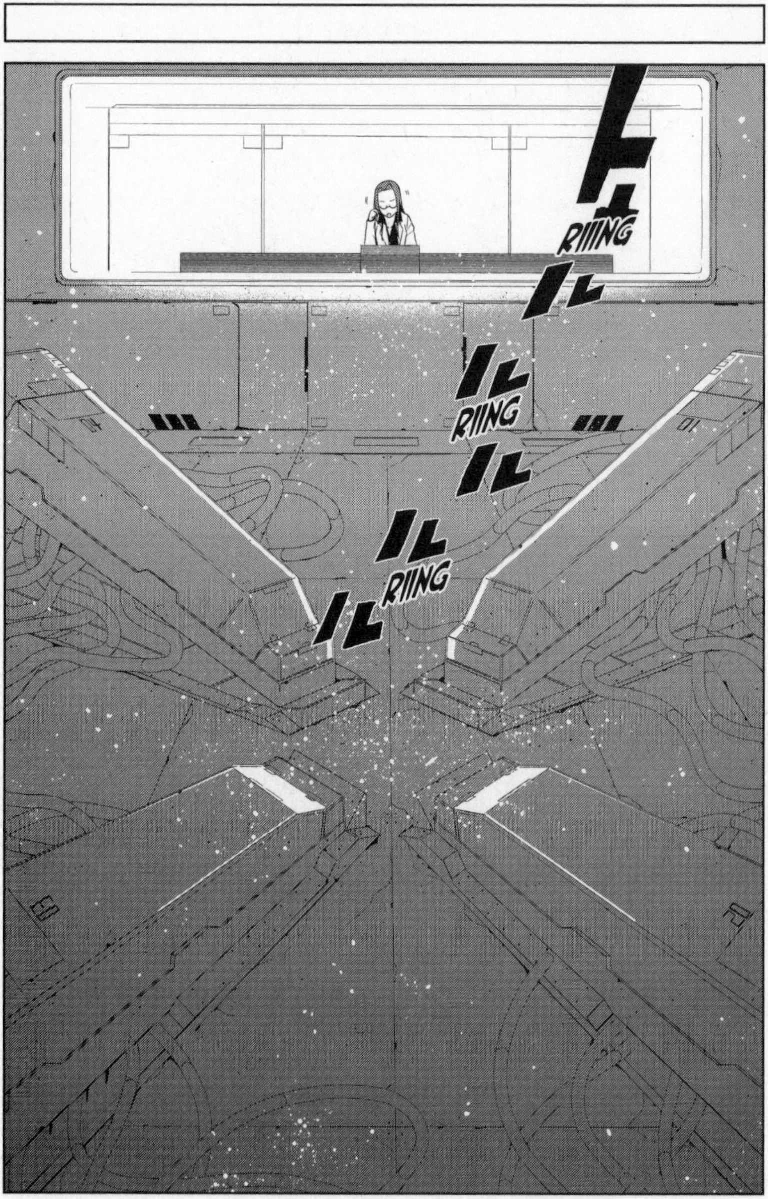
RIIING
RIIING
RIIING

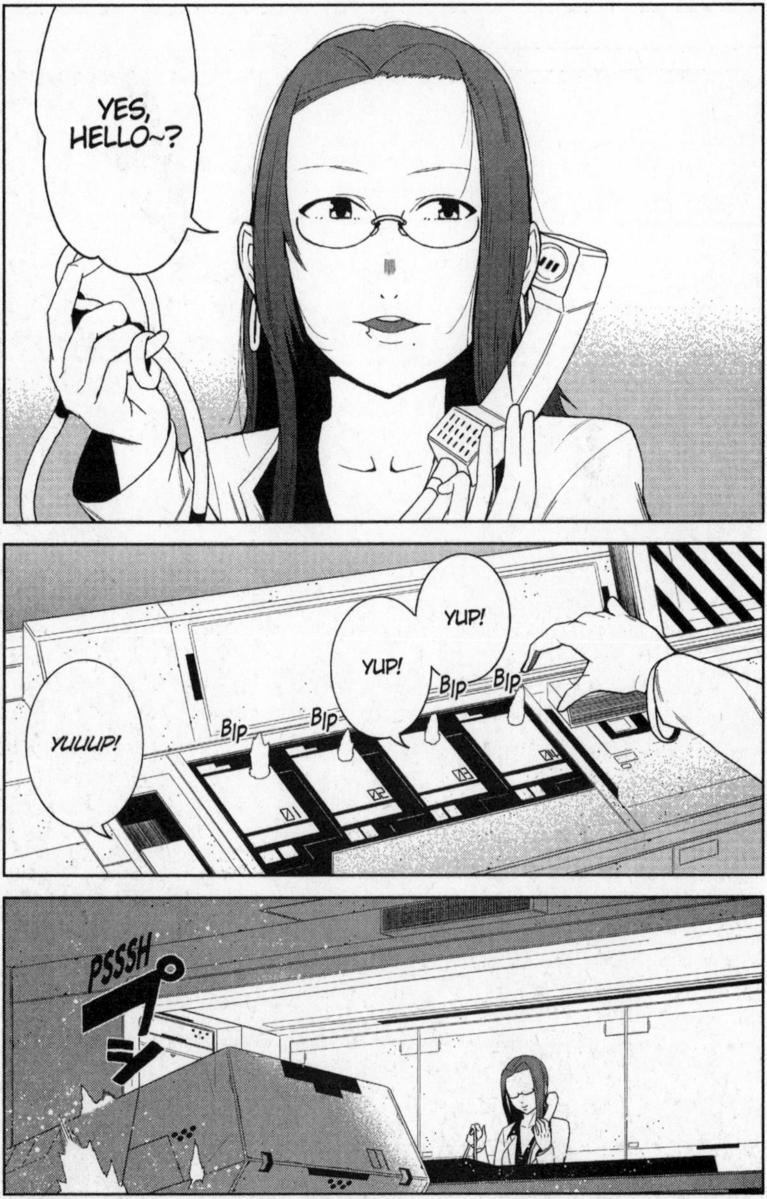
YES, HELLO~?
YUP!
YUP!
BIP BIP BIP BIP
YUUUP!
PSSSH

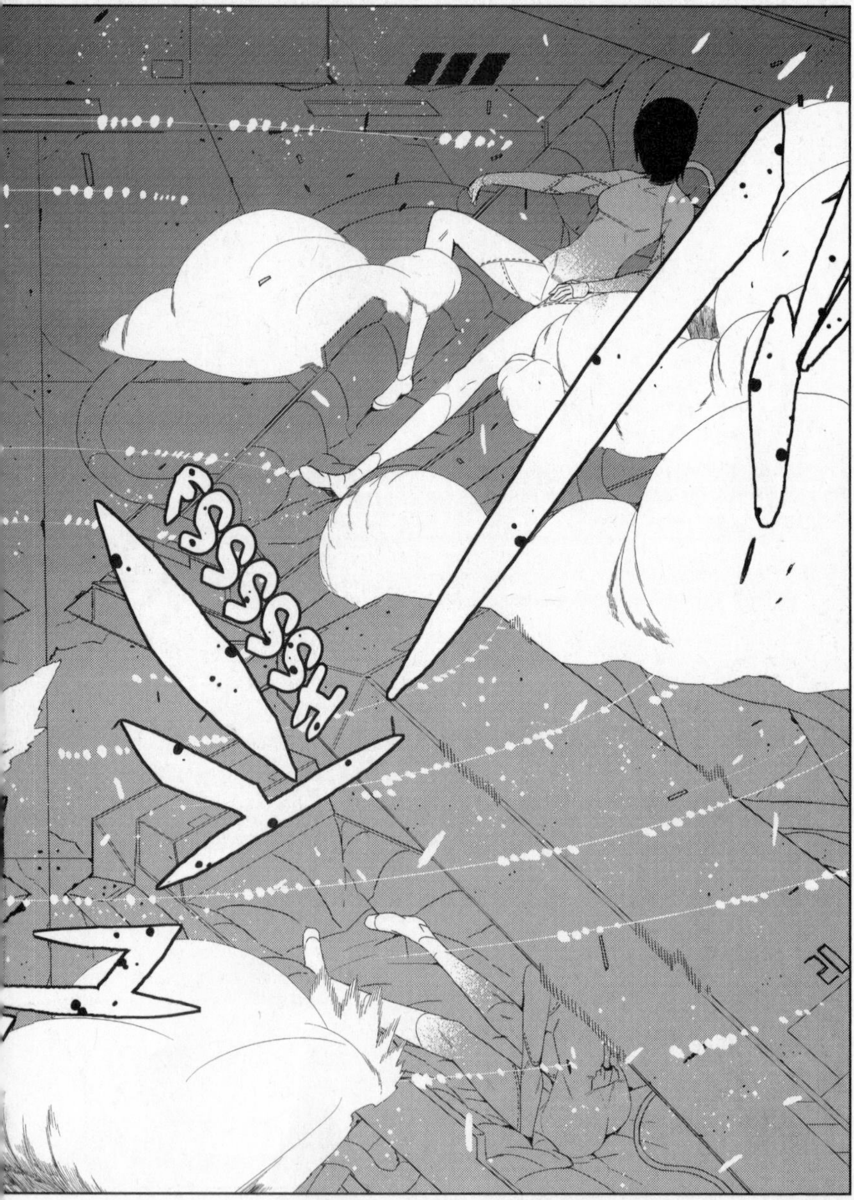
FSSSSH

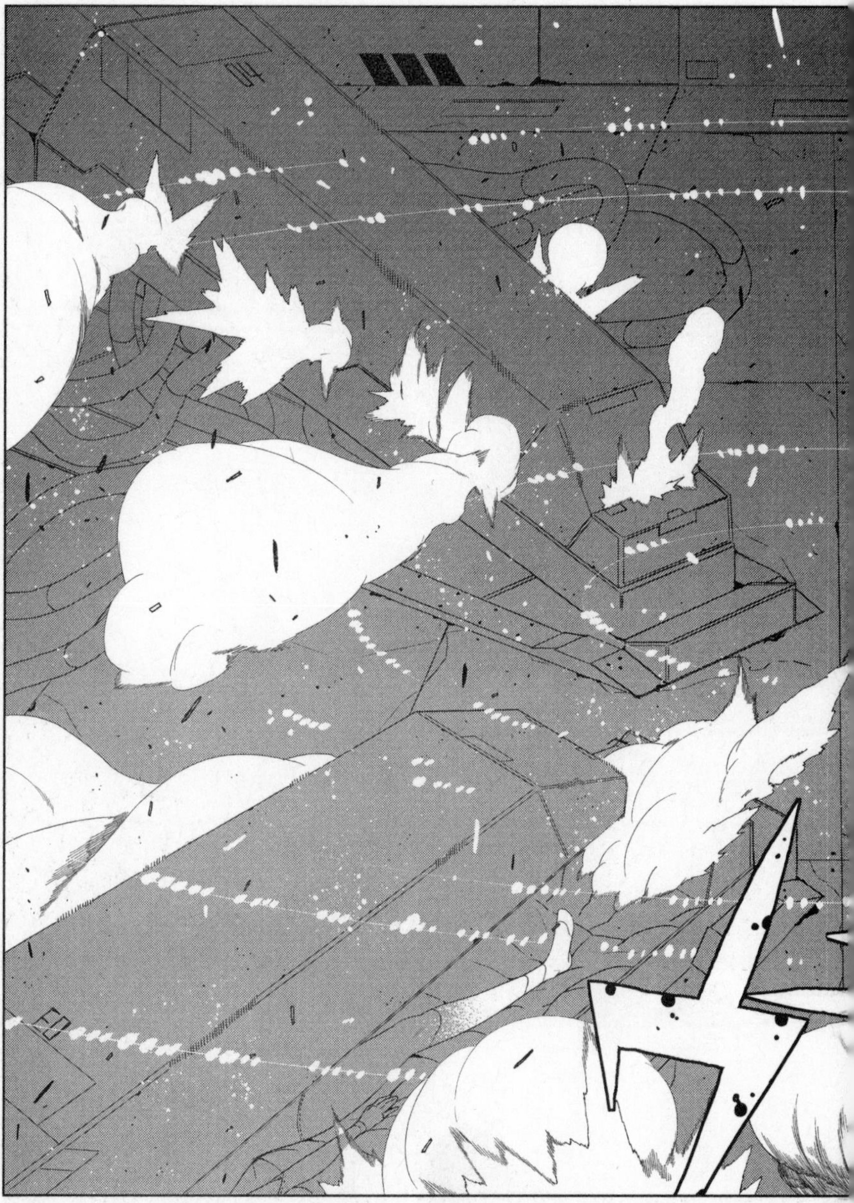

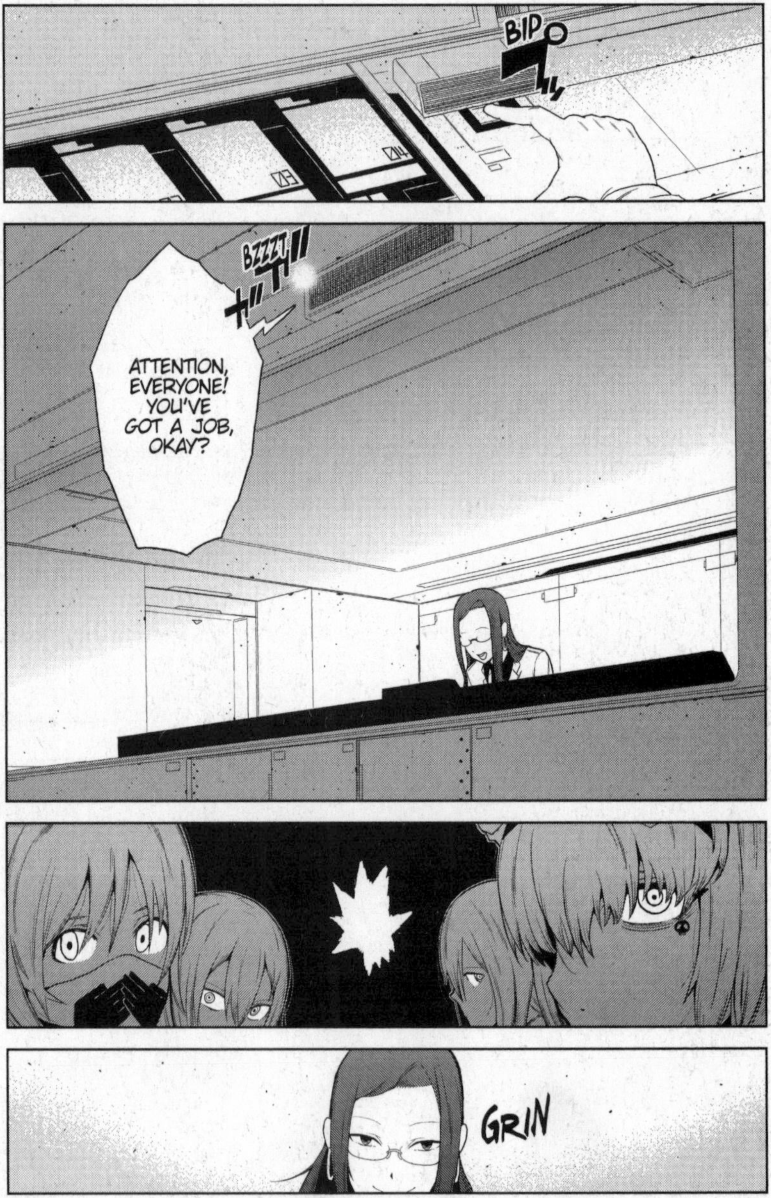
BIP
BZZZT
ATTENTION, EVERYONE! YOU'VE GOT A JOB, OKAY?
GRIN

a certain
SCIENTIFIC
ACCELERATOR

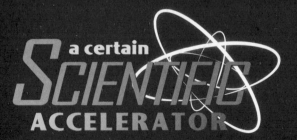

とある科学の一方通行

とある魔術の禁書目録外伝

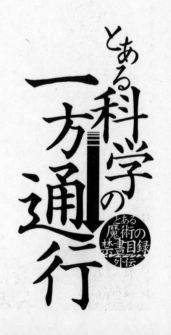

CHAPTER 7

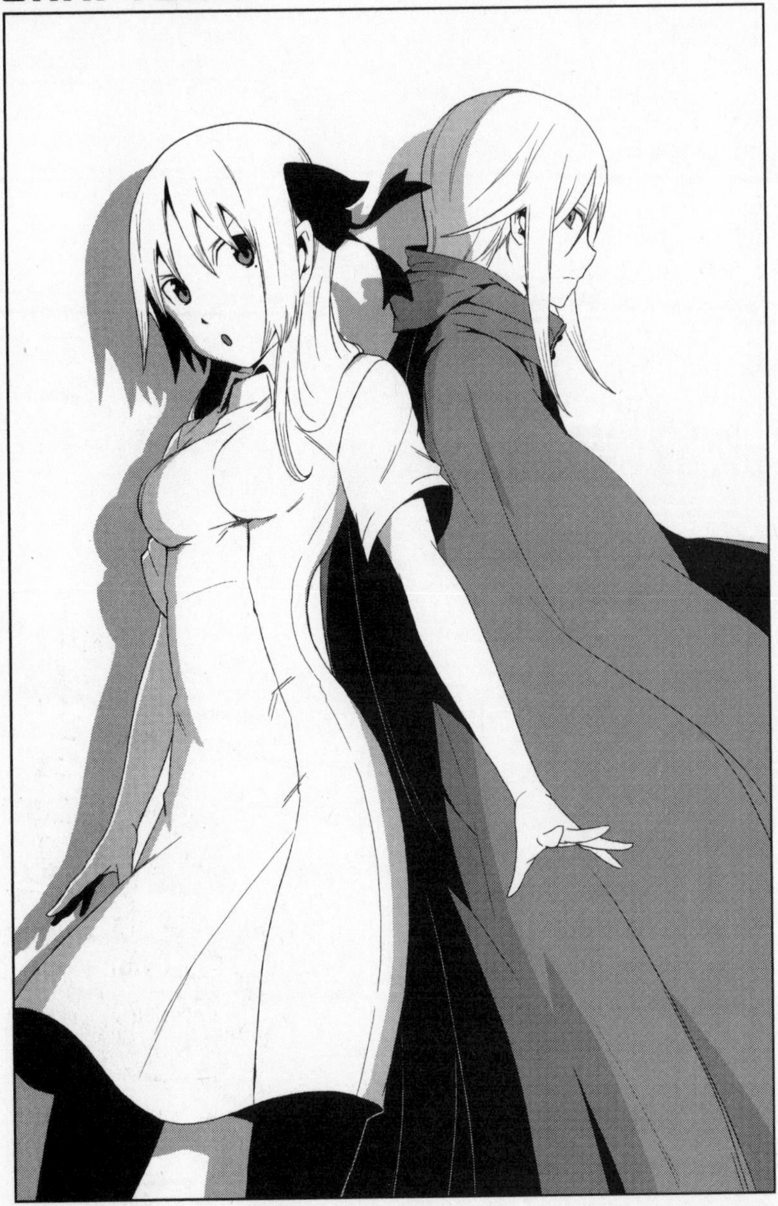

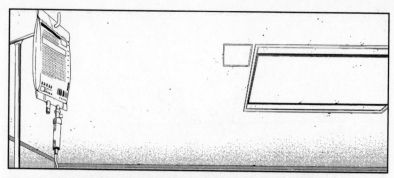

BEEP

BEEP

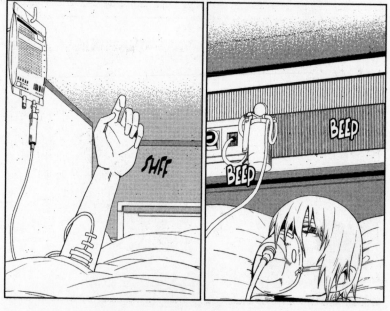

SHFF

BEEP

BEEP

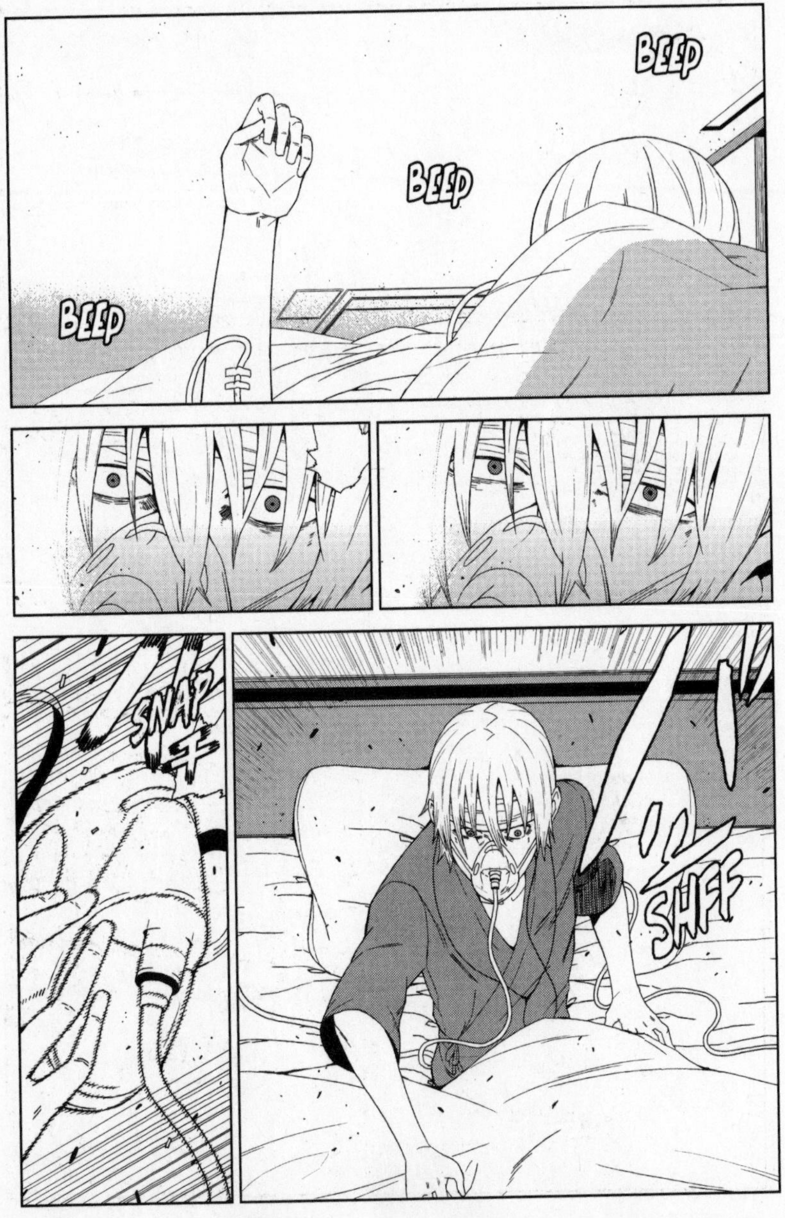
BEEP
BEEP
BEEP
SHFF
SNAP

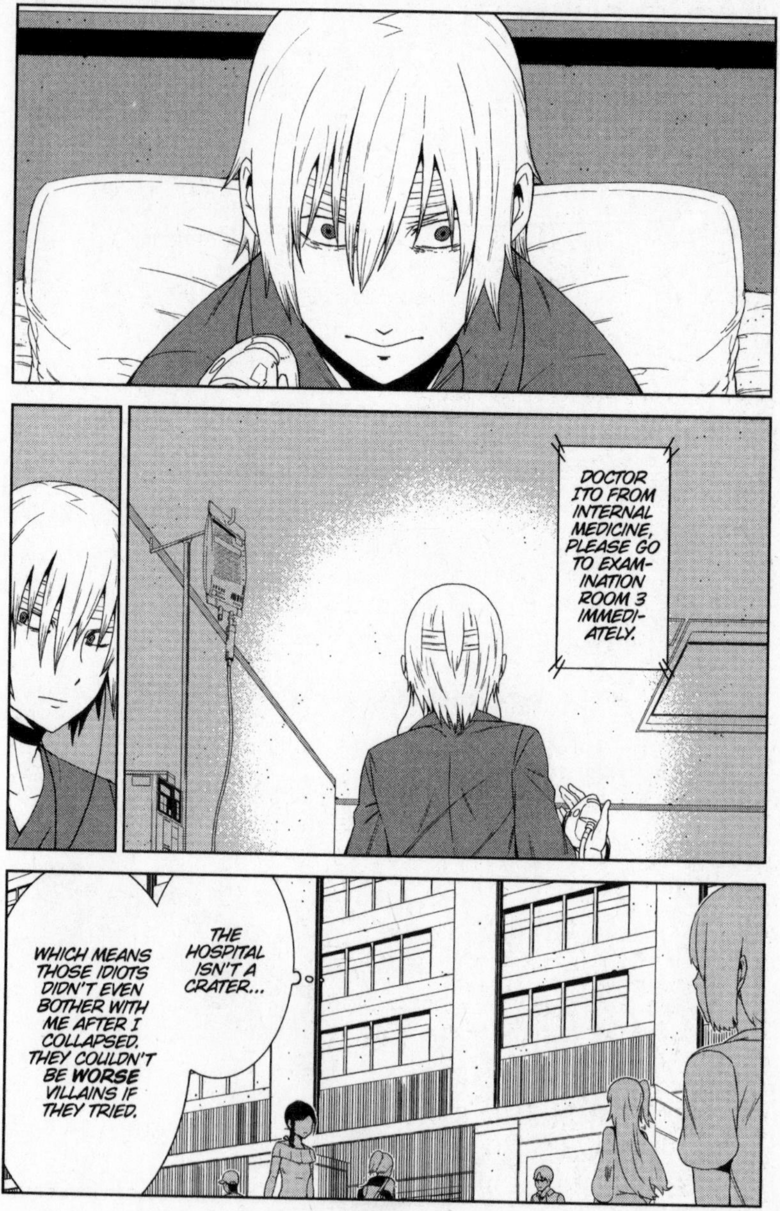
DOCTOR ITO FROM INTERNAL MEDICINE, PLEASE GO TO EXAMINATION ROOM 3 IMMEDIATELY.
THE HOSPITAL ISN'T A CRATER...
WHICH MEANS THOSE IDIOTS DIDN'T EVEN BOTHER WITH ME AFTER I COLLAPSED. THEY COULDN'T BE **WORSE** VILLAINS IF THEY TRIED.

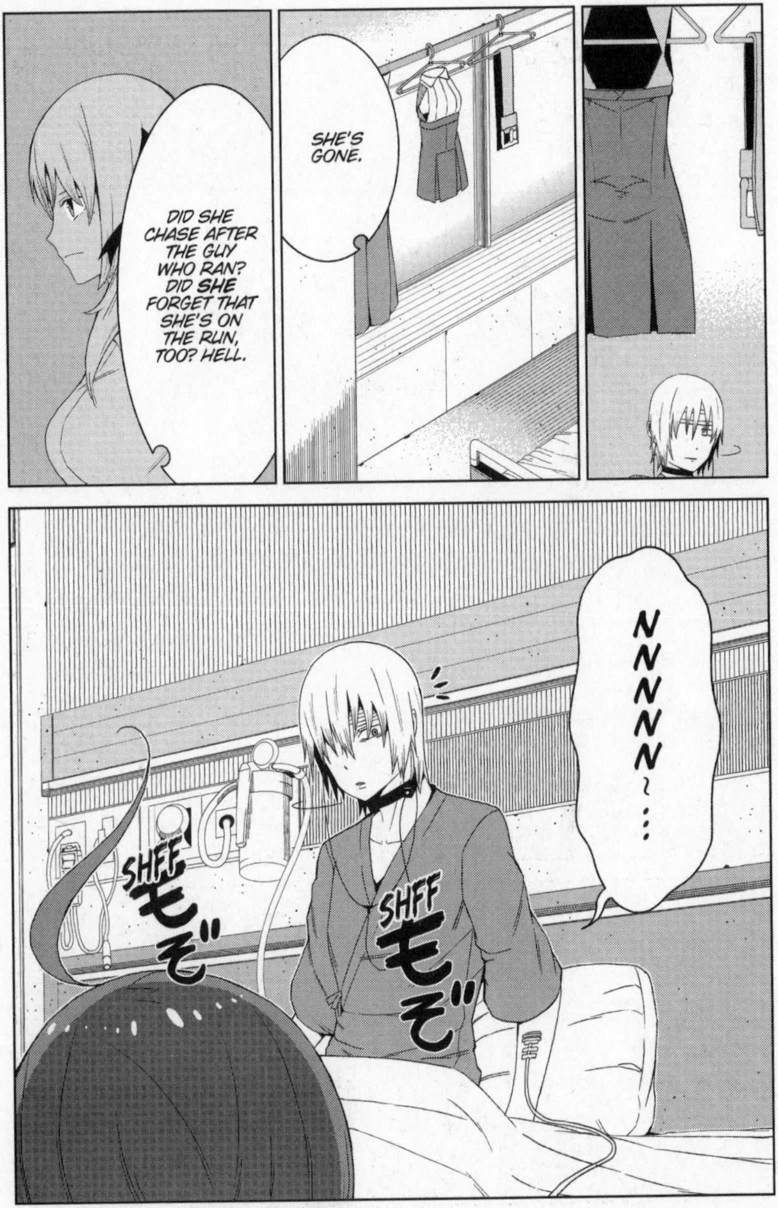
SHE'S GONE.
DID SHE CHASE AFTER THE GUY WHO RAN? DID SHE FORGET THAT SHE'S ON THE RUN, TOO? HELL.
NNNNN~...
SHFF もぞ
SHFF もぞ

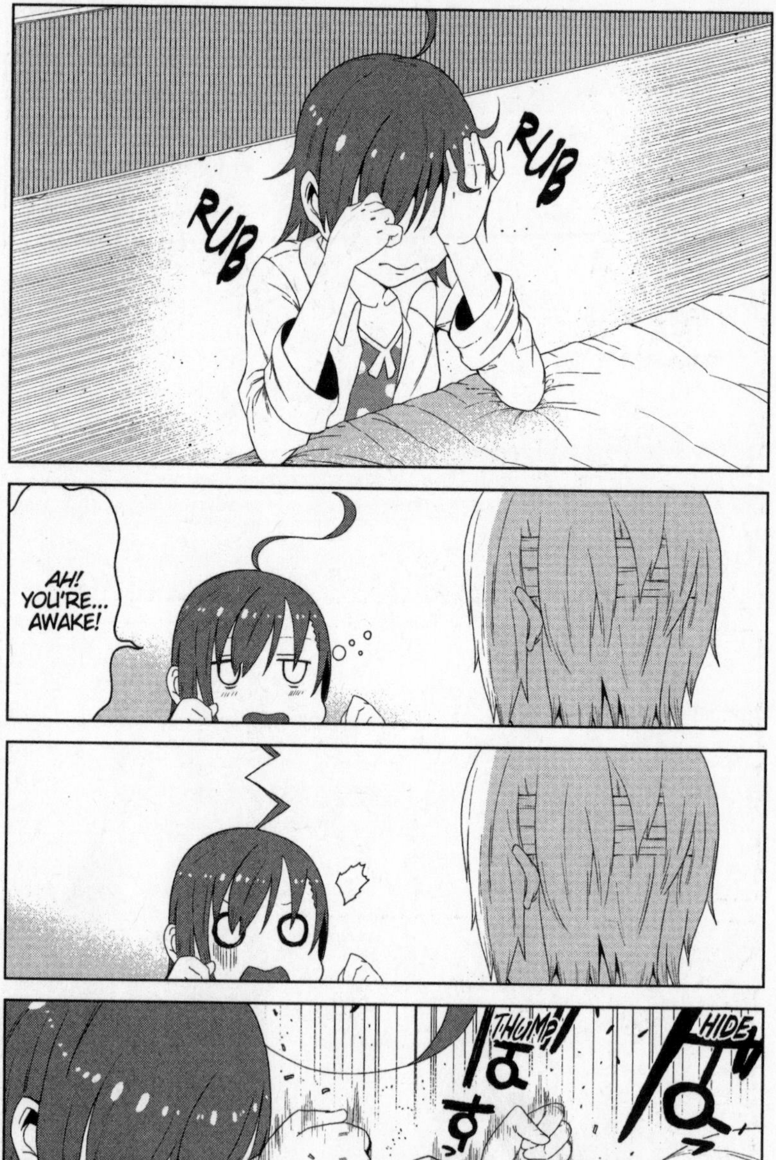
RUB
RUB
AH! YOU'RE... AWAKE!
HIDE
THUMP!

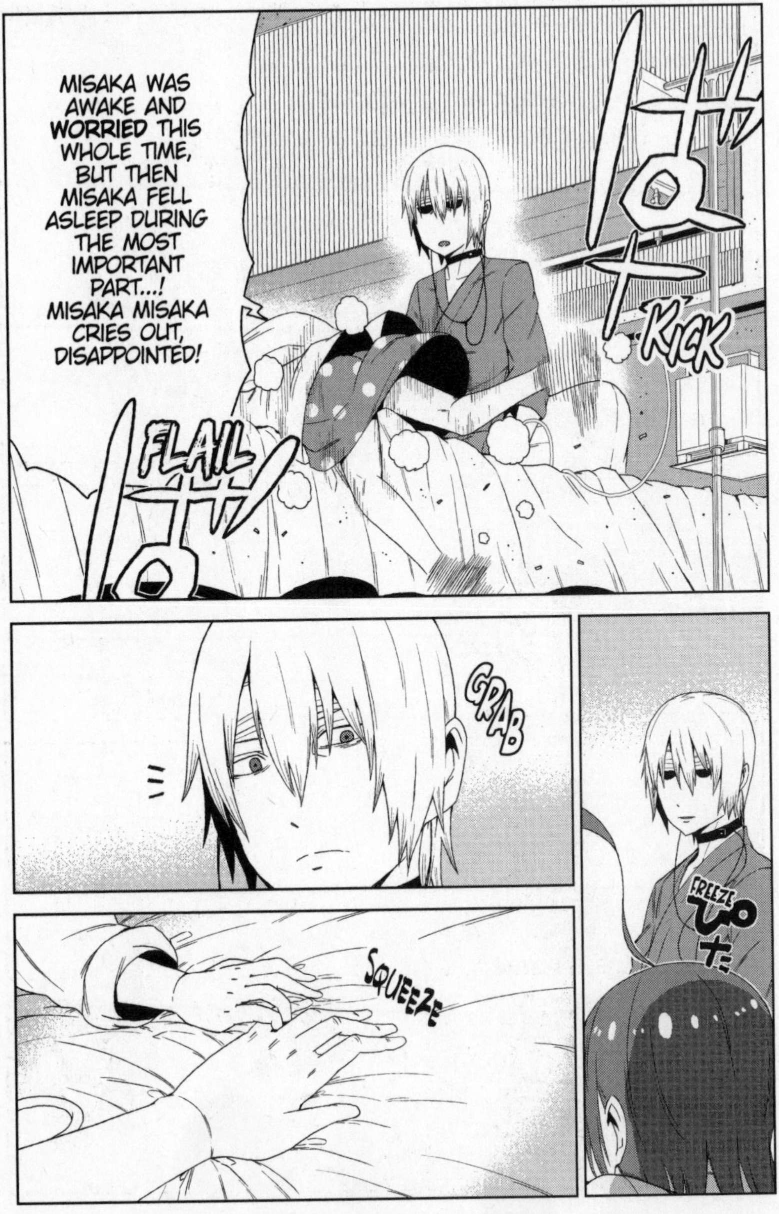
KICK
MISAKA WAS AWAKE AND WORRIED THIS WHOLE TIME, BUT THEN MISAKA FELL ASLEEP DURING THE MOST IMPORTANT PART...! MISAKA MISAKA CRIES OUT, DISAPPOINTED!
FLAIL
FREEZE
GRAB
SQUEEZE

ARE YOU... OKAY?

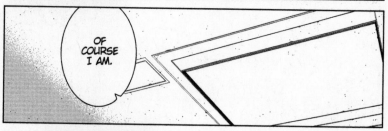

OF COURSE I AM.

FIDGET

FIDGET

WH-WHAT DO YOU WANT TO EAT? MISAKA MISAKA ASKS THIS DESPITE BEING AFRAID THAT YOU'LL WANT AN APPLE, SINCE MISAKA DOESN'T KNOW HOW TO PEEL ONE.

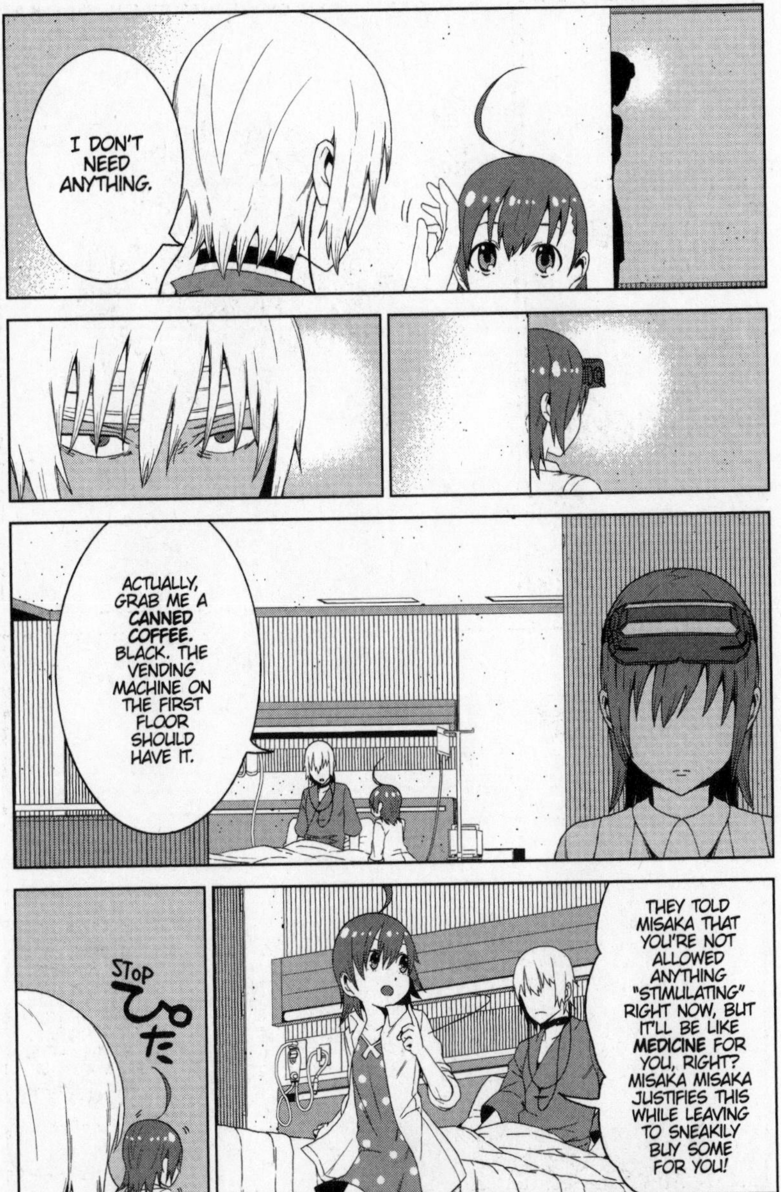
I DON'T NEED ANYTHING.
ACTUALLY, GRAB ME A CANNED COFFEE. BLACK. THE VENDING MACHINE ON THE FIRST FLOOR SHOULD HAVE IT.
THEY TOLD MISAKA THAT YOU'RE NOT ALLOWED ANYTHING "STIMULATING" RIGHT NOW, BUT IT'LL BE LIKE MEDICINE FOR YOU, RIGHT? MISAKA MISAKA JUSTIFIES THIS WHILE LEAVING TO SNEAKILY BUY SOME FOR YOU!
STOP
ぴた

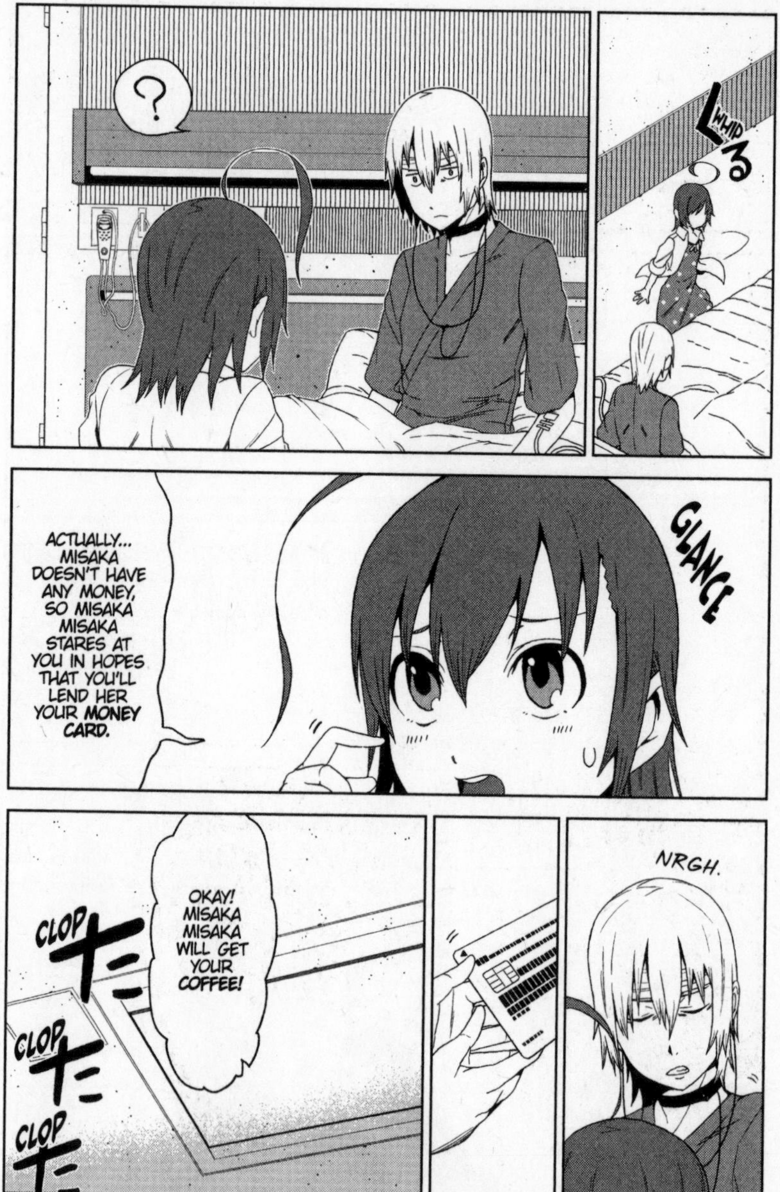
?
WHIP
る
GLANCE
ACTUALLY... MISAKA DOESN'T HAVE ANY MONEY, SO MISAKA MISAKA STARES AT YOU IN HOPES THAT YOU'LL LEND HER YOUR MONEY CARD.
NRGH.
OKAY! MISAKA MISAKA WILL GET YOUR COFFEE!
CLOP
CLOP
CLOP

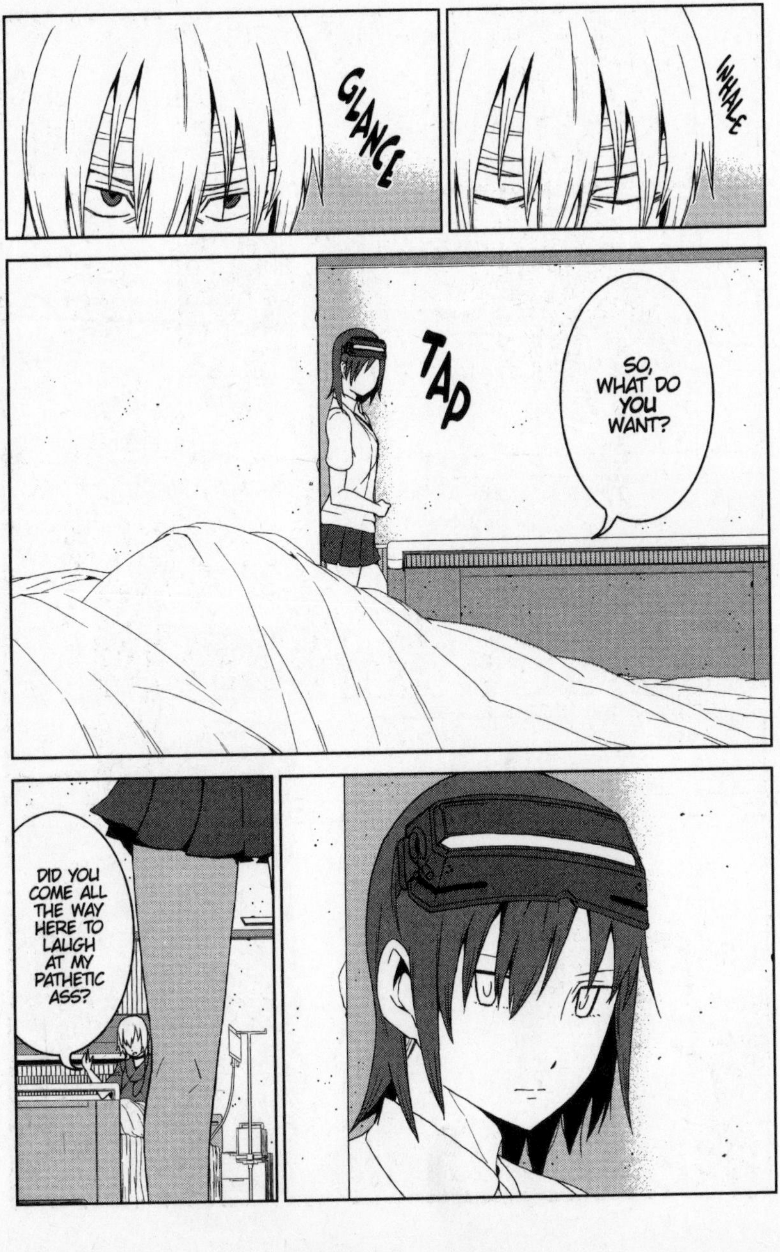
GLANCE
INHALE
TAP
SO, WHAT DO YOU WANT?
DID YOU COME ALL THE WAY HERE TO LAUGH AT MY PATHETIC ASS?

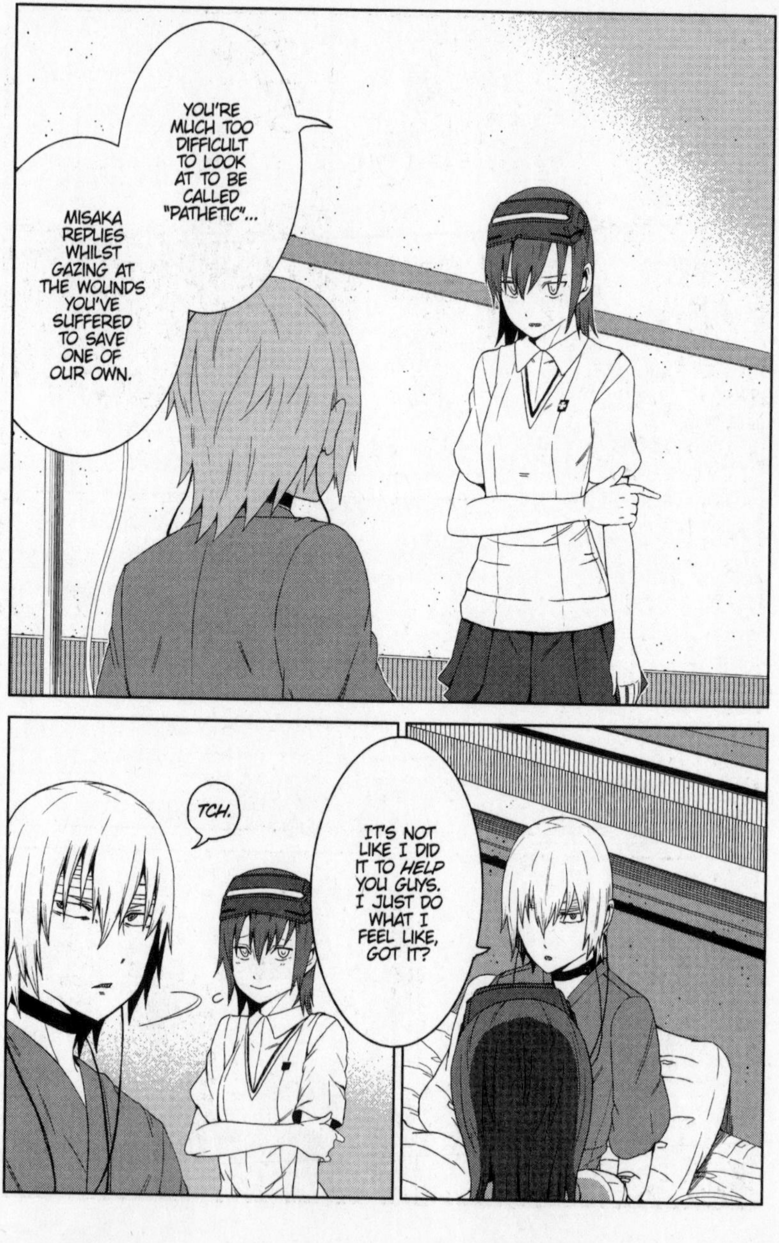
YOU'RE MUCH TOO DIFFICULT TO LOOK AT TO BE CALLED "PATHETIC"...
MISAKA REPLIES WHILST GAZING AT THE WOUNDS YOU'VE SUFFERED TO SAVE ONE OF OUR OWN.
IT'S NOT LIKE I DID IT TO *HELP* YOU GUYS. I JUST DO WHAT I FEEL LIKE, GOT IT?
TCH.

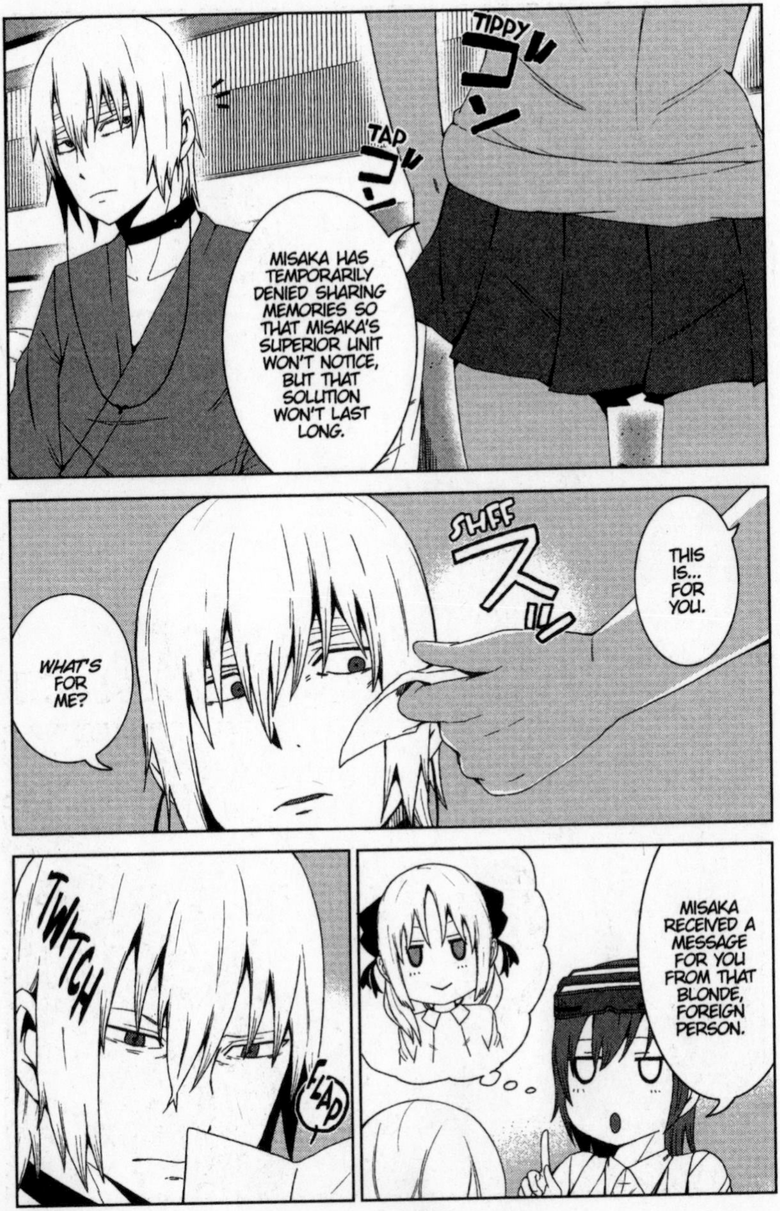
TIPPY
TAP
MISAKA HAS TEMPORARILY DENIED SHARING MEMORIES SO THAT MISAKA'S SUPERIOR UNIT WON'T NOTICE, BUT THAT SOLUTION WON'T LAST LONG.
SHFF
THIS IS... FOR YOU.
WHAT'S FOR ME?
MISAKA RECEIVED A MESSAGE FOR YOU FROM THAT BLONDE, FOREIGN PERSON.
FLAP
TWITCH

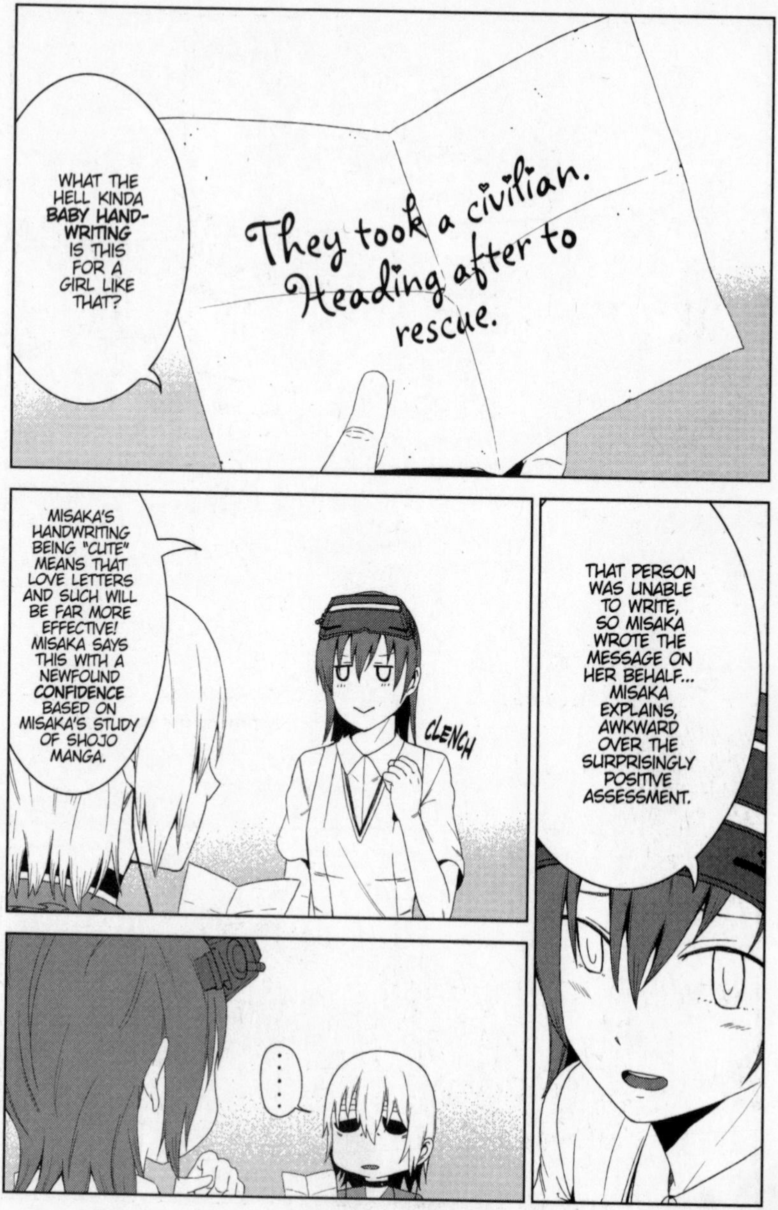
They took a civilian. Heading after to rescue.
WHAT THE HELL KINDA BABY HAND-WRITING IS THIS FOR A GIRL LIKE THAT?
THAT PERSON WAS UNABLE TO WRITE, SO MISAKA WROTE THE MESSAGE ON HER BEHALF... MISAKA EXPLAINS, AWKWARD OVER THE SURPRISINGLY POSITIVE ASSESSMENT.
MISAKA'S HANDWRITING BEING "CUTE" MEANS THAT LOVE LETTERS AND SUCH WILL BE FAR MORE EFFECTIVE! MISAKA SAYS THIS WITH A NEWFOUND CONFIDENCE BASED ON MISAKA'S STUDY OF SHOJO MANGA.
CLENCH
......

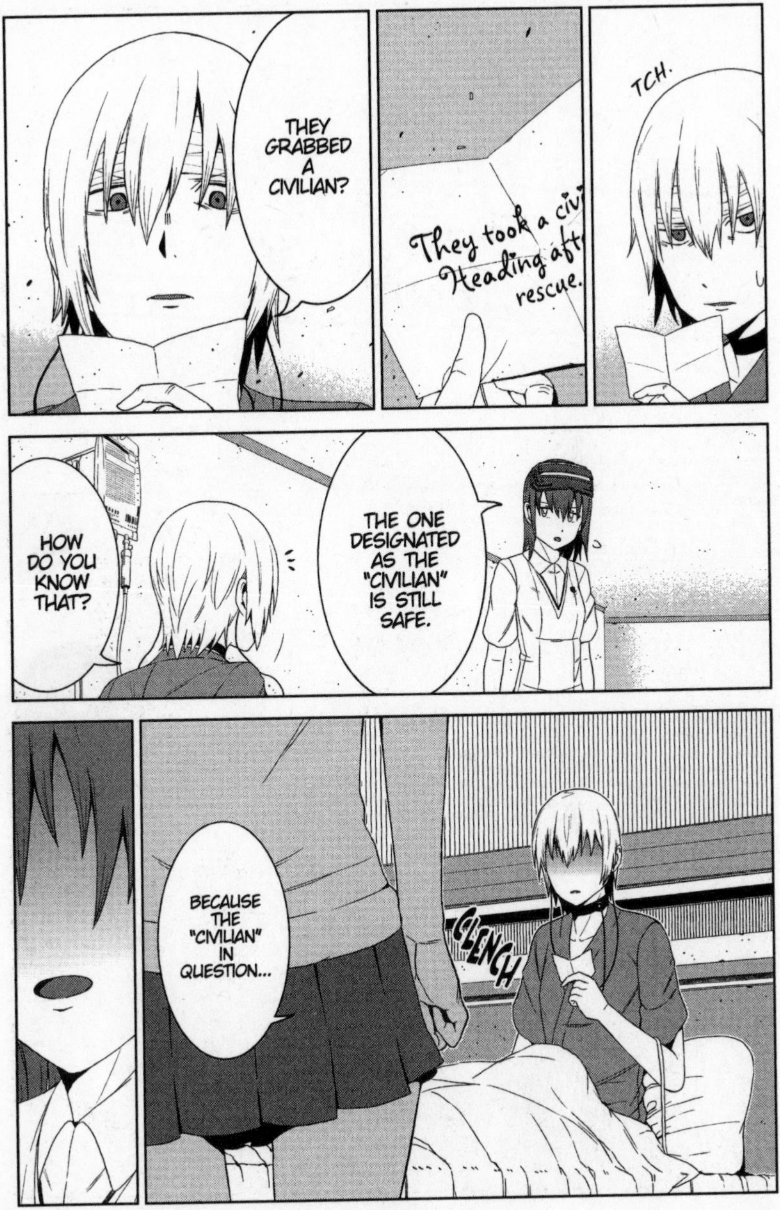
TCH.
They took a civi
Heading aft
rescue.
THEY GRABBED A CIVILIAN?
THE ONE DESIGNATED AS THE "CIVILIAN" IS STILL SAFE.
HOW DO YOU KNOW THAT?
CLENCH
BECAUSE THE "CIVILIAN" IN QUESTION...

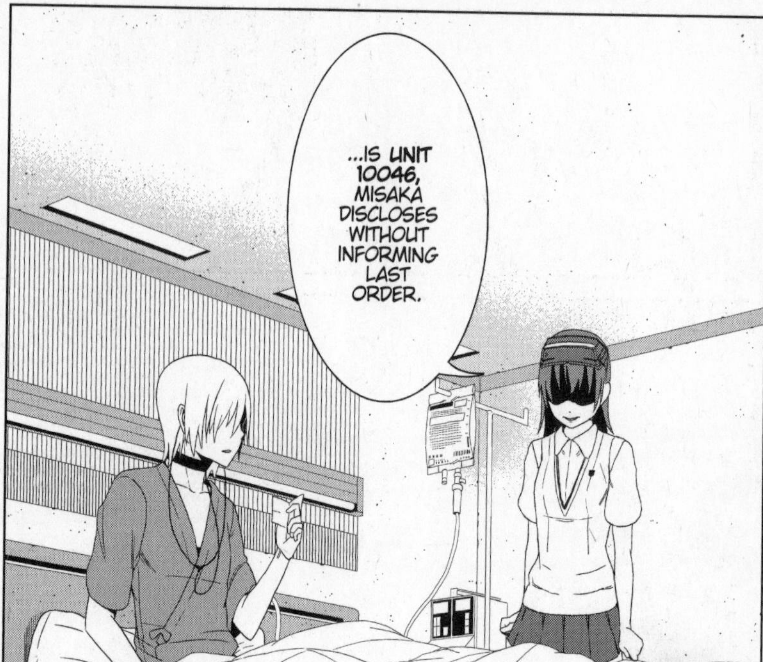
...IS UNIT 10046, MISAKA DISCLOSES WITHOUT INFORMING LAST ORDER.

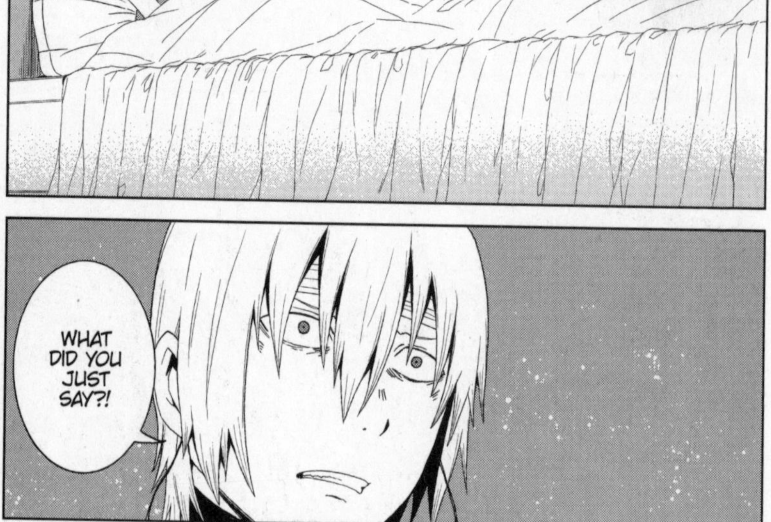
WHAT DID YOU JUST SAY?!

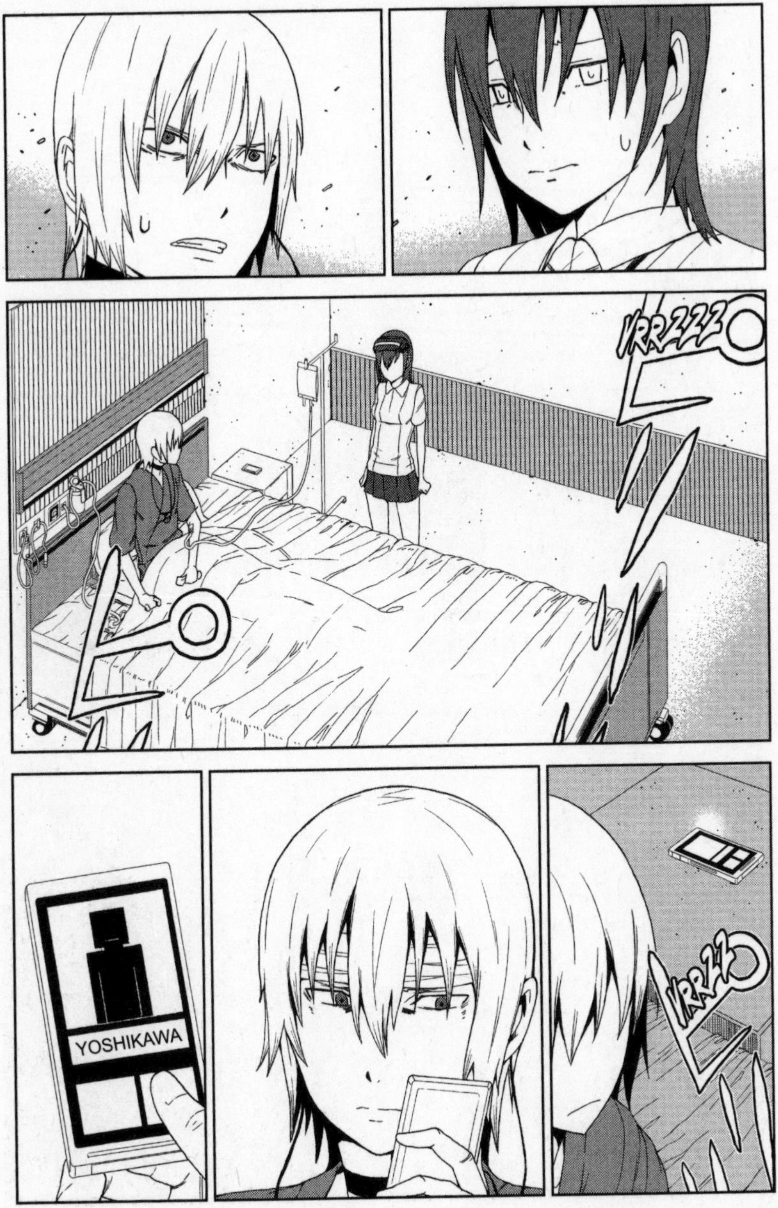
VRRZZZO
YOSHIKAWA
VRRZZO

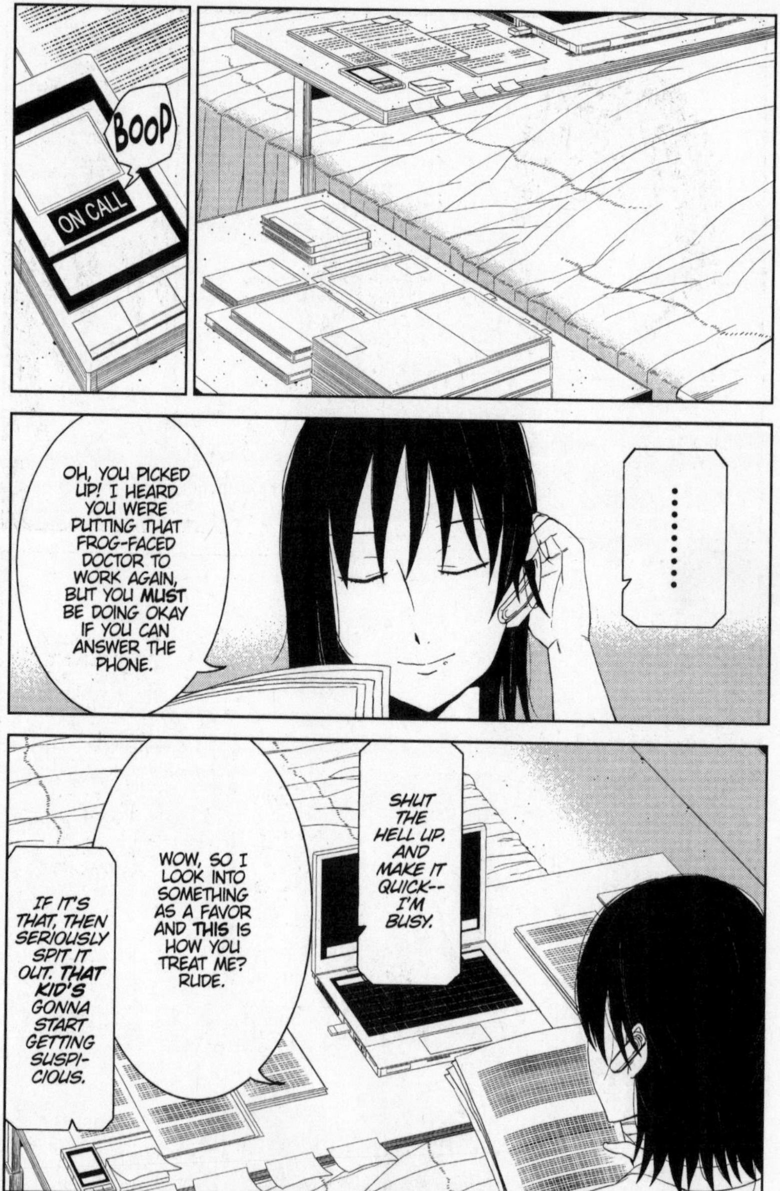
BOOP
ON CALL
......
OH, YOU PICKED UP! I HEARD YOU WERE PUTTING THAT FROG-FACED DOCTOR TO WORK AGAIN, BUT YOU MUST BE DOING OKAY IF YOU CAN ANSWER THE PHONE.
SHUT THE HELL UP. AND MAKE IT QUICK--I'M BUSY.
WOW, SO I LOOK INTO SOMETHING AS A FAVOR AND THIS IS HOW YOU TREAT ME? RUDE.
IF IT'S THAT, THEN SERIOUSLY SPIT IT OUT. THAT KID'S GONNA START GETTING SUSPI-CIOUS.

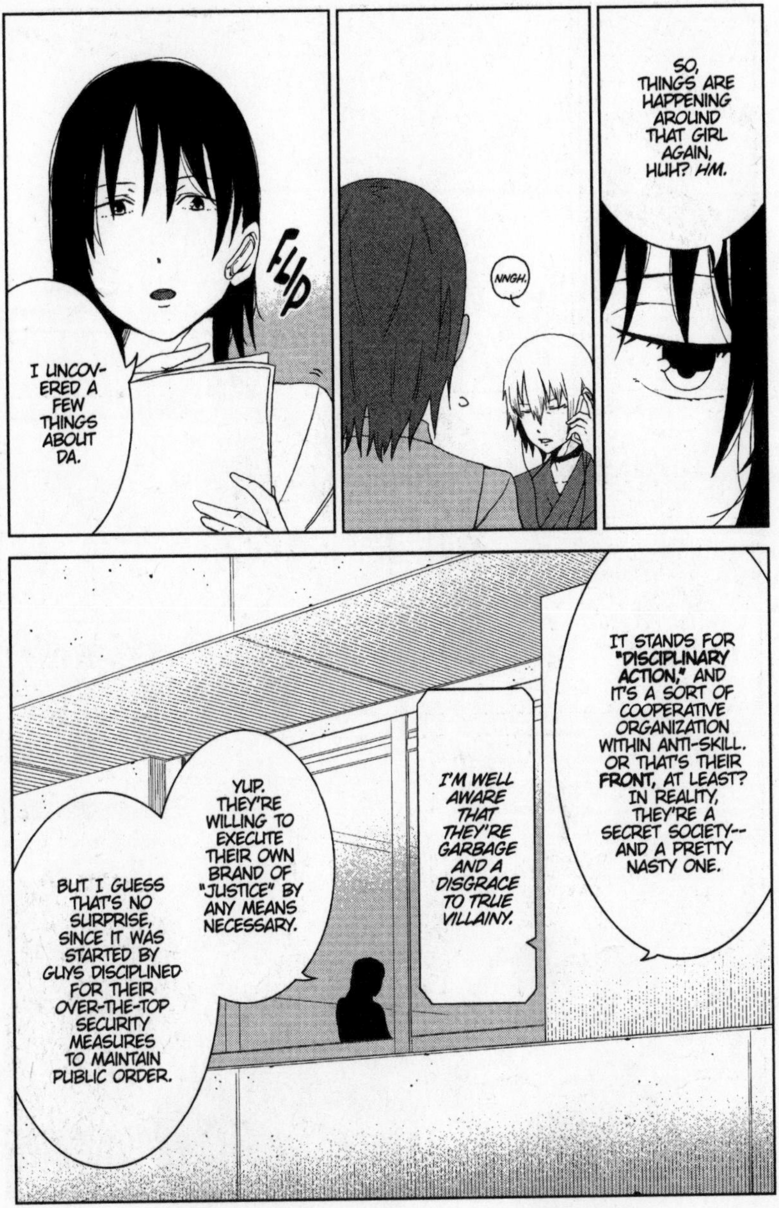
SO, THINGS ARE HAPPENING AROUND THAT GIRL AGAIN, HUH? *HM.*
NNGH.
FLIP
I UNCOVERED A FEW THINGS ABOUT DA.
IT STANDS FOR **"DISCIPLINARY ACTION,"** AND IT'S A SORT OF COOPERATIVE ORGANIZATION WITHIN ANTI-SKILL. OR THAT'S THEIR **FRONT,** AT LEAST? IN REALITY, THEY'RE A SECRET SOCIETY-- AND A PRETTY NASTY ONE.
I'M WELL AWARE THAT THEY'RE GARBAGE AND A DISGRACE TO TRUE VILLAINY.
YUP. THEY'RE WILLING TO EXECUTE THEIR OWN BRAND OF "JUSTICE" BY ANY MEANS NECESSARY.
BUT I GUESS THAT'S NO SURPRISE, SINCE IT WAS STARTED BY GUYS DISCIPLINED FOR THEIR OVER-THE-TOP SECURITY MEASURES TO MAINTAIN PUBLIC ORDER.

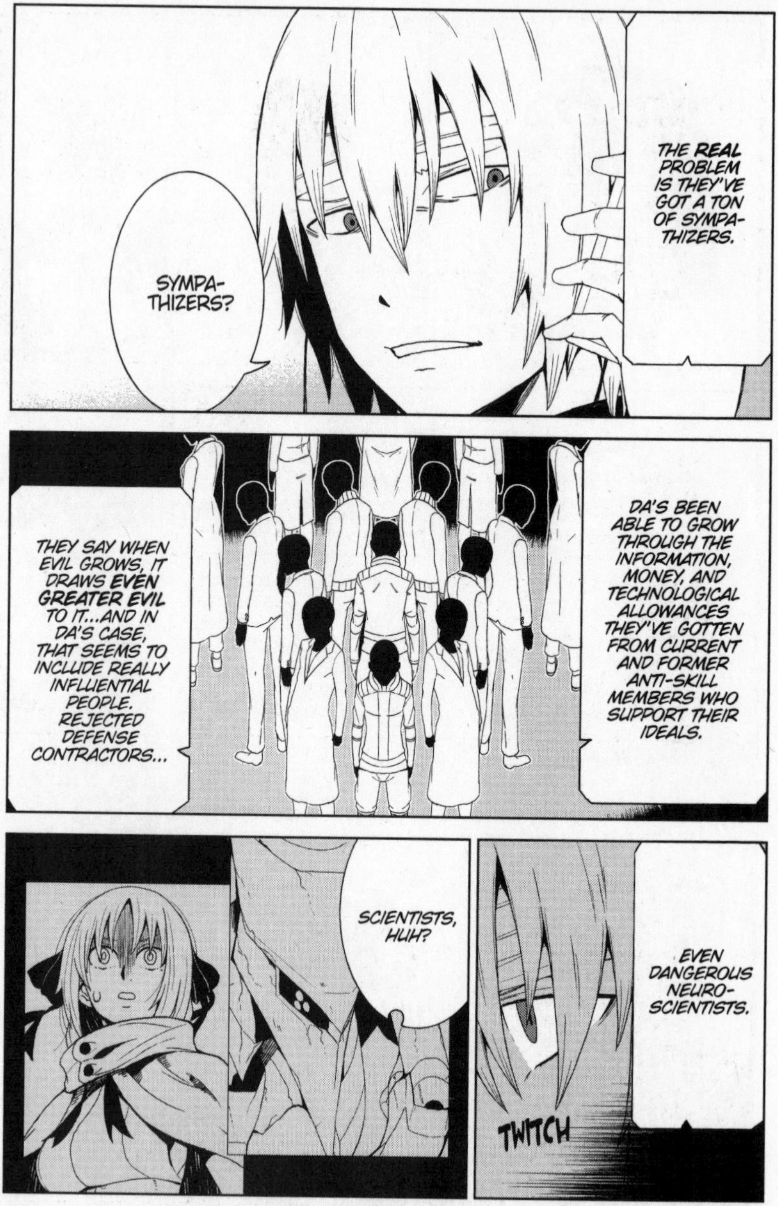
THE REAL PROBLEM IS THEY'VE GOT A TON OF SYMPA-THIZERS.
SYMPA-THIZERS?
DA'S BEEN ABLE TO GROW THROUGH THE INFORMATION, MONEY, AND TECHNOLOGICAL ALLOWANCES THEY'VE GOTTEN FROM CURRENT AND FORMER ANTI-SKILL MEMBERS WHO SUPPORT THEIR IDEALS.
THEY SAY WHEN EVIL GROWS, IT DRAWS EVEN GREATER EVIL TO IT...AND IN DA'S CASE, THAT SEEMS TO INCLUDE REALLY INFLUENTIAL PEOPLE. REJECTED DEFENSE CONTRACTORS...
EVEN DANGEROUS NEURO-SCIENTISTS.
TWITCH
SCIENTISTS, HUH?

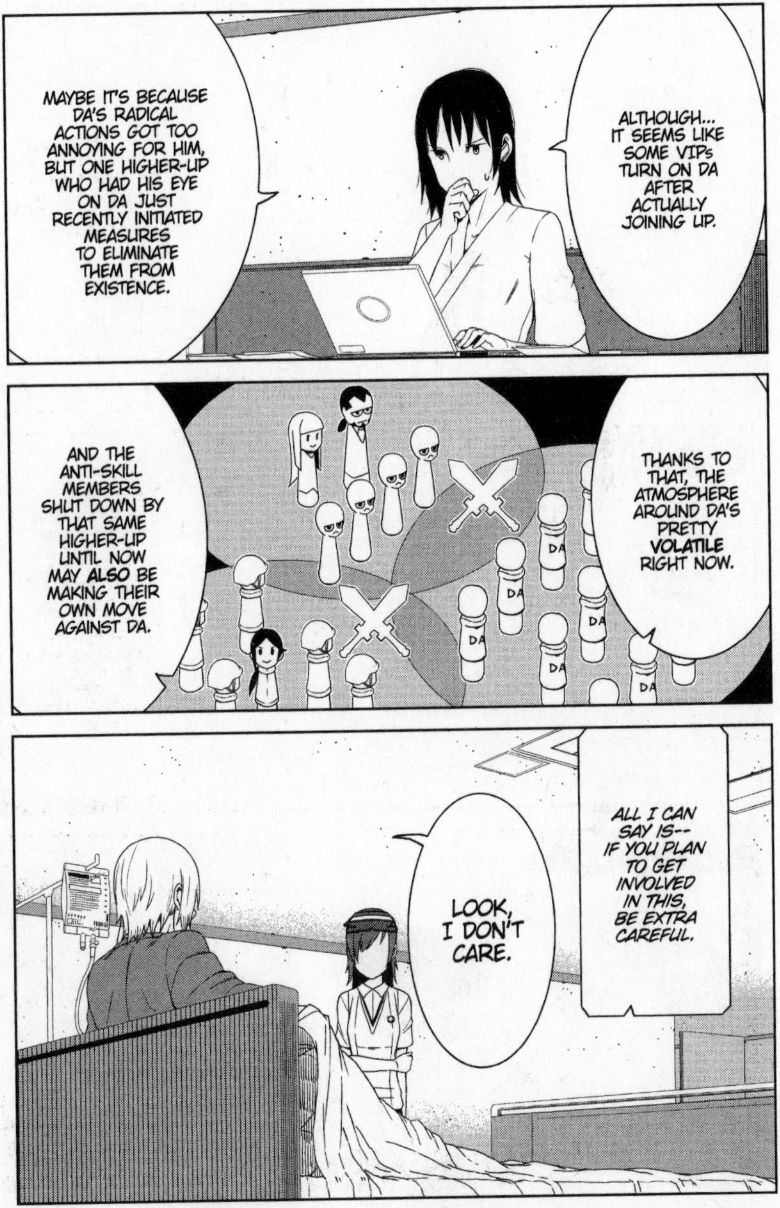
ALTHOUGH... IT SEEMS LIKE SOME VIPs TURN ON DA AFTER ACTUALLY JOINING UP.
MAYBE IT'S BECAUSE DA'S RADICAL ACTIONS GOT TOO ANNOYING FOR HIM, BUT ONE HIGHER-UP WHO HAD HIS EYE ON DA JUST RECENTLY INITIATED MEASURES TO ELIMINATE THEM FROM EXISTENCE.
THANKS TO THAT, THE ATMOSPHERE AROUND DA'S PRETTY **VOLATILE** RIGHT NOW.
AND THE ANTI-SKILL MEMBERS SHUT DOWN BY THAT SAME HIGHER-UP UNTIL NOW MAY **ALSO** BE MAKING THEIR OWN MOVE AGAINST DA.
ALL I CAN SAY IS-- IF YOU PLAN TO GET INVOLVED IN THIS, BE EXTRA CAREFUL.
LOOK, I DON'T CARE.

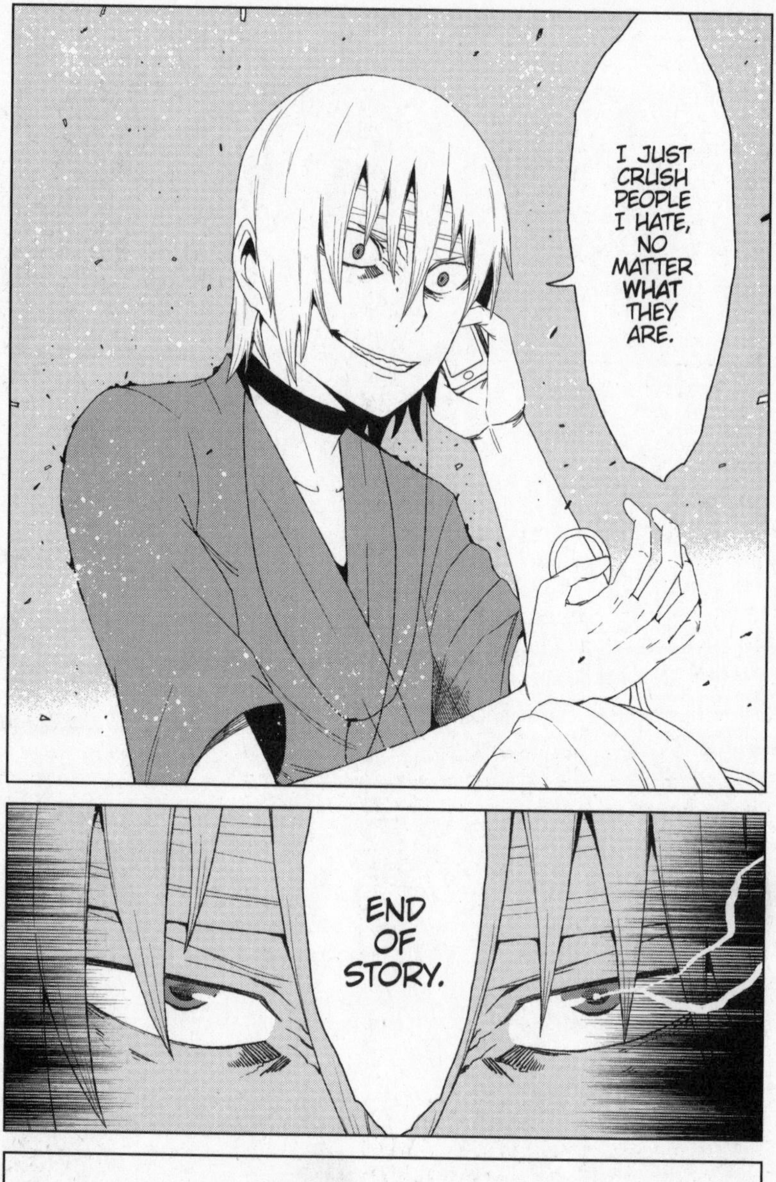
I JUST CRUSH PEOPLE I HATE, NO MATTER WHAT THEY ARE.
END OF STORY.

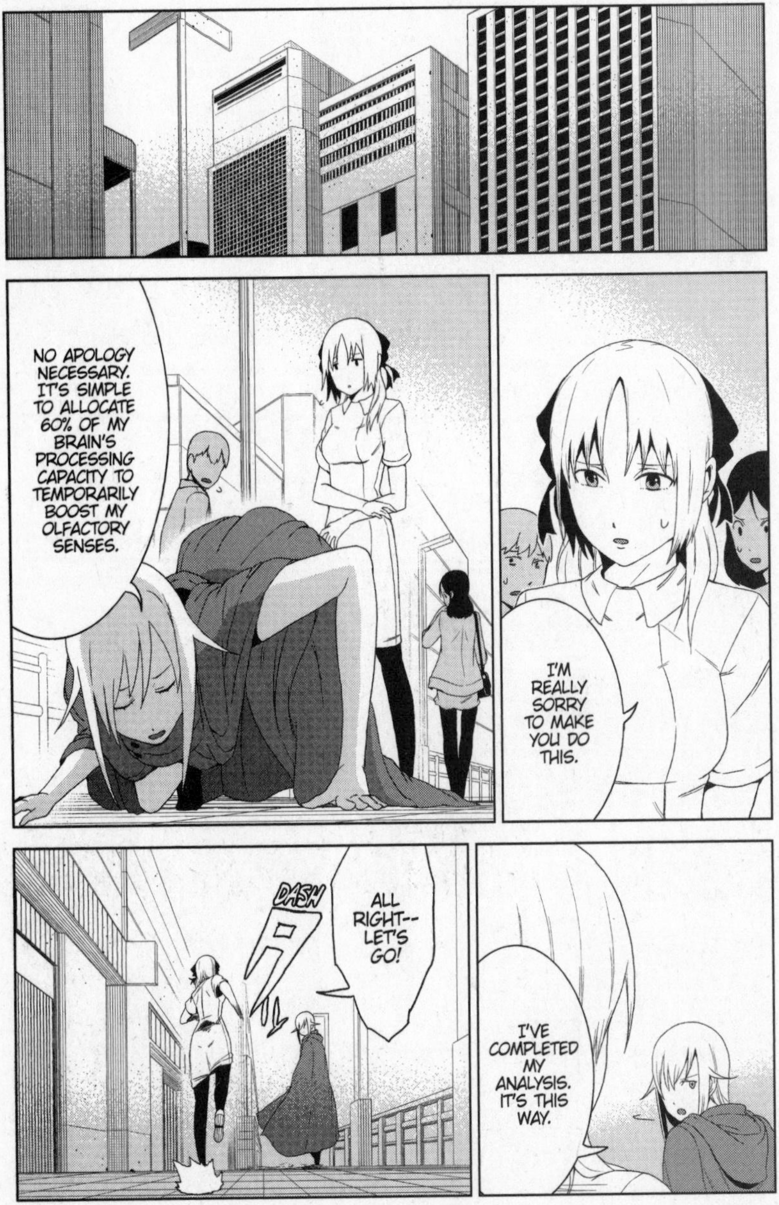
I'M REALLY SORRY TO MAKE YOU DO THIS.
NO APOLOGY NECESSARY. IT'S SIMPLE TO ALLOCATE 60% OF MY BRAIN'S PROCESSING CAPACITY TO TEMPORARILY BOOST MY OLFACTORY SENSES.
I'VE COMPLETED MY ANALYSIS. IT'S THIS WAY.
ALL RIGHT-- LET'S GO!
DASH

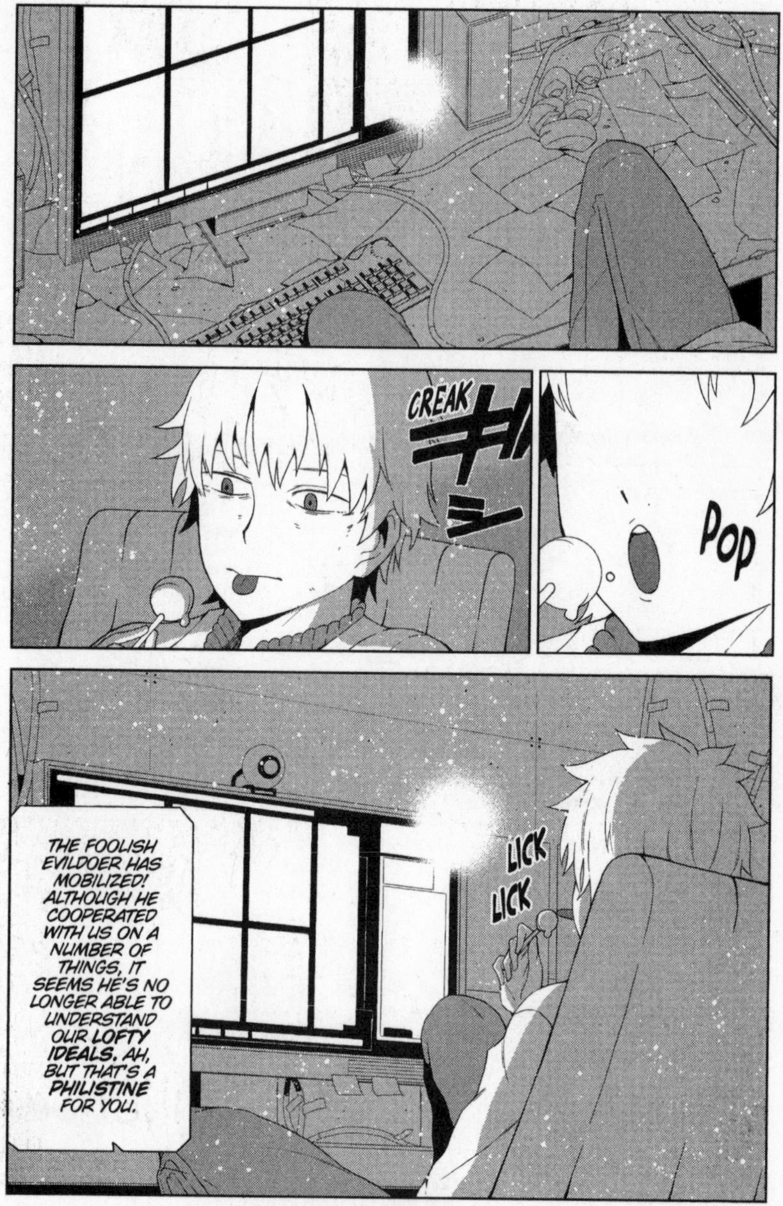
CREAK
POP
THE FOOLISH EVILDOER HAS MOBILIZED! ALTHOUGH HE COOPERATED WITH US ON A NUMBER OF THINGS, IT SEEMS HE'S NO LONGER ABLE TO UNDERSTAND OUR LOFTY IDEALS. AH, BUT THAT'S A PHILISTINE FOR YOU.
LICK LICK

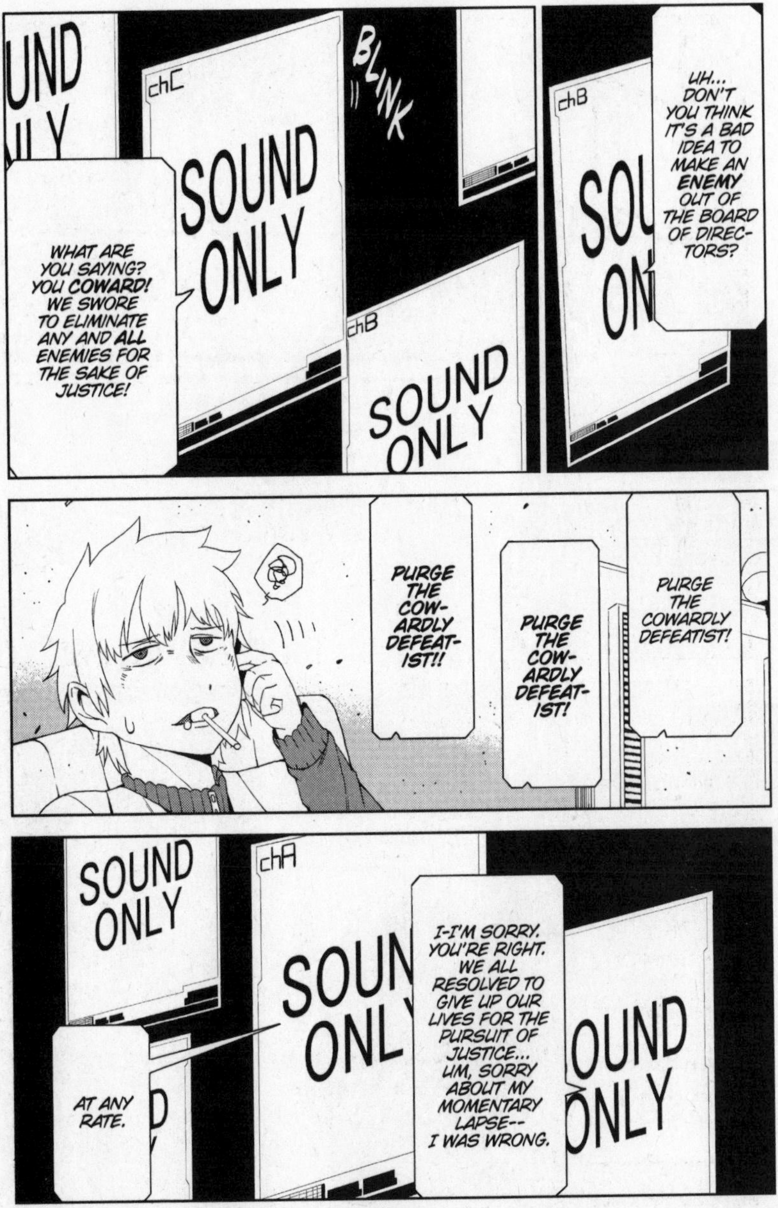
chB
SOUND ONLY
UH... DON'T YOU THINK IT'S A BAD IDEA TO MAKE AN ENEMY OUT OF THE BOARD OF DIREC-TORS?
BLINK
chC
SOUND ONLY
WHAT ARE YOU SAYING? YOU COWARD! WE SWORE TO ELIMINATE ANY AND ALL ENEMIES FOR THE SAKE OF JUSTICE!
chB
SOUND ONLY
PURGE THE COWARDLY DEFEATIST!
PURGE THE COW-ARDLY DEFEAT-IST!
PURGE THE COW-ARDLY DEFEAT-IST!!
SOUND ONLY
I-I'M SORRY. YOU'RE RIGHT. WE ALL RESOLVED TO GIVE UP OUR LIVES FOR THE PURSUIT OF JUSTICE... UM, SORRY ABOUT MY MOMENTARY LAPSE-- I WAS WRONG.
chA
SOUND ONLY
SOUND ONLY
AT ANY RATE.

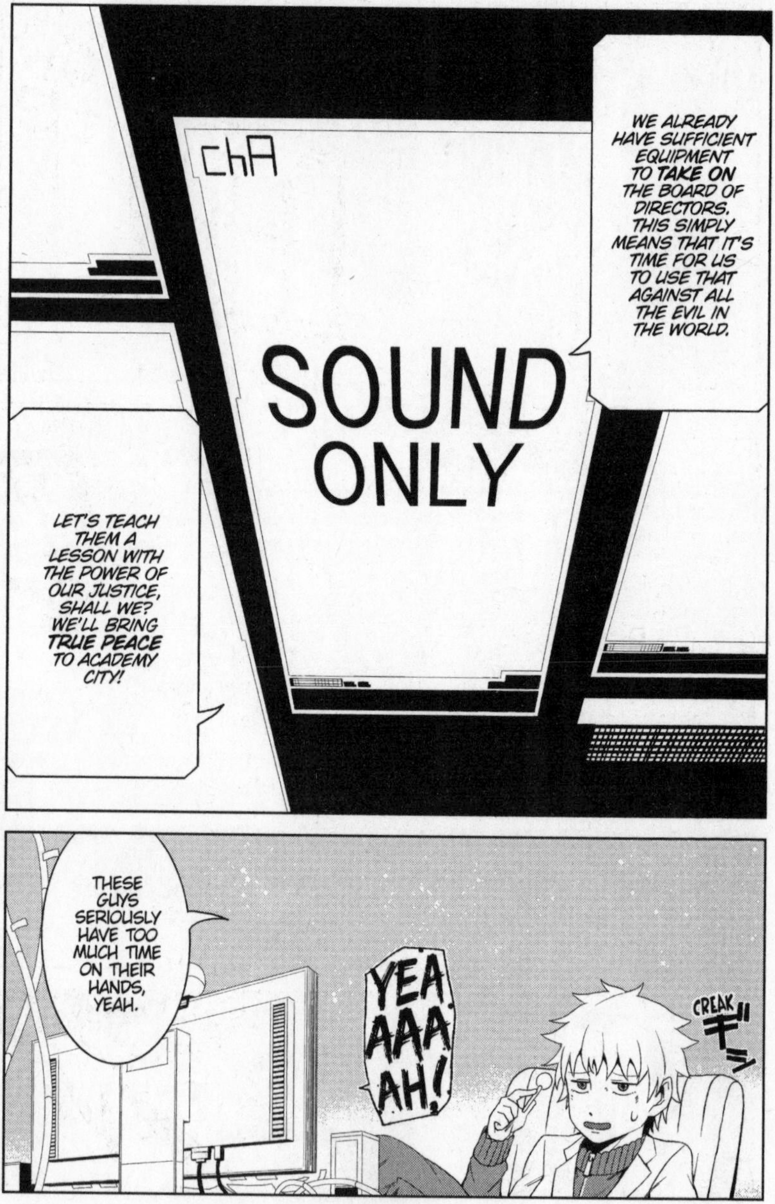
ChA
SOUND ONLY
WE ALREADY HAVE SUFFICIENT EQUIPMENT TO TAKE ON THE BOARD OF DIRECTORS. THIS SIMPLY MEANS THAT IT'S TIME FOR US TO USE THAT AGAINST ALL THE EVIL IN THE WORLD.
LET'S TEACH THEM A LESSON WITH THE POWER OF OUR JUSTICE, SHALL WE? WE'LL BRING TRUE PEACE TO ACADEMY CITY!
CREAK
YEAAAAAH!
THESE GUYS SERIOUSLY HAVE TOO MUCH TIME ON THEIR HANDS, YEAH.

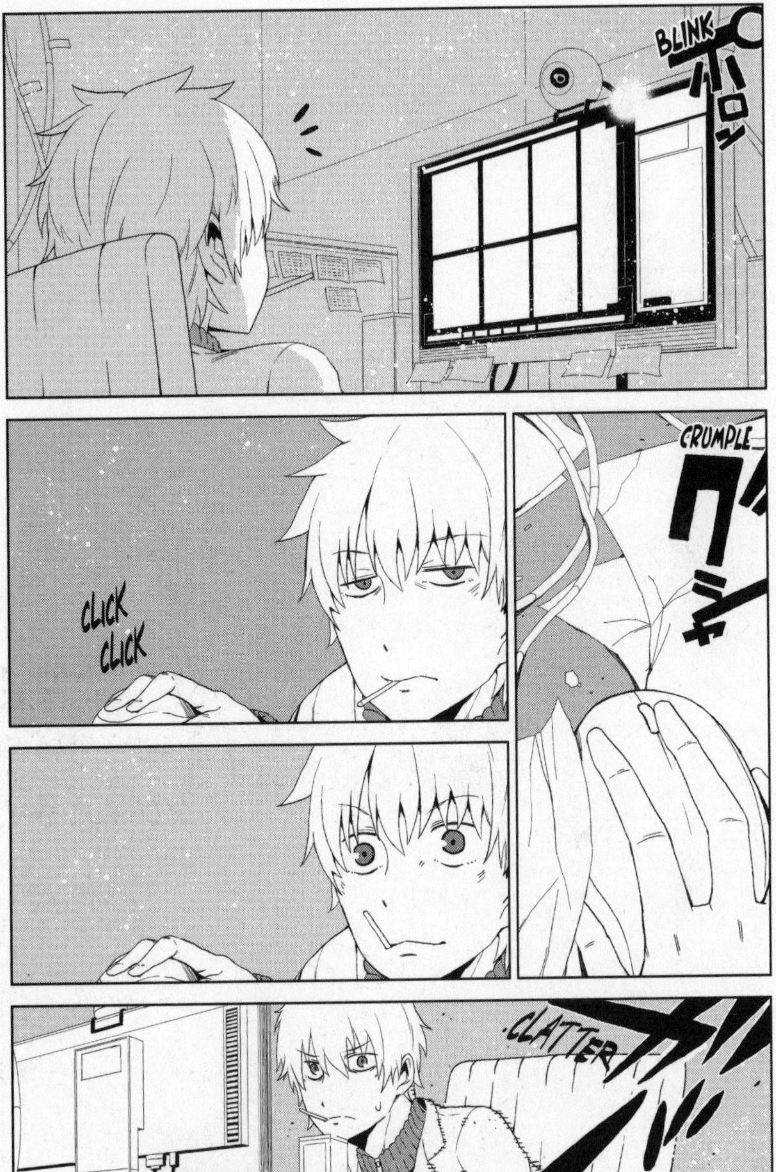

BLINK
ポロン
CRUMPLE
クシャ
CLICK
CLICK
CLATTER
ガタッ

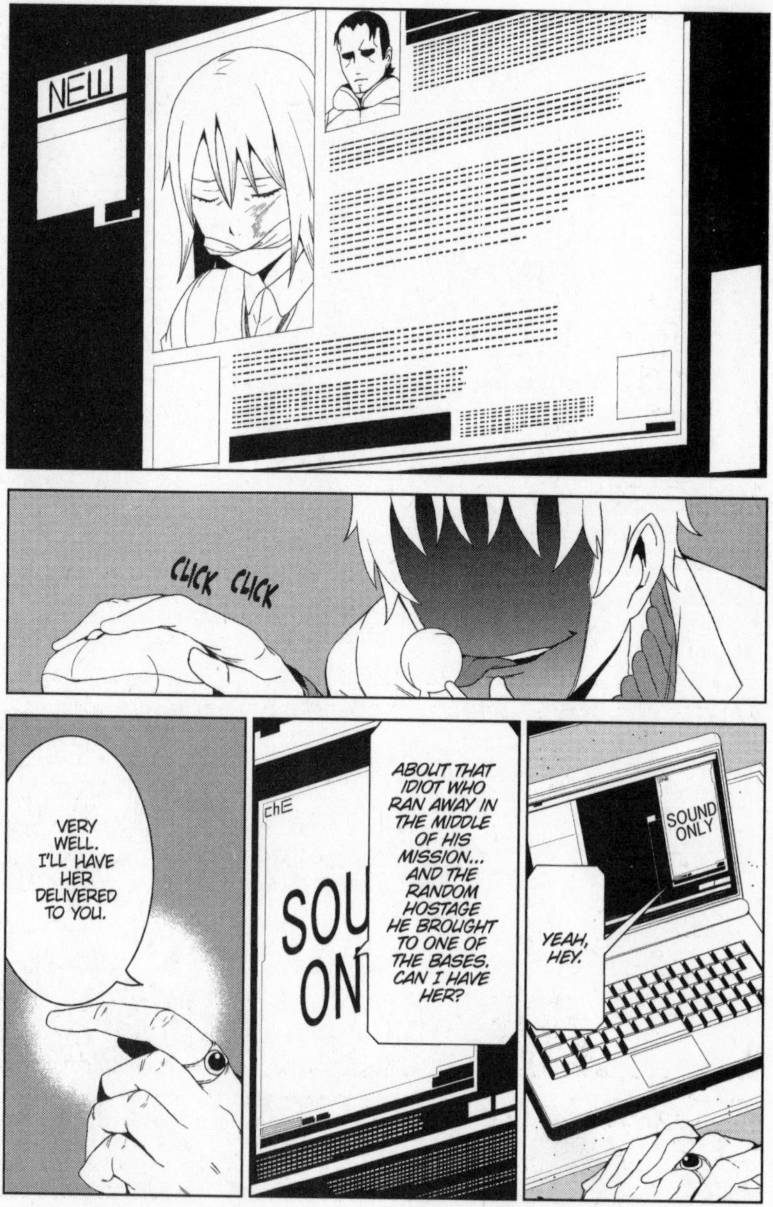
NEW
CLICK CLICK
YEAH, HEY.
SOUND ONLY
ABOUT THAT IDIOT WHO RAN AWAY IN THE MIDDLE OF HIS MISSION... AND THE RANDOM HOSTAGE HE BROUGHT TO ONE OF THE BASES. CAN I HAVE HER?
VERY WELL. I'LL HAVE HER DELIVERED TO YOU.

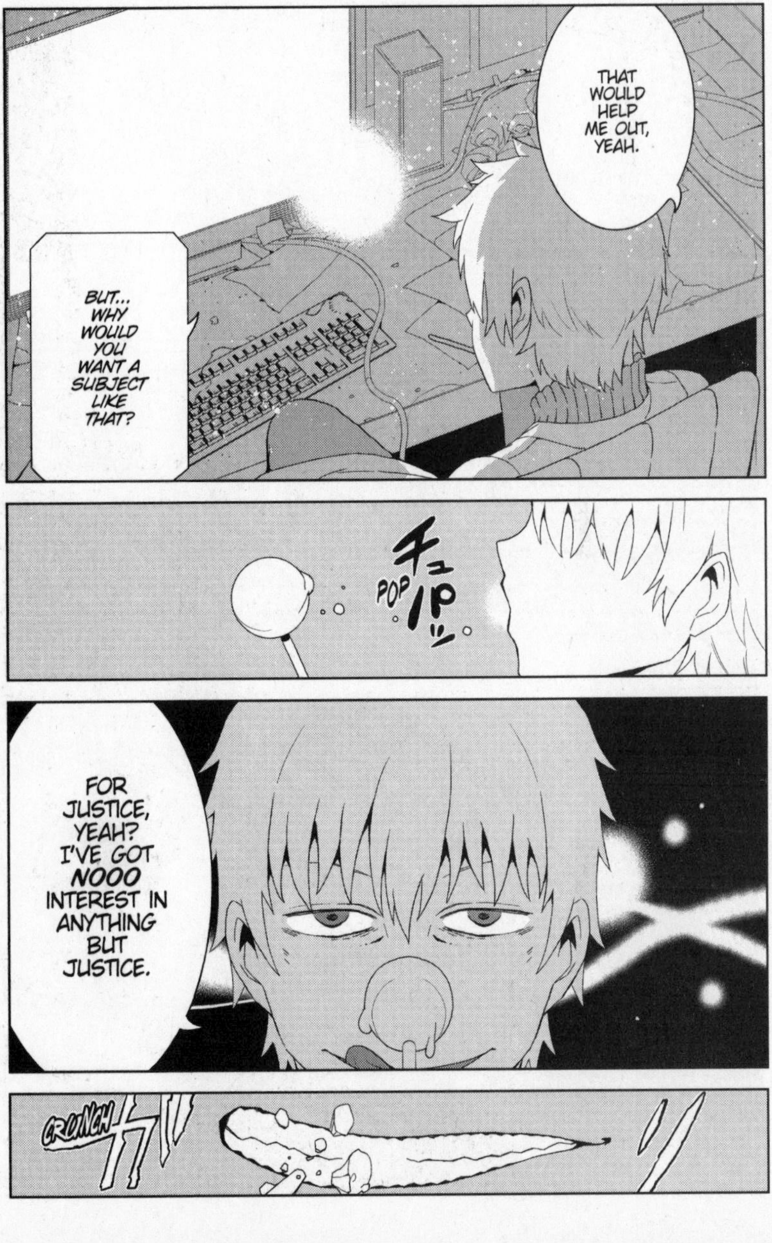
THAT WOULD HELP ME OUT, YEAH.
BUT... WHY WOULD YOU WANT A SUBJECT LIKE THAT?
チュパッ
POP
FOR JUSTICE, YEAH? I'VE GOT **NOOO** INTEREST IN ANYTHING BUT JUSTICE.
CRUNCH

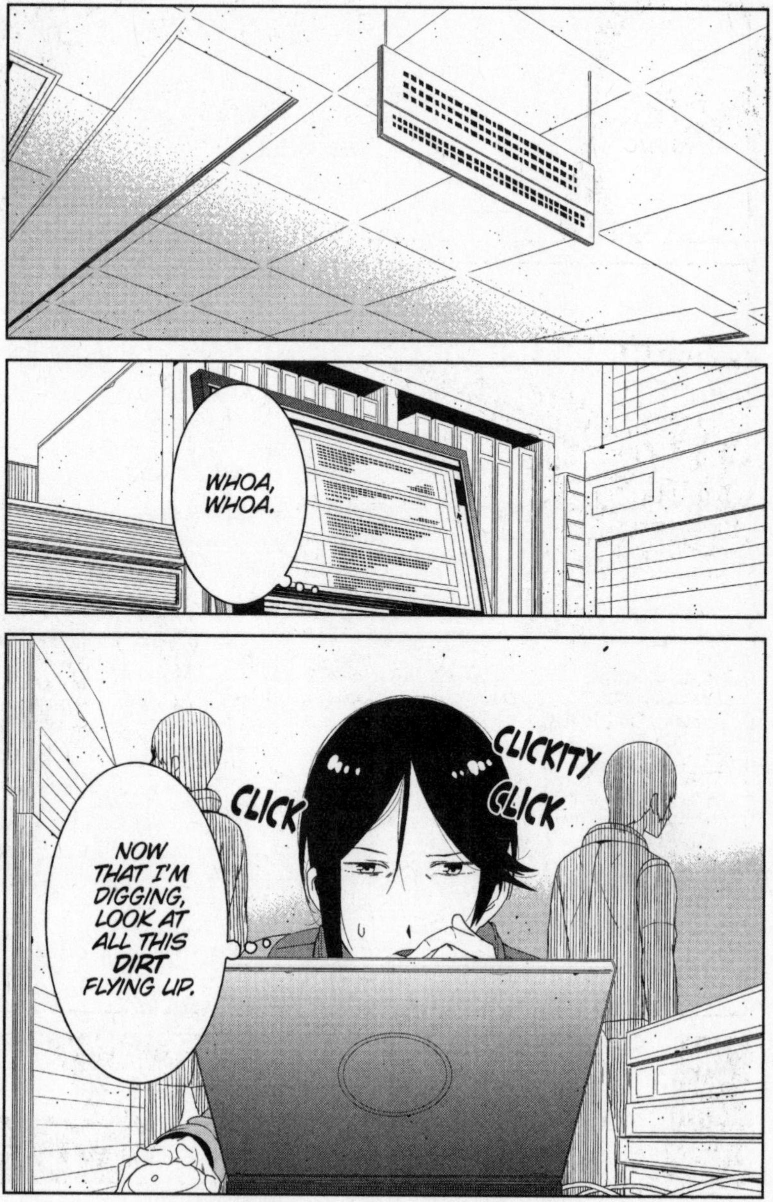
WHOA, WHOA.
CLICKITY CLICK
CLICK
NOW THAT I'M DIGGING, LOOK AT ALL THIS DIRT FLYING UP.

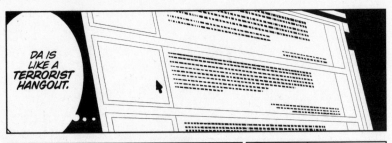

DA IS LIKE A **TERRORIST HANGOUT.**

...

BUT WHY WOULD ALL THIS INFORMATION SUDDENLY SHOW UP WHEN I WASN'T ABLE TO FIND IT EARLIER?

AND FROM WHAT I CAN MAKE OF ALL THIS, DA HAS EQUIPMENT THAT EASILY SURPASSES ANTI-SKILL'S MOST POWERFUL TECH...

WELL, NO ONE HAS ANY IDEA HOW THAT MACHINE PACKED WITH A **CORPSE** WAS USING A LEVEL 4 "ABILITY." THESE GUYS HAVE TO BE PRETTY DANGEROUS.

CLICK CLICK

HUH?!

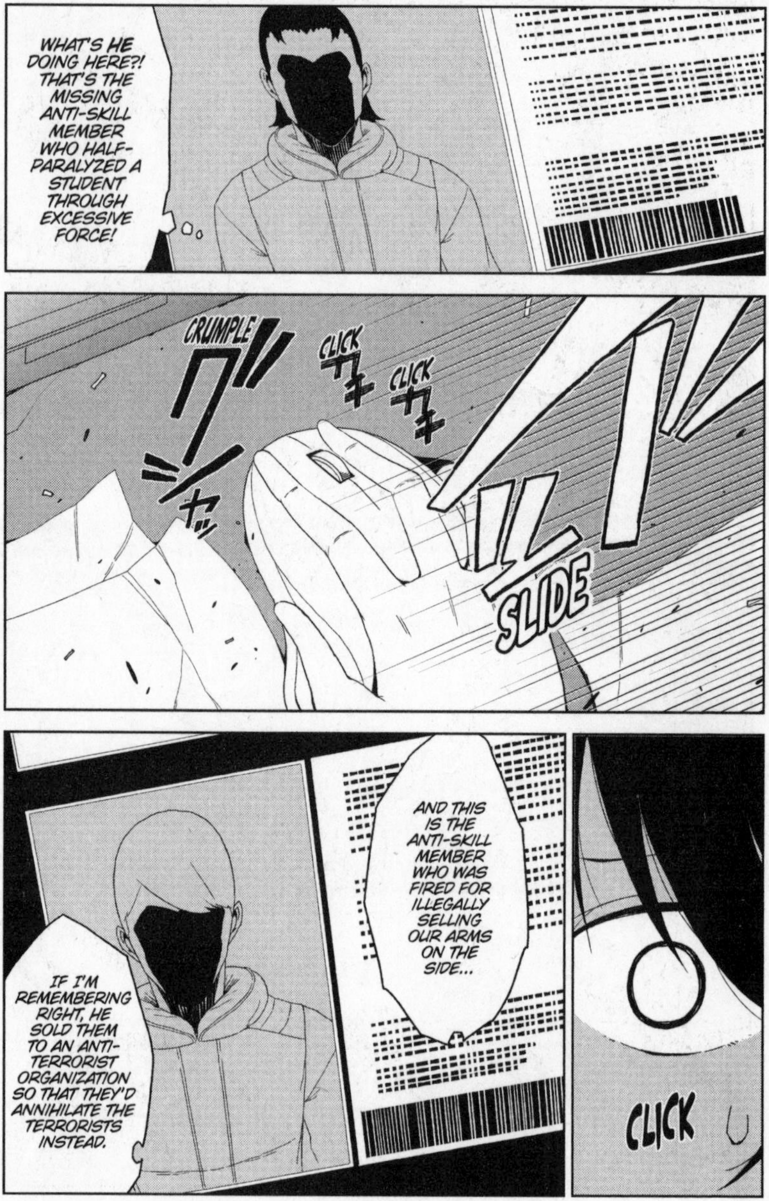
WHAT'S HE DOING HERE?! THAT'S THE MISSING ANTI-SKILL MEMBER WHO HALF-PARALYZED A STUDENT THROUGH EXCESSIVE FORCE!
SLIDE
CLICK
CLICK
CRUMPLE
CLICK
AND THIS IS THE ANTI-SKILL MEMBER WHO WAS FIRED FOR ILLEGALLY SELLING OUR ARMS ON THE SIDE...
IF I'M REMEMBERING RIGHT, HE SOLD THEM TO AN ANTI-TERRORIST ORGANIZATION SO THAT THEY'D ANNIHILATE THE TERRORISTS INSTEAD.

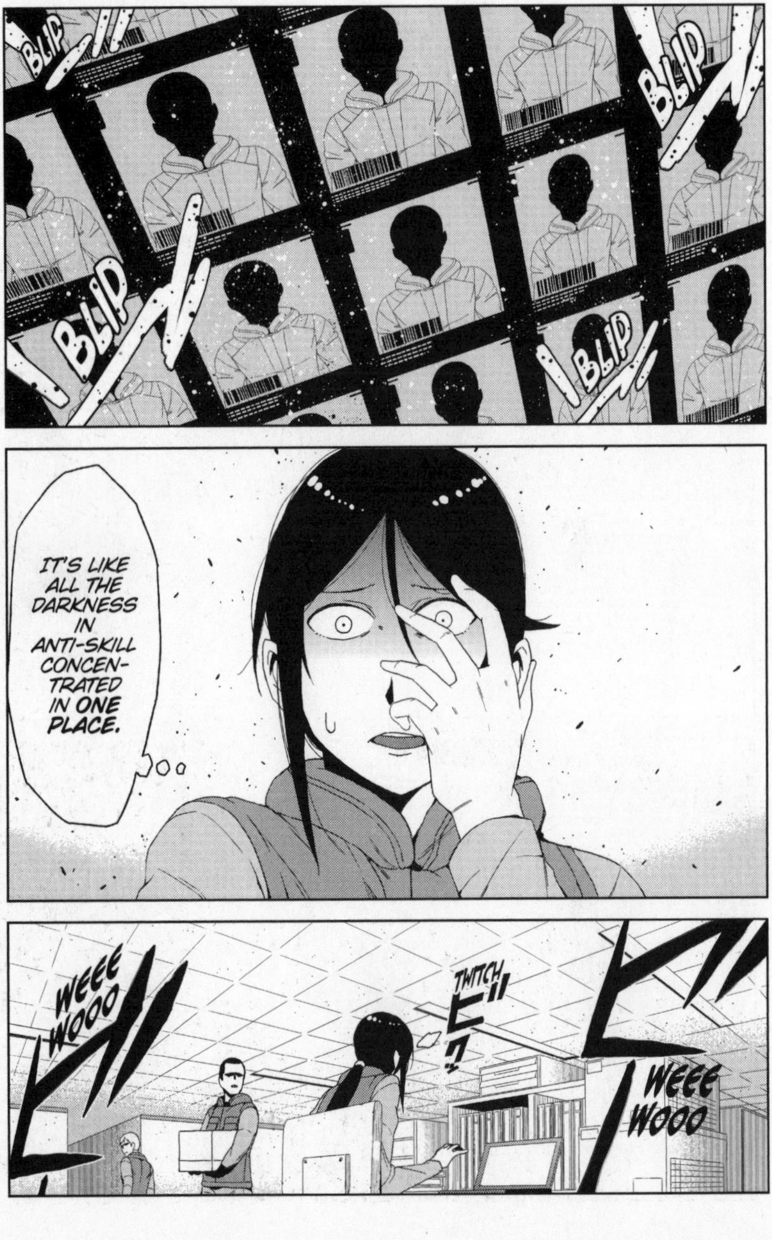
BLIP
BLIP
BLIP
BLIP
IT'S LIKE ALL THE DARKNESS IN ANTI-SKILL CONCENTRATED IN ONE PLACE.
WEEE WOOO
TWITCH
WEEE WOOO

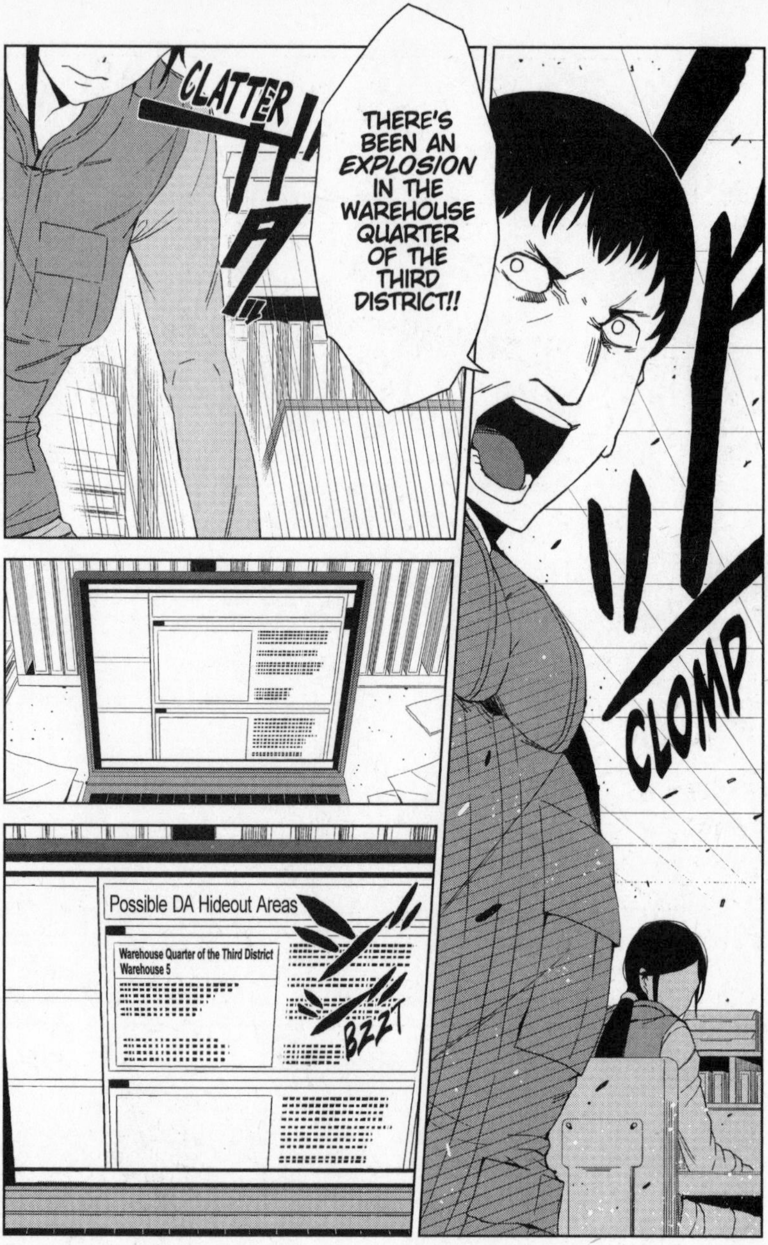
CLATTER
THERE'S BEEN AN EXPLOSION IN THE WAREHOUSE QUARTER OF THE THIRD DISTRICT!!
CLOMP
Possible DA Hideout Areas
Warehouse Quarter of the Third District
Warehouse 5
BZZT

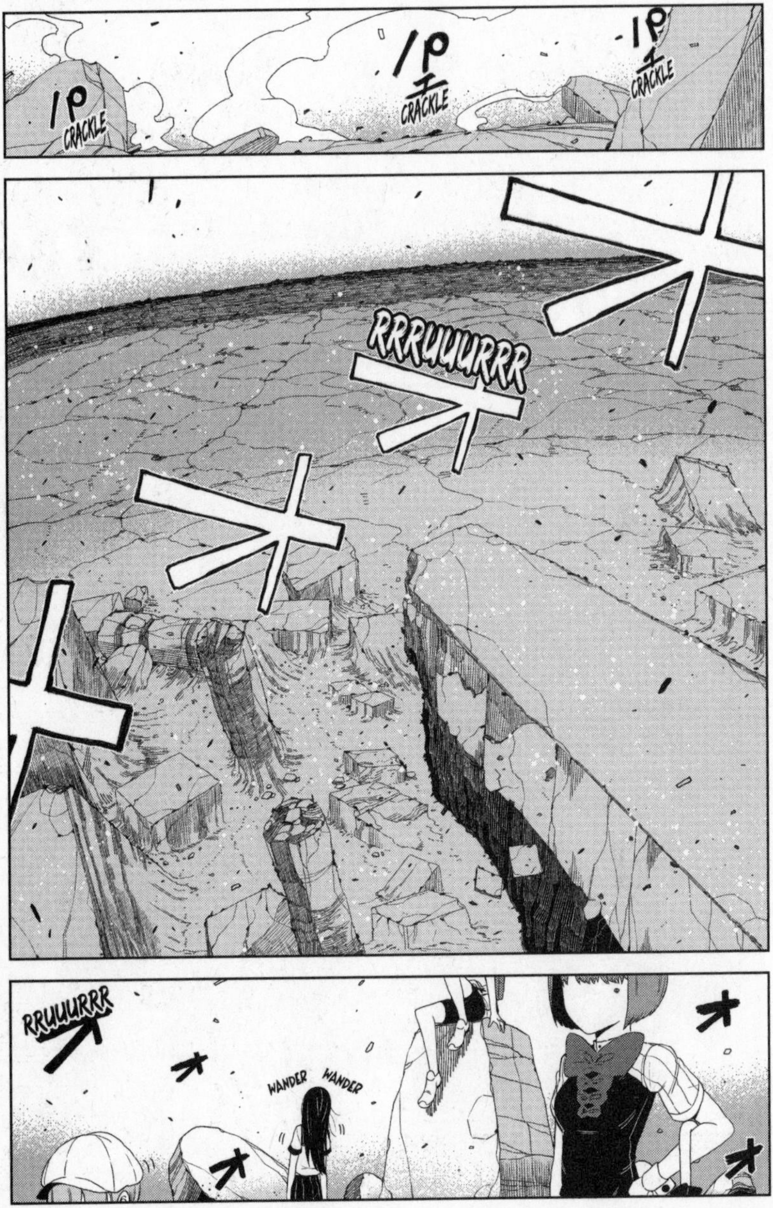
CRACKLE
CRACKLE
CRACKLE
RRRUUUURRR
RRUUURRR
WANDER WANDER

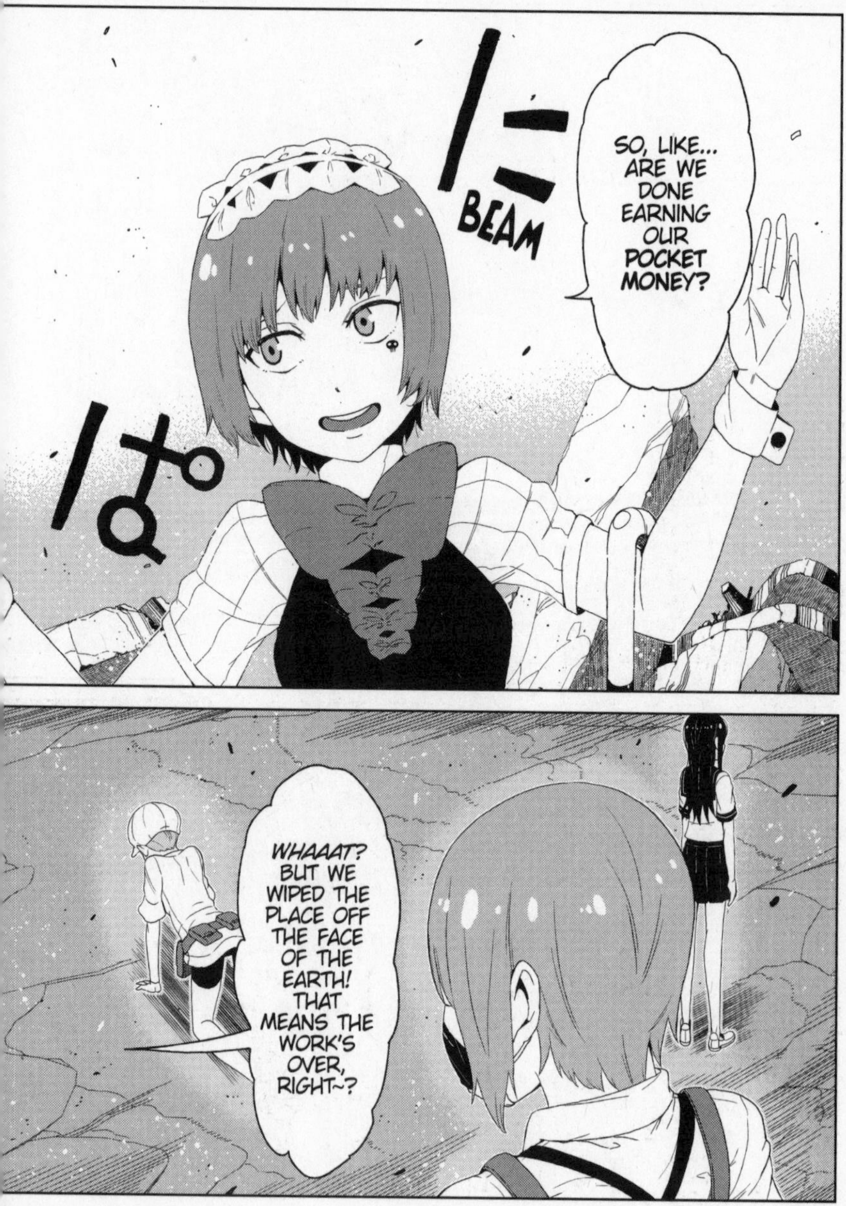
SO, LIKE... ARE WE DONE EARNING OUR POCKET MONEY?
BEAM
WHAAAT? BUT WE WIPED THE PLACE OFF THE FACE OF THE EARTH! THAT MEANS THE WORK'S OVER, RIGHT~?

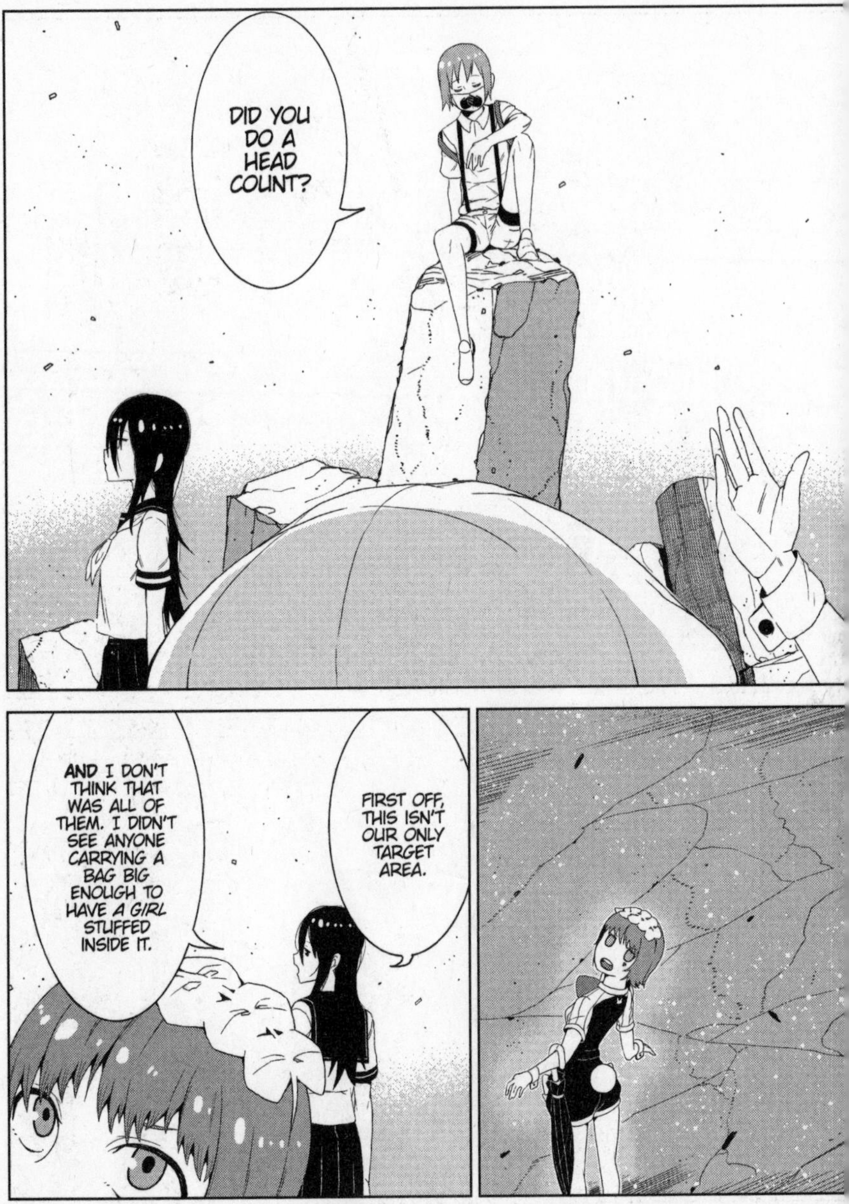
DID YOU DO A HEAD COUNT?
FIRST OFF, THIS ISN'T OUR ONLY TARGET AREA.
AND I DON'T THINK THAT WAS ALL OF THEM. I DIDN'T SEE ANYONE CARRYING A BAG BIG ENOUGH TO HAVE A GIRL STUFFED INSIDE IT.

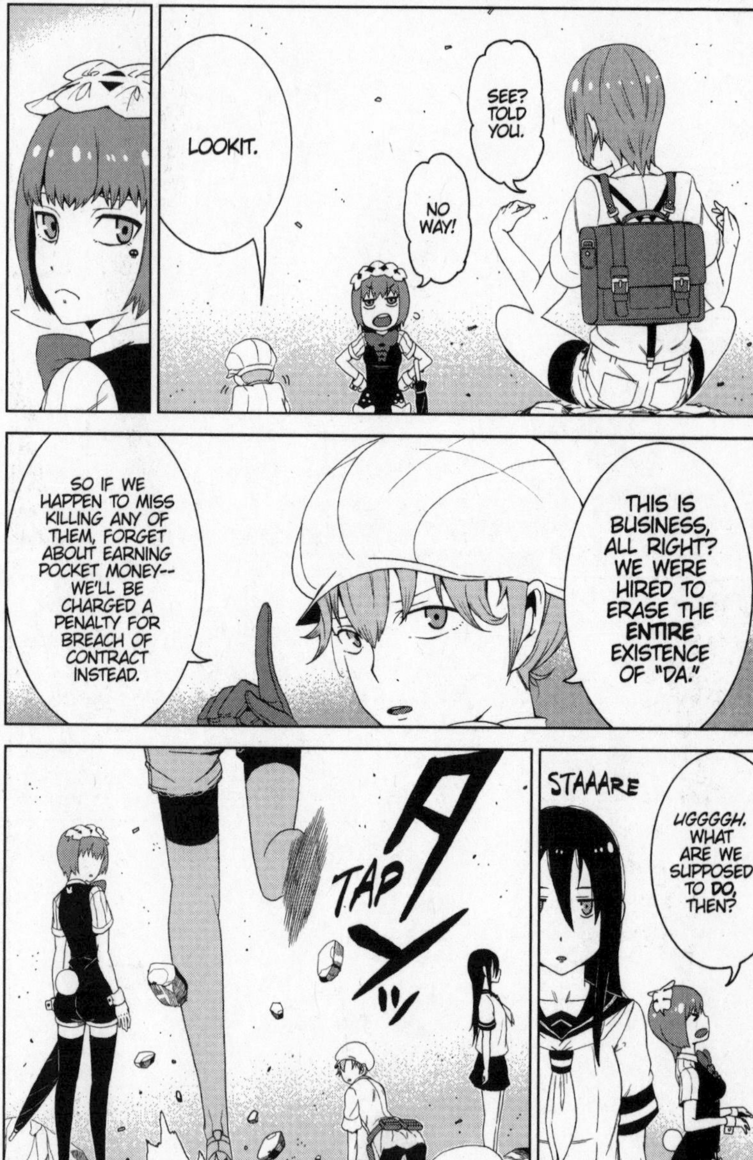
SEE? TOLD YOU.
NO WAY!
LOOKIT.
THIS IS BUSINESS, ALL RIGHT? WE WERE HIRED TO ERASE THE ENTIRE EXISTENCE OF "DA."
SO IF WE HAPPEN TO MISS KILLING ANY OF THEM, FORGET ABOUT EARNING POCKET MONEY--WE'LL BE CHARGED A PENALTY FOR BREACH OF CONTRACT INSTEAD.
STAAARE
UGGGGH. WHAT ARE WE SUPPOSED TO DO, THEN?
TAP

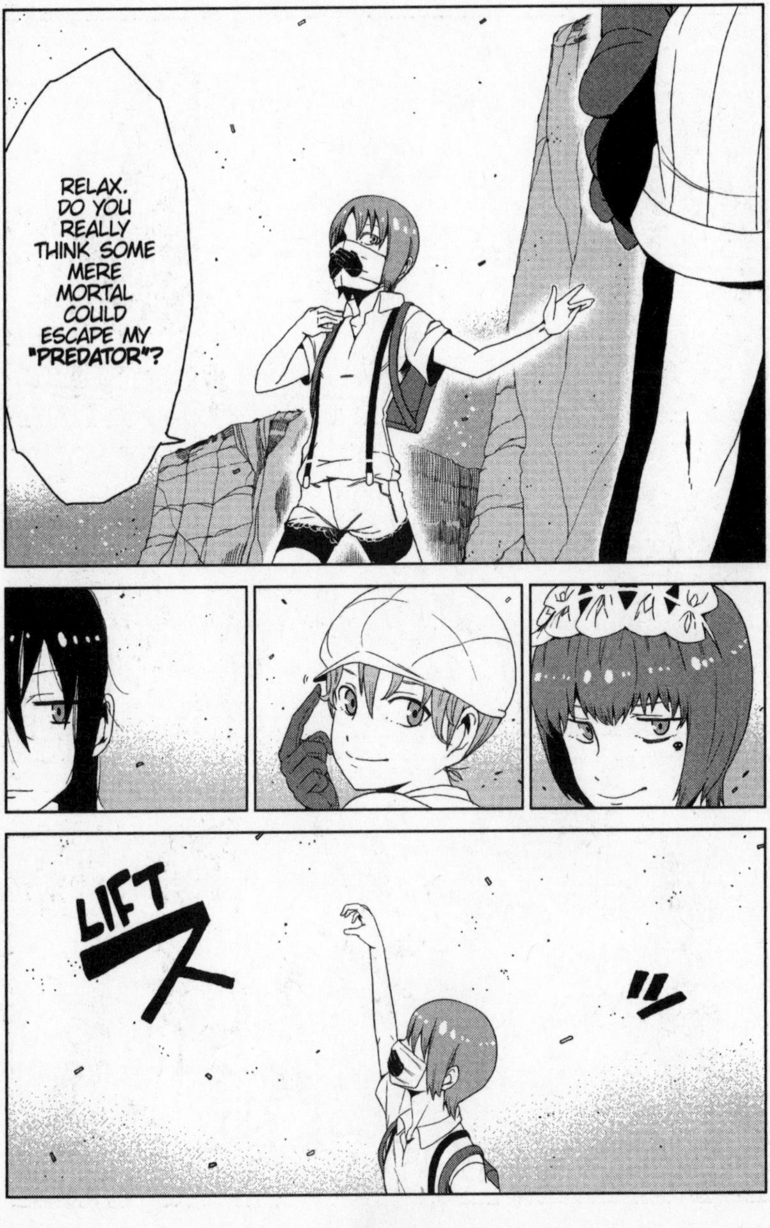
RELAX. DO YOU REALLY THINK SOME MERE MORTAL COULD ESCAPE MY "PREDATOR"?
LIFT

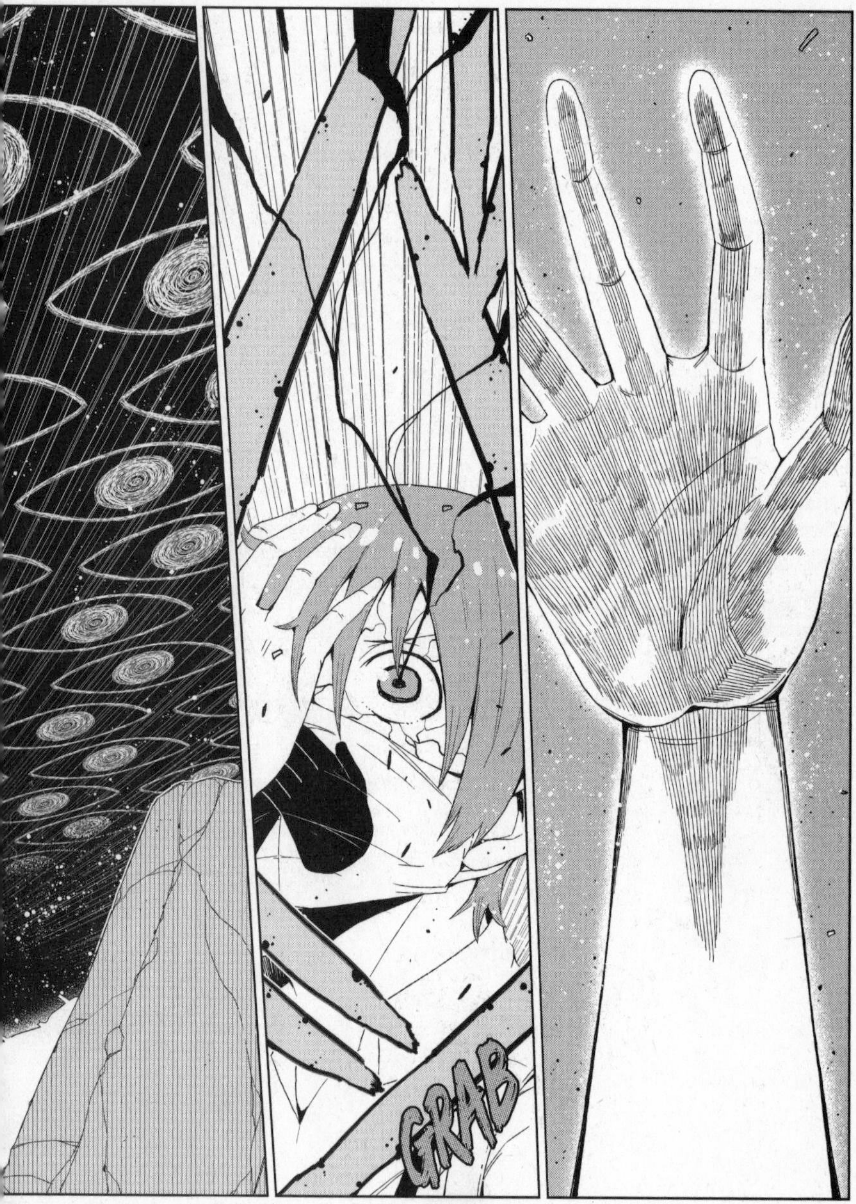
GRAB

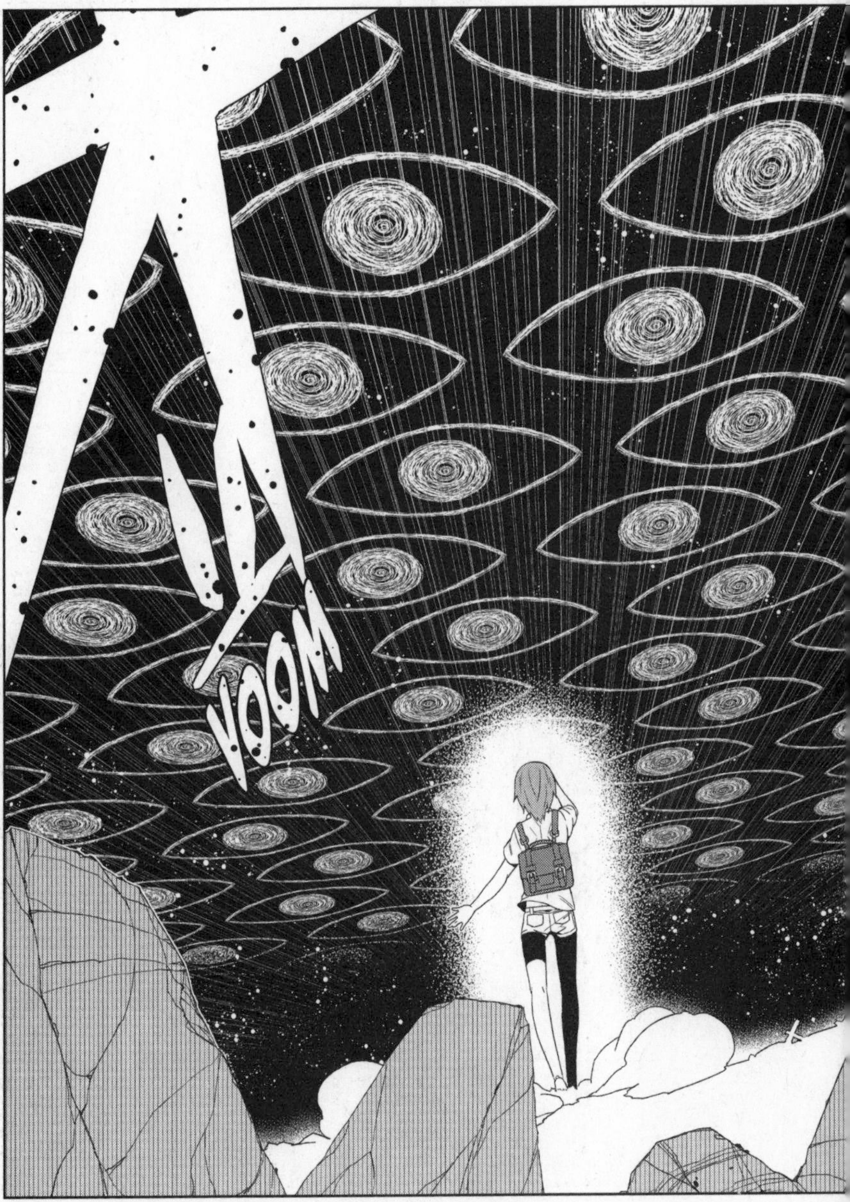
VOOM

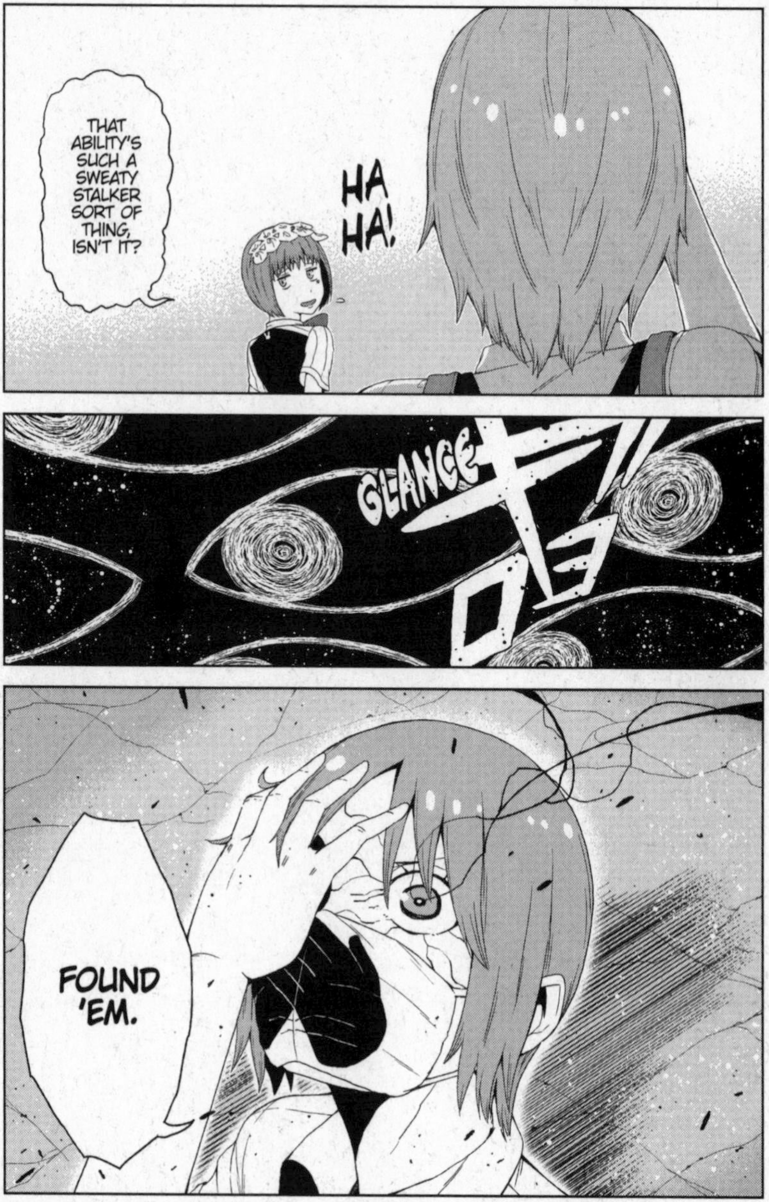
HA HA!
THAT ABILITY'S SUCH A SWEATY STALKER SORT OF THING, ISN'T IT?
GLANCE
ギョロ
FOUND 'EM.

a certain
SCIENTIFIC
ACCELERATOR

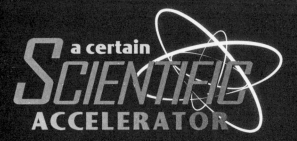

とある科学の一方通行

とある魔術の禁書目録外伝

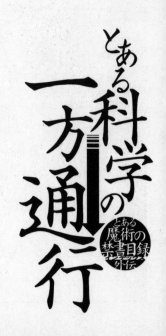

CHAPTER 8

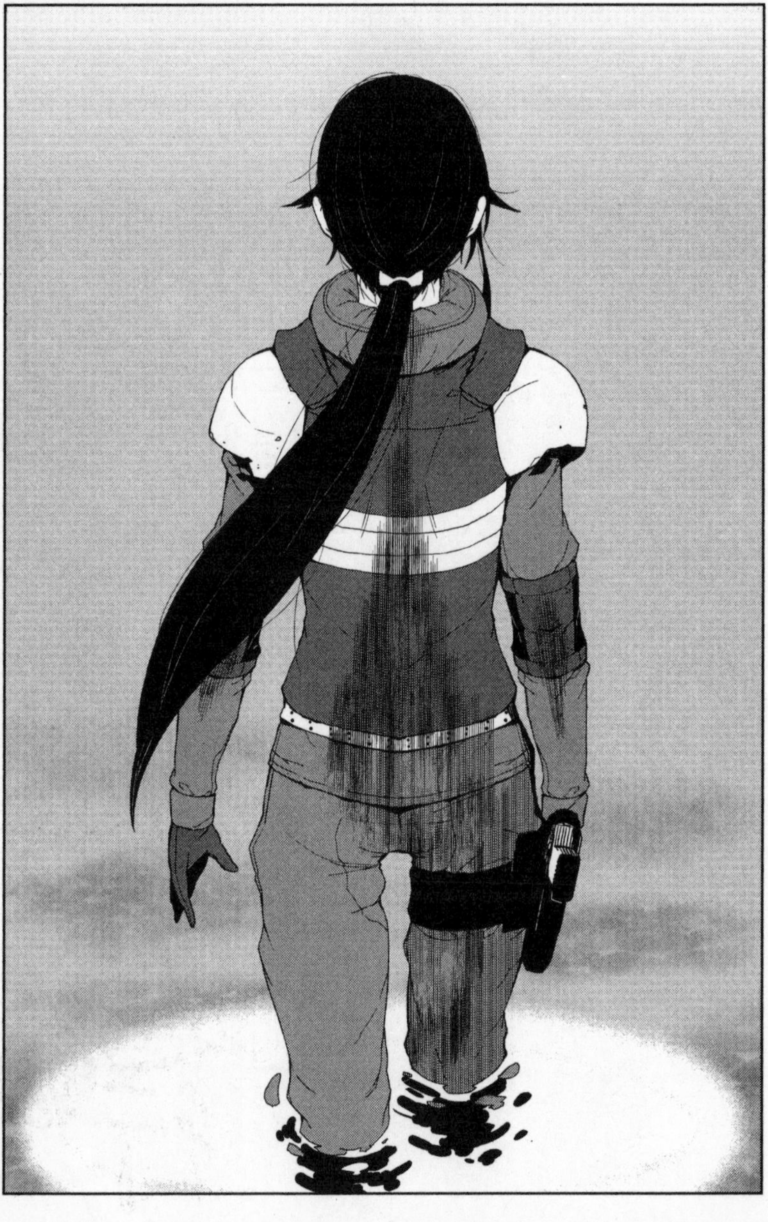

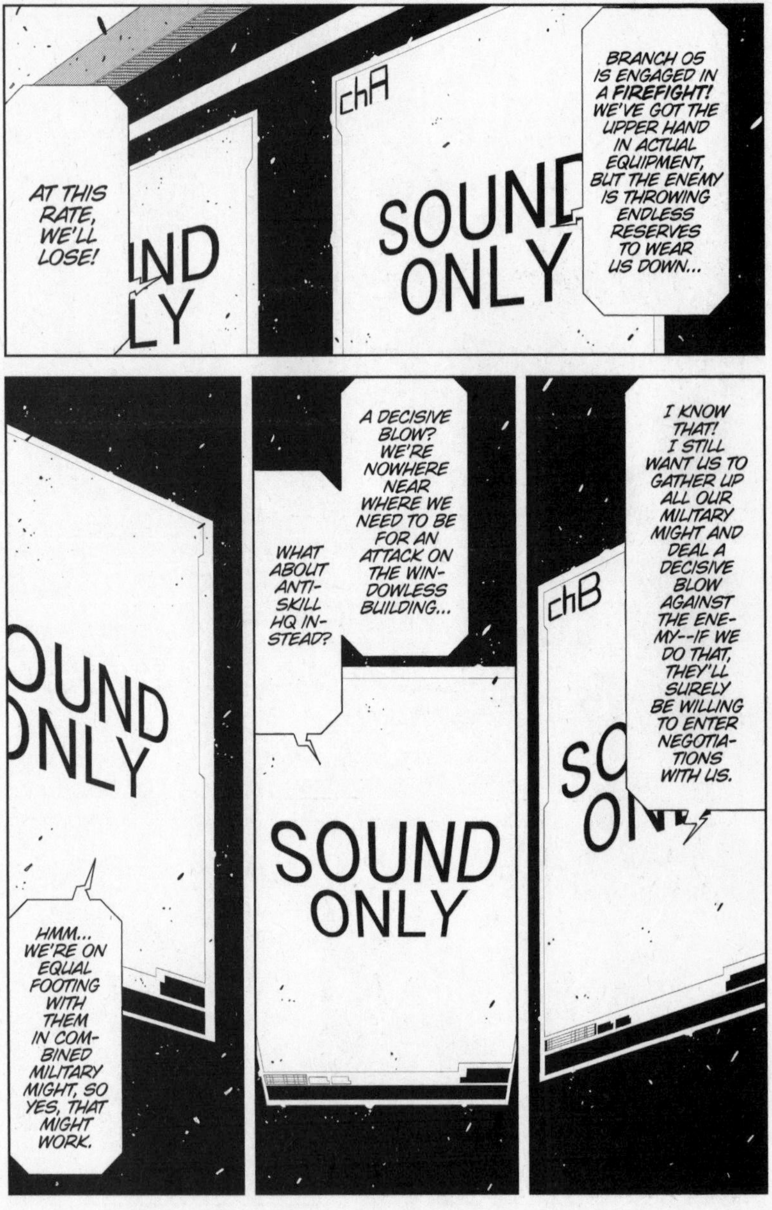
BRANCH 05 IS ENGAGED IN A FIREFIGHT! WE'VE GOT THE UPPER HAND IN ACTUAL EQUIPMENT, BUT THE ENEMY IS THROWING ENDLESS RESERVES TO WEAR US DOWN...
chA
SOUND ONLY
AT THIS RATE, WE'LL LOSE!
I KNOW THAT! I STILL WANT US TO GATHER UP ALL OUR MILITARY MIGHT AND DEAL A DECISIVE BLOW AGAINST THE ENEMY--IF WE DO THAT, THEY'LL SURELY BE WILLING TO ENTER NEGOTIATIONS WITH US.
chB
A DECISIVE BLOW? WE'RE NOWHERE NEAR WHERE WE NEED TO BE FOR AN ATTACK ON THE WINDOWLESS BUILDING...
WHAT ABOUT ANTI-SKILL HQ INSTEAD?
SOUND ONLY
HMM... WE'RE ON EQUAL FOOTING WITH THEM IN COMBINED MILITARY MIGHT, SO YES, THAT MIGHT WORK.

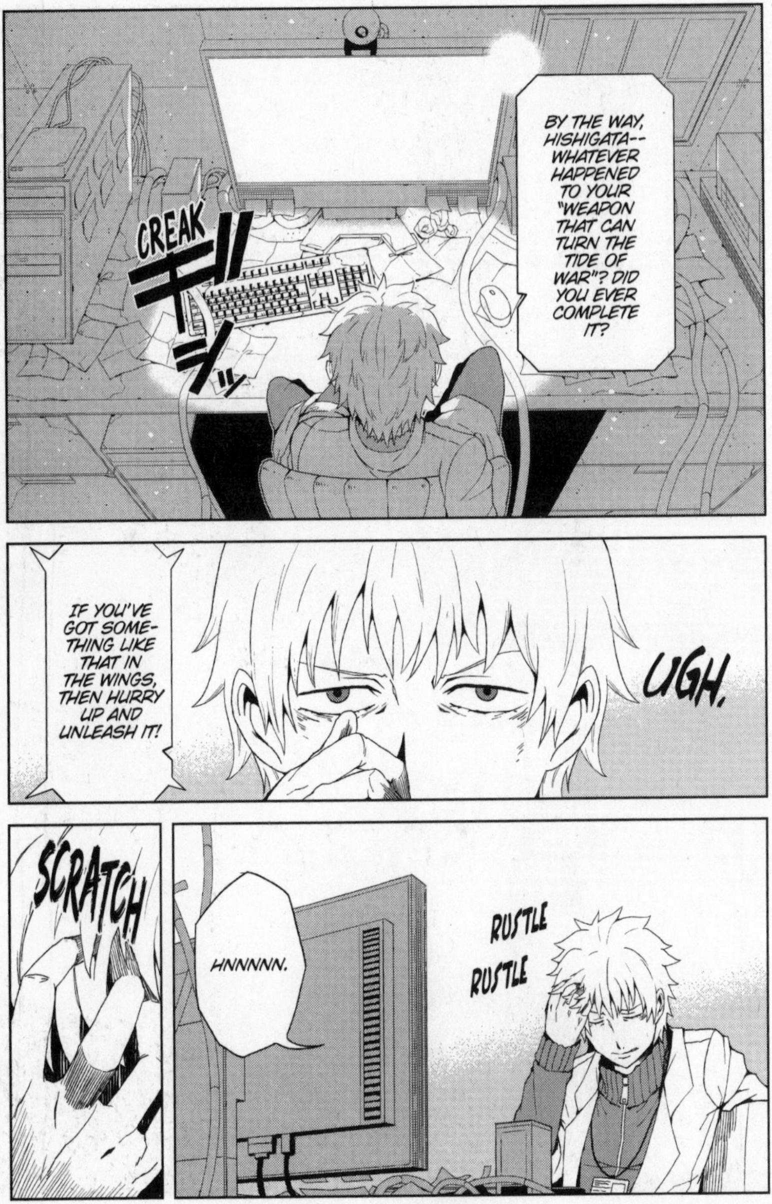
BY THE WAY, HISHIGATA-- WHATEVER HAPPENED TO YOUR "WEAPON THAT CAN TURN THE TIDE OF WAR"? DID YOU EVER COMPLETE IT?
CREAK
UGH.
IF YOU'VE GOT SOME-THING LIKE THAT IN THE WINGS, THEN HURRY UP AND UNLEASH IT!
RUSTLE
RUSTLE
HNNNNN.
SCRATCH

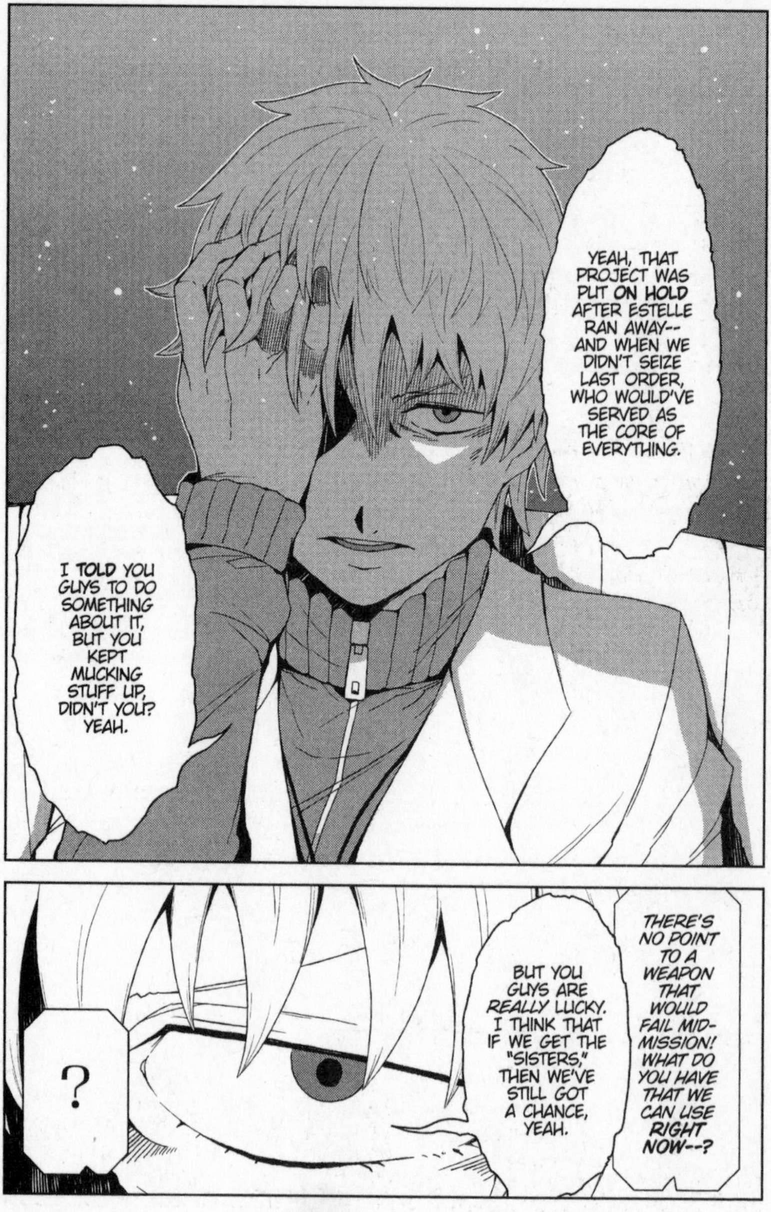
YEAH, THAT PROJECT WAS PUT ON HOLD AFTER ESTELLE RAN AWAY-- AND WHEN WE DIDN'T SEIZE LAST ORDER, WHO WOULD'VE SERVED AS THE CORE OF EVERYTHING.
I TOLD YOU GUYS TO DO SOMETHING ABOUT IT, BUT YOU KEPT MUCKING STUFF UP, DIDN'T YOU? YEAH.
THERE'S NO POINT TO A WEAPON THAT WOULD FAIL MID-MISSION! WHAT DO YOU HAVE THAT WE CAN USE RIGHT NOW--?
BUT YOU GUYS ARE REALLY LUCKY. I THINK THAT IF WE GET THE "SISTERS," THEN WE'VE STILL GOT A CHANCE, YEAH.
?

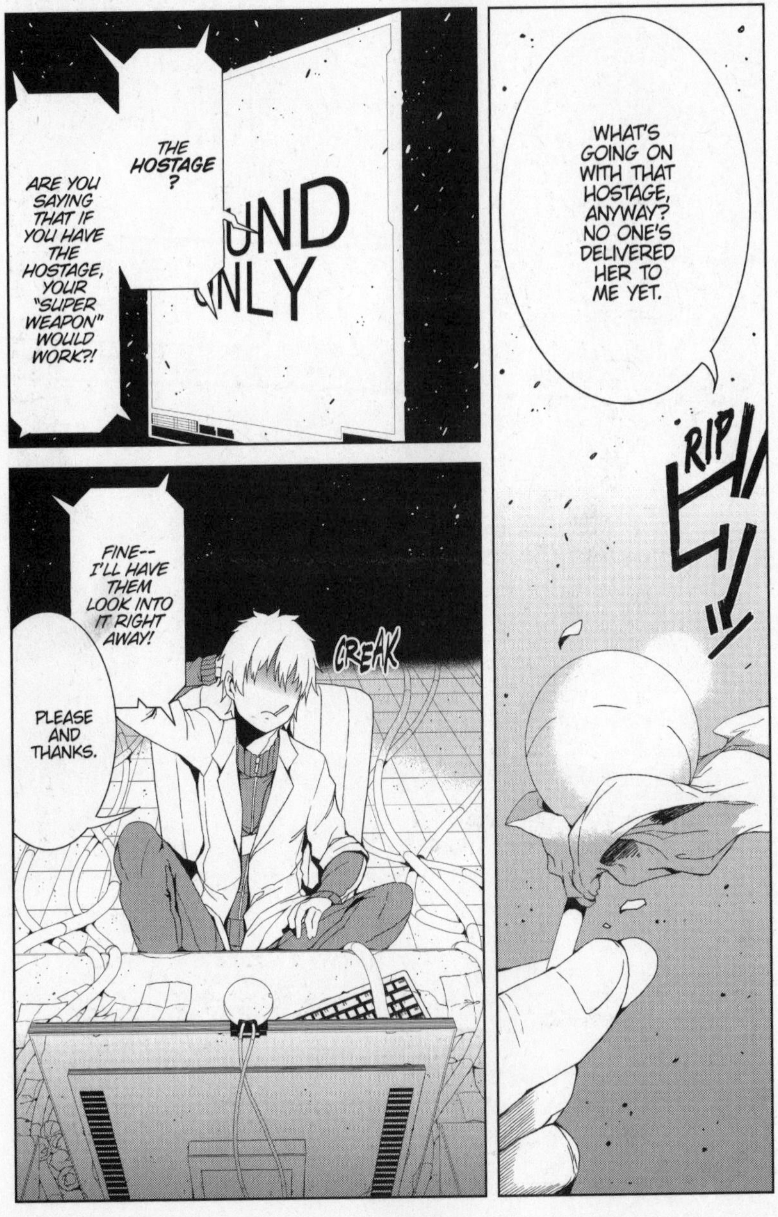
WHAT'S GOING ON WITH THAT HOSTAGE, ANYWAY? NO ONE'S DELIVERED HER TO ME YET.
RIP
THE HOSTAGE?
ARE YOU SAYING THAT IF YOU HAVE THE HOSTAGE, YOUR "SUPER WEAPON" WOULD WORK?!
UND
NLY
FINE-- I'LL HAVE THEM LOOK INTO IT RIGHT AWAY!
CREAK
PLEASE AND THANKS.

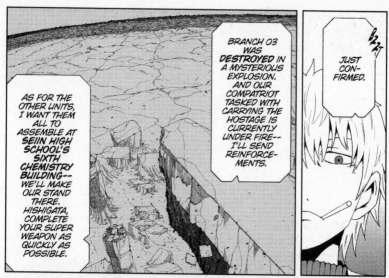

BZZT
JUST CON-FIRMED.
BRANCH 03 WAS DESTROYED IN A MYSTERIOUS EXPLOSION. AND OUR COMPATRIOT TASKED WITH CARRYING THE HOSTAGE IS CURRENTLY UNDER FIRE-- I'LL SEND REINFORCE-MENTS.
AS FOR THE OTHER UNITS, I WANT THEM ALL TO ASSEMBLE AT SEIIN HIGH SCHOOL'S SIXTH CHEMISTRY BUILDING-- WE'LL MAKE OUR STAND THERE. HISHIGATA, COMPLETE YOUR SUPER WEAPON AS QUICKLY AS POSSIBLE.
THE SIXTH CHEMISTRY BUILDING, EH...? A FORTIFIED BUILDING LIKE THAT WOULD BE A FITTING STAGE FOR OUR COUNTER-ATTACK.
CLACK

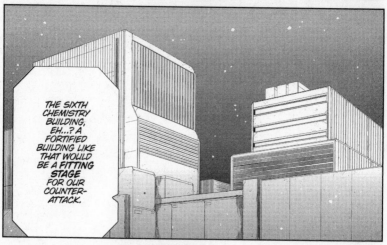

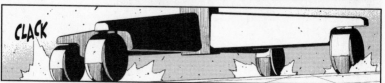

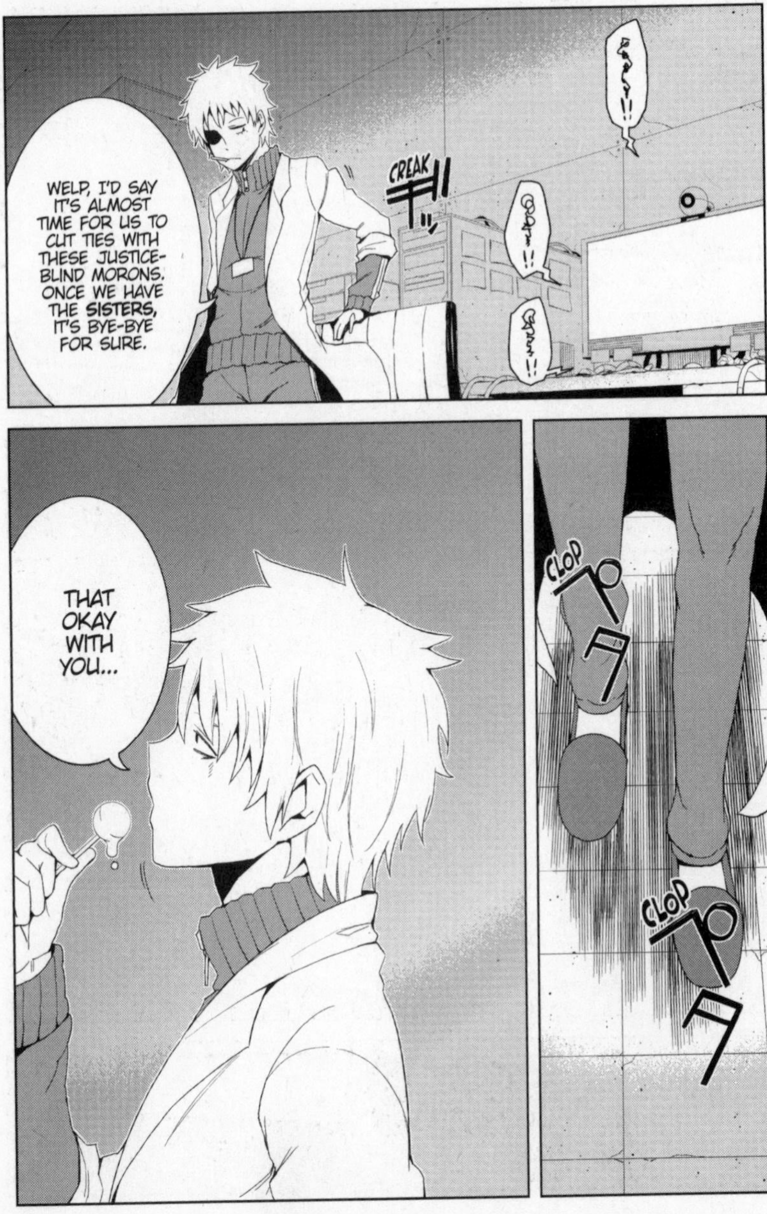
CREAK
WELP, I'D SAY IT'S ALMOST TIME FOR US TO CUT TIES WITH THESE JUSTICE-BLIND MORONS. ONCE WE HAVE THE **SISTERS**, IT'S BYE-BYE FOR SURE.
CLOP
CLOP
THAT OKAY WITH YOU...

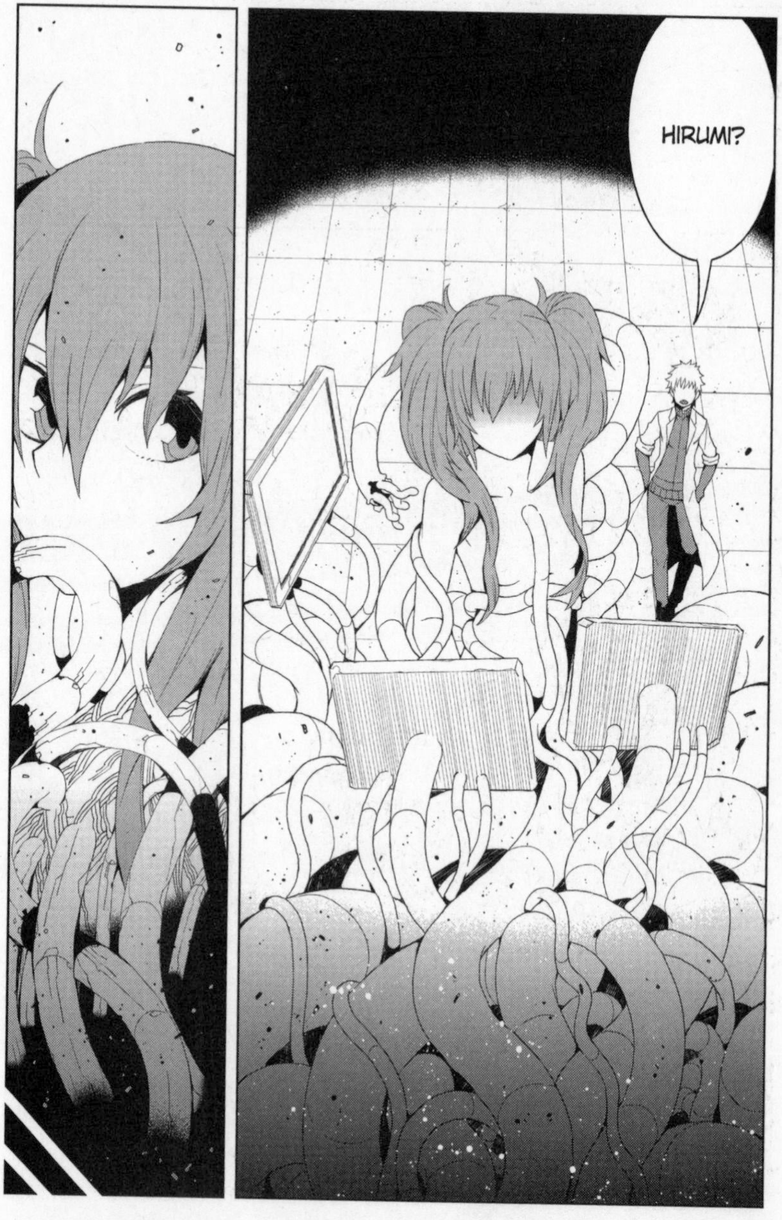
HIRUMI?

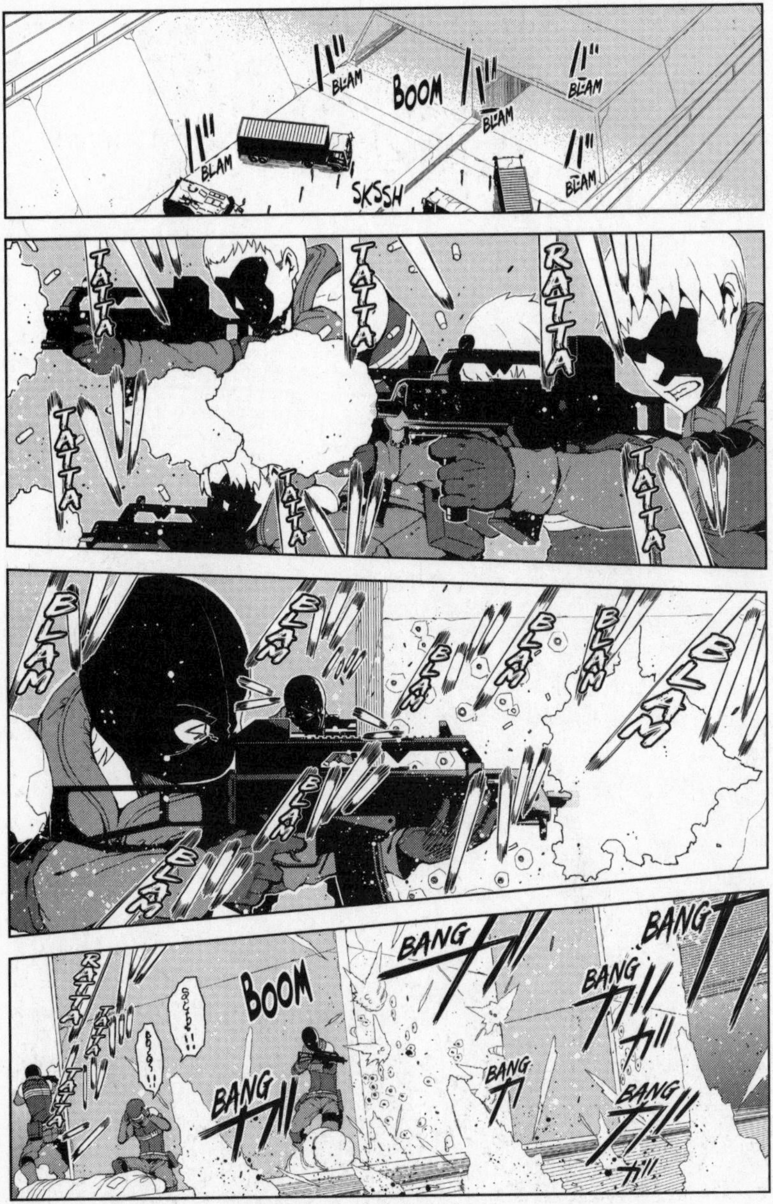
BLAM
BLAM
BOOM
BLAM
BLAM
BLAM
SKSSH
RATTA
TATTA
TATTA
TATTA
TATTA
TATTA
BLAM
BLAM
BLAM
BLAM
BLAM
BLAM
BLAM
BLAM
BANG
BANG
BANG
BANG
BANG
BOOM
BANG
RATTA
TATTA
TATTA

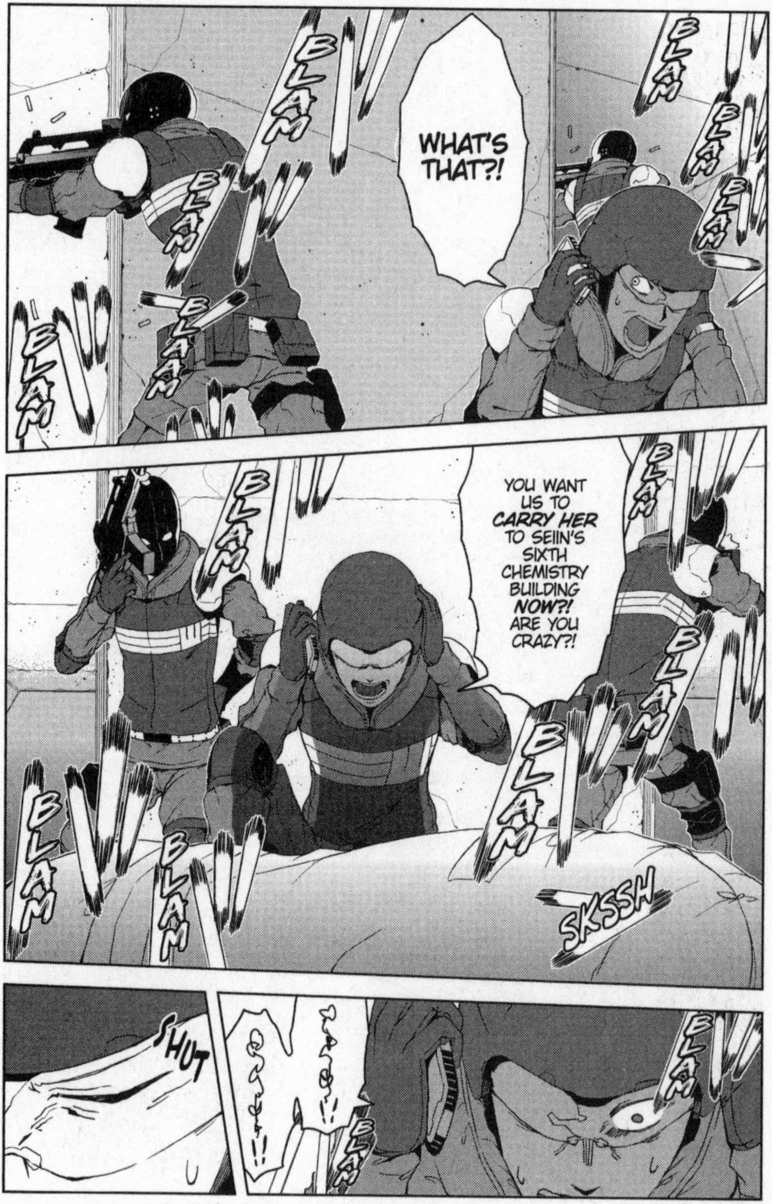
BLAM
BLAM
BLAM
WHAT'S THAT?!
BLAM
BLAM
BLAM
BLAM
YOU WANT US TO CARRY HER TO SEIIN'S SIXTH CHEMISTRY BUILDING NOW?! ARE YOU CRAZY?!
BLAM
BLAM
BLAM
BLAM
SKSSH
BLAM
BLAM
SHUT

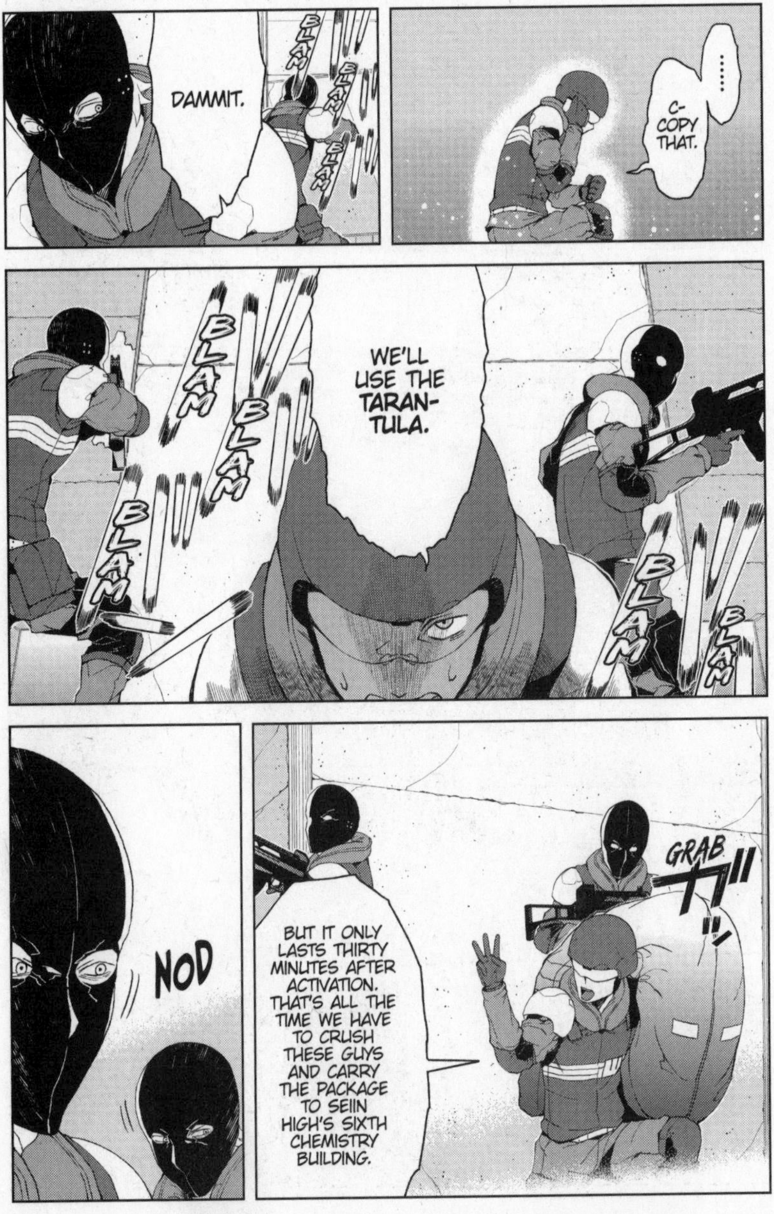
......
C-COPY THAT.
BLAM BLAM BLAM BLAM
DAMMIT.
BLAM BLAM BLAM BLAM
WE'LL USE THE TARAN-TULA.
BLAM BLAM BLAM
GRAB
BUT IT ONLY LASTS THIRTY MINUTES AFTER ACTIVATION. THAT'S ALL THE TIME WE HAVE TO CRUSH THESE GUYS AND CARRY THE PACKAGE TO SEIIN HIGH'S SIXTH CHEMISTRY BUILDING.
NOD

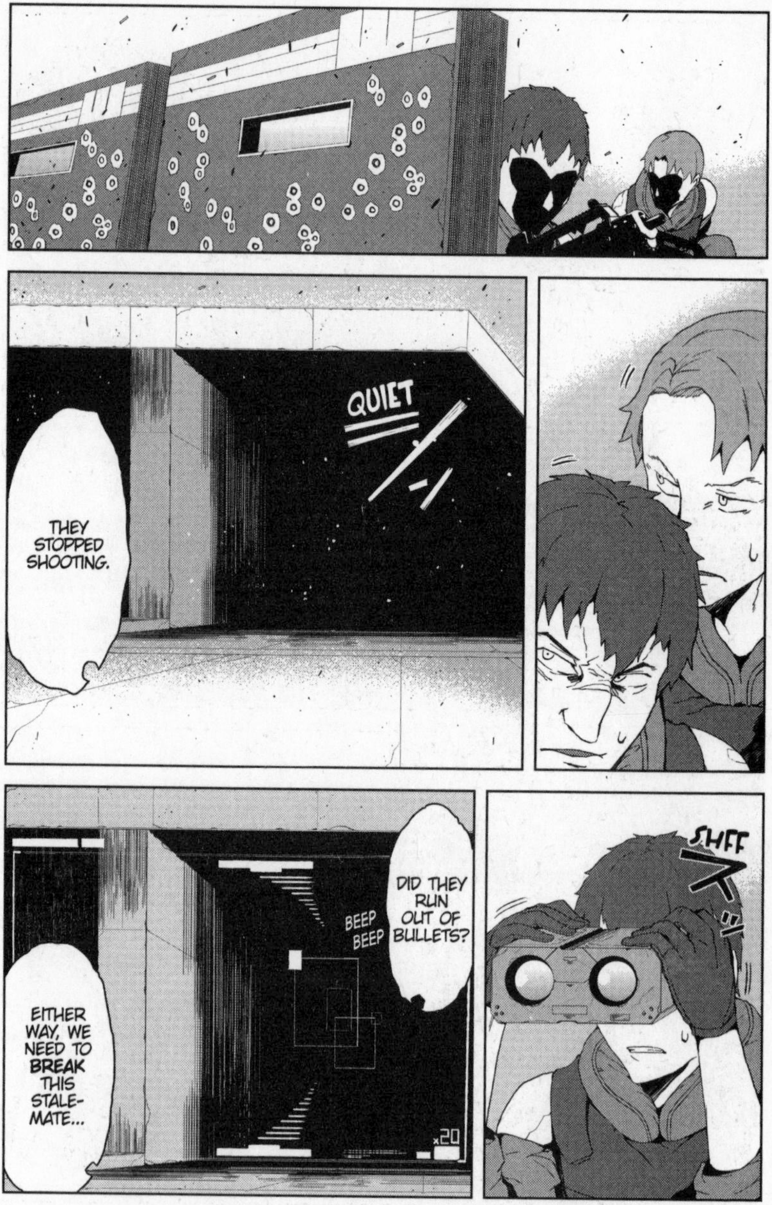
QUIET
THEY STOPPED SHOOTING.
DID THEY RUN OUT OF BULLETS?
BEEP BEEP
EITHER WAY, WE NEED TO BREAK THIS STALE-MATE...
×20
SHFF

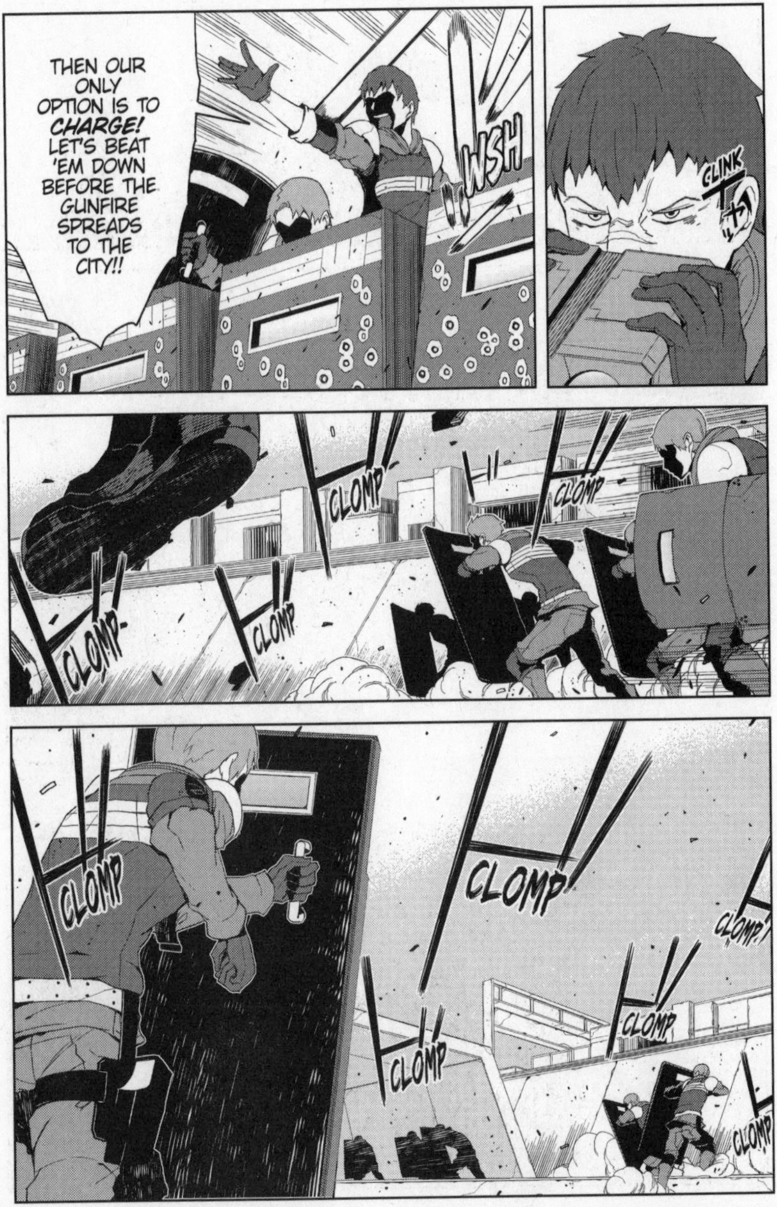
THEN OUR ONLY OPTION IS TO CHARGE! LET'S BEAT 'EM DOWN BEFORE THE GUNFIRE SPREADS TO THE CITY!!
WSH
CLINK
CLOMP
CLOMP
CLOMP
CLOMP
CLOMP
CLOMP
CLOMP
CLOMP
CLOMP
CLOMP

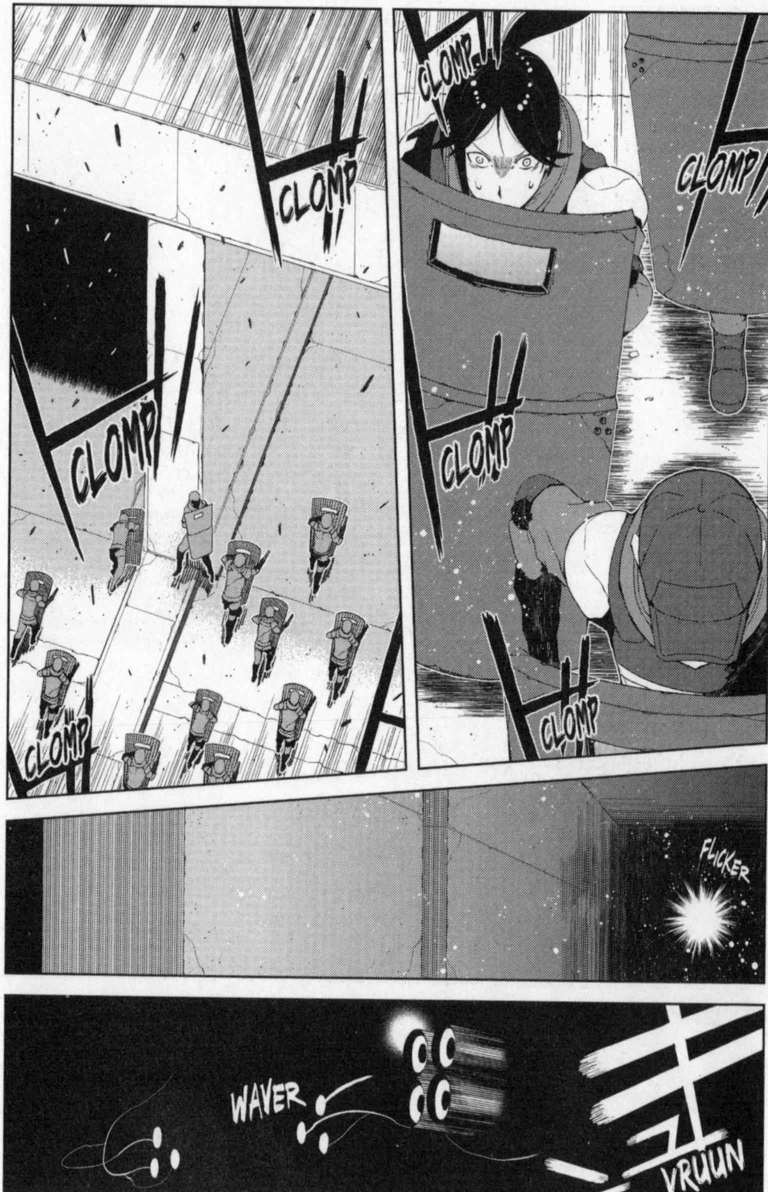
CLOMP
CLOMP
CLOMP
CLOMP
CLOMP
CLOMP
CLOMP
FLICKER
VRUUN
WAVER

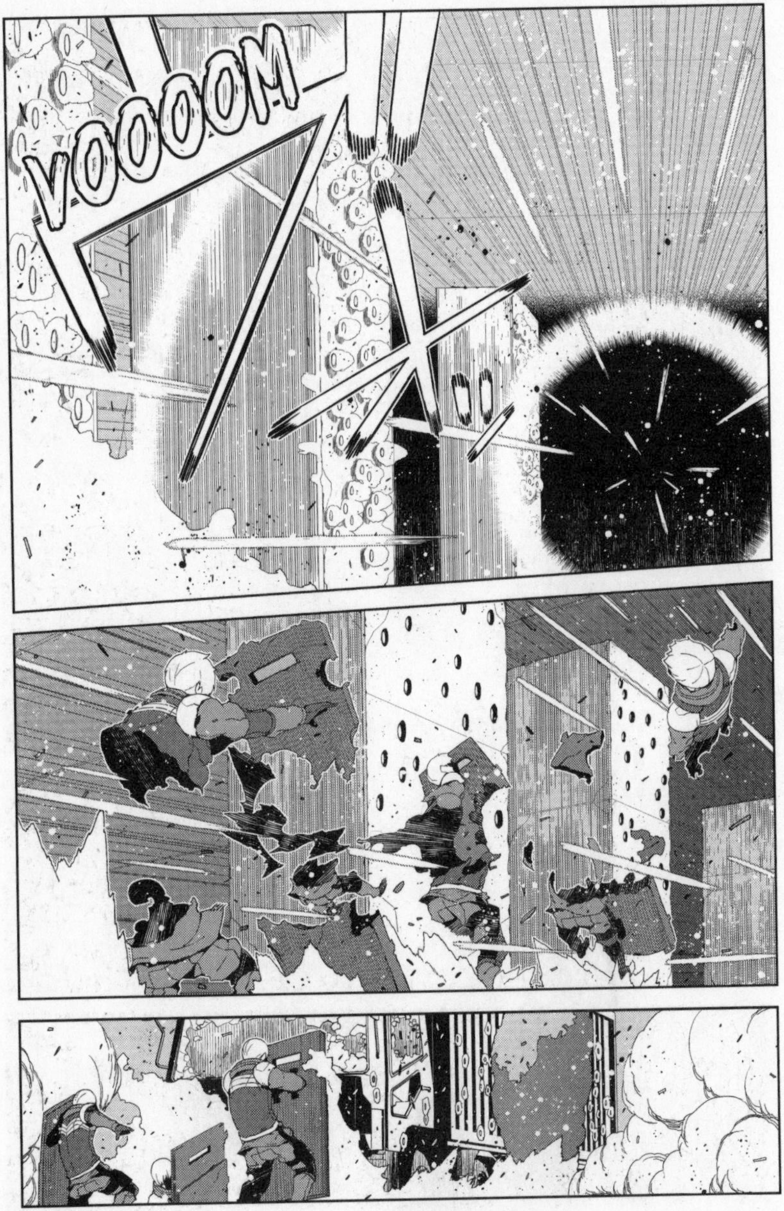
VOOOOM

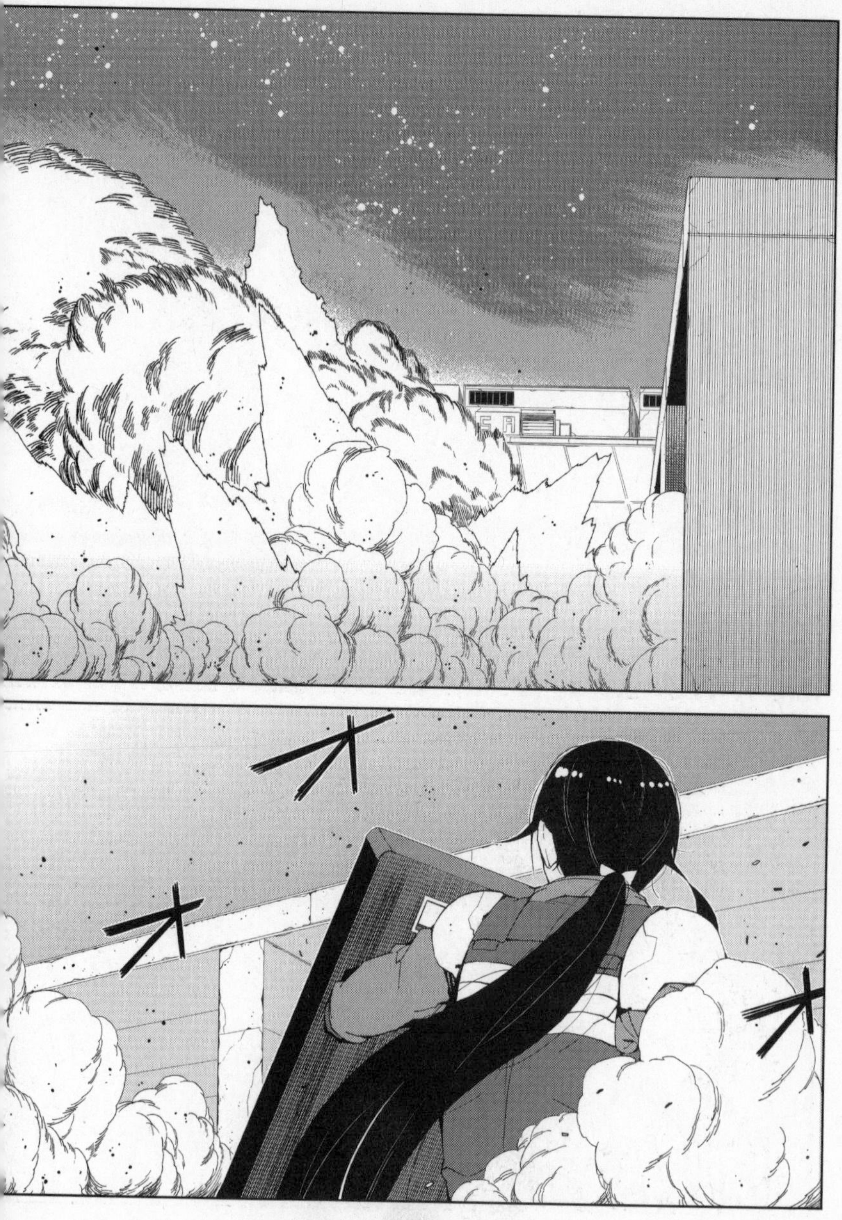
オ
オ
オ

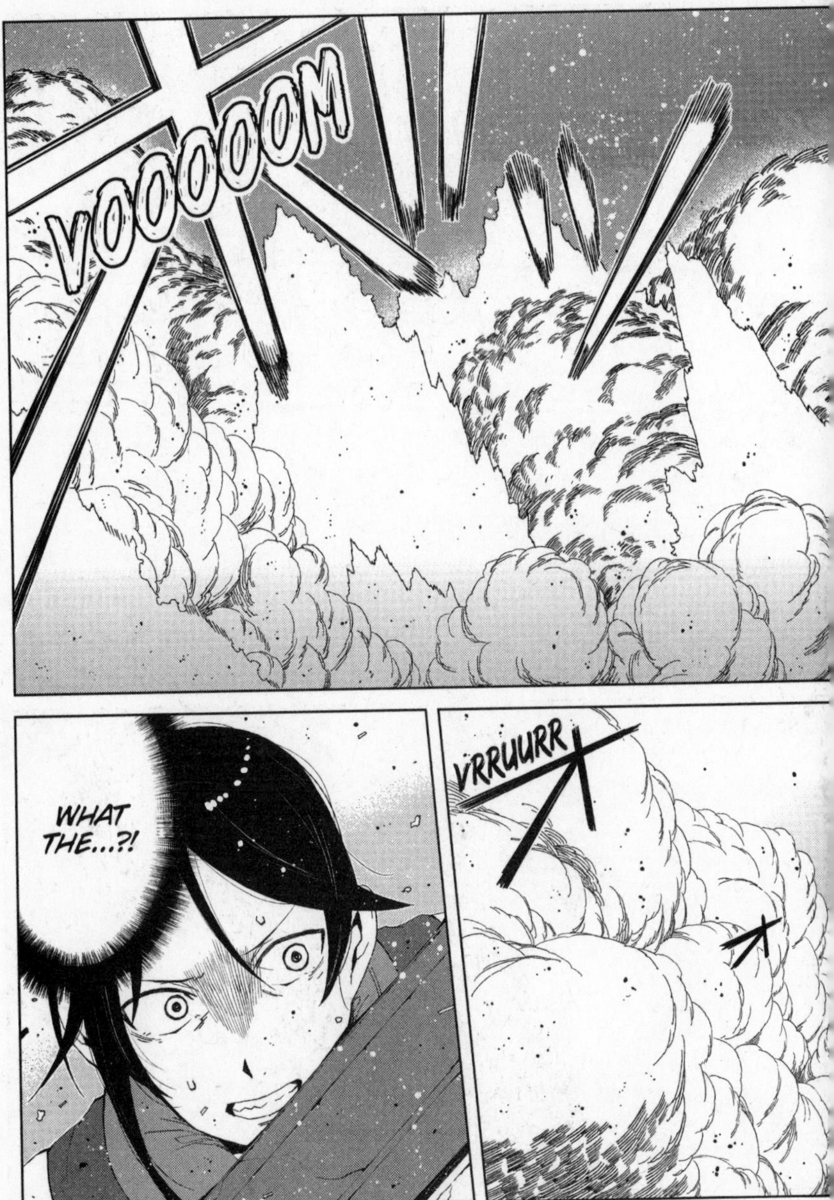
VOOOOOM
VRRUURR
WHAT THE...?!

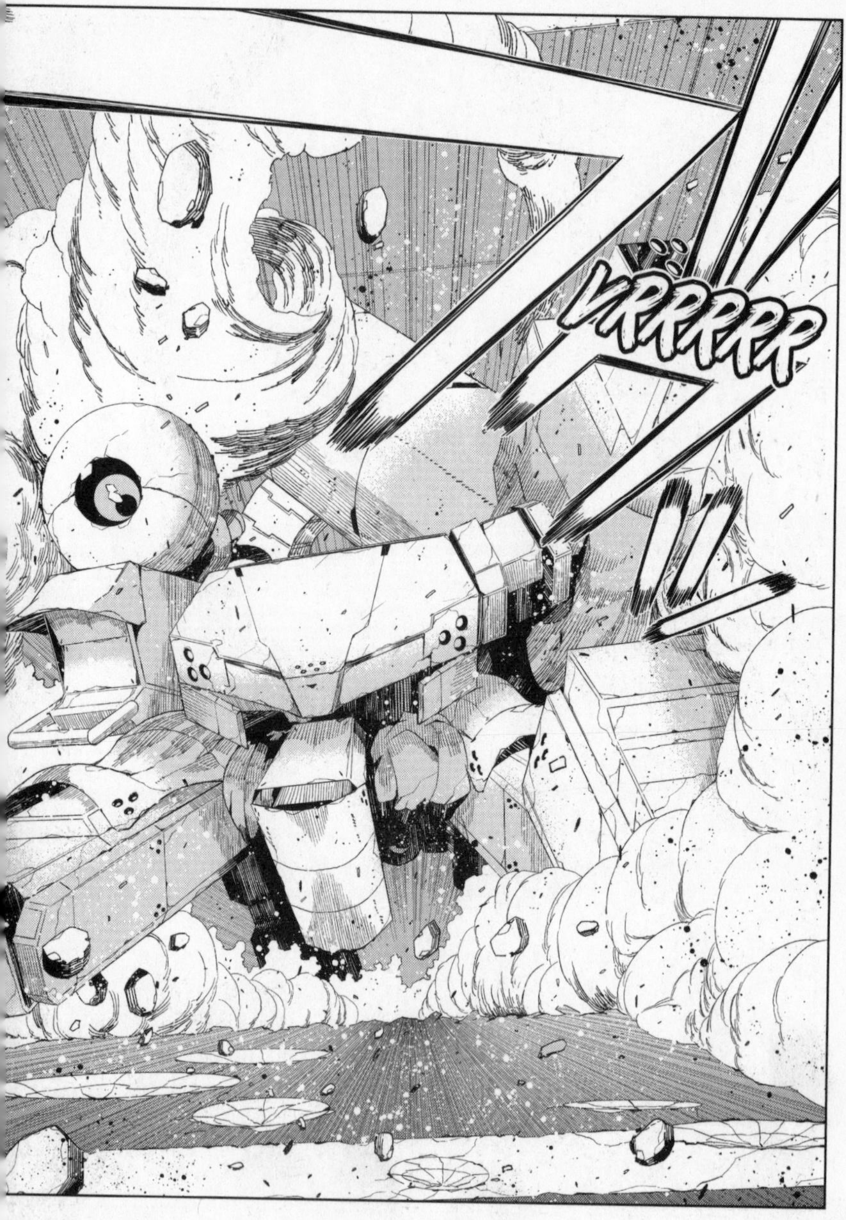
VRRRRRR

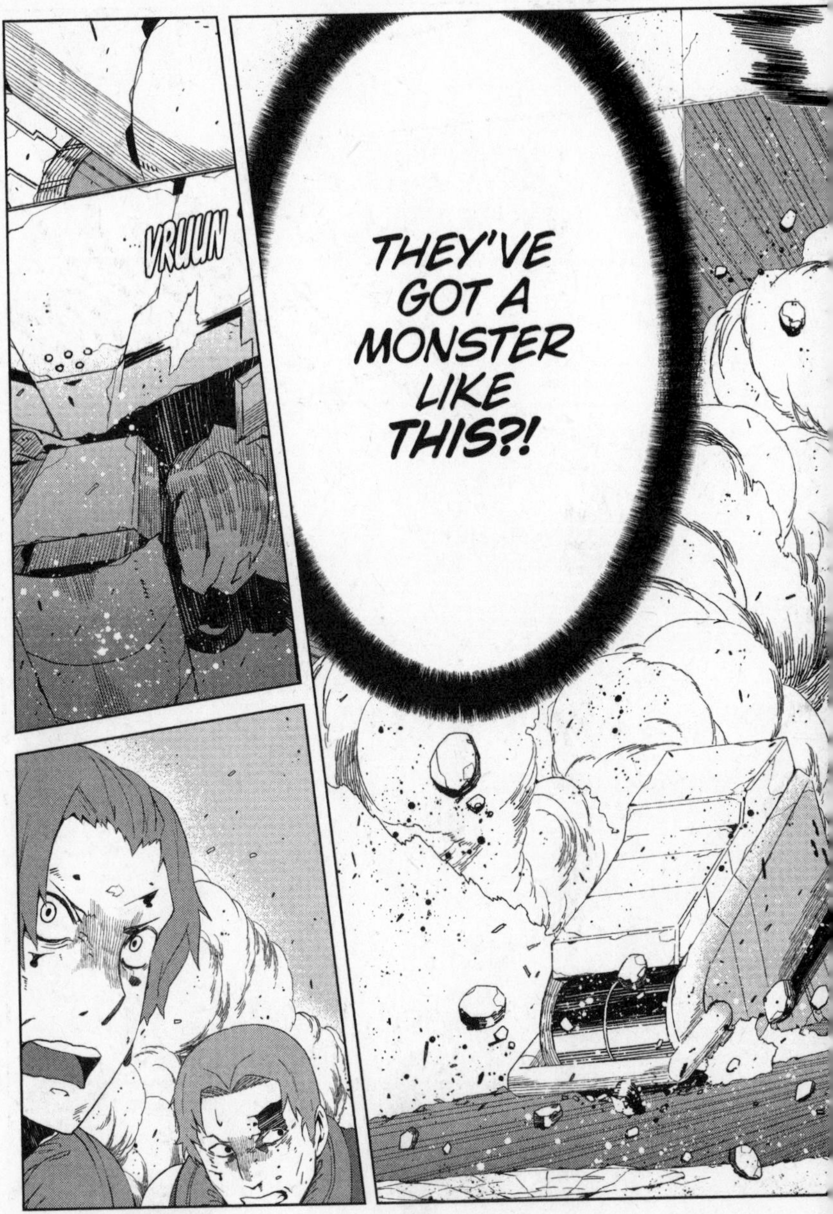
THEY'VE GOT A MONSTER LIKE THIS?!
VRUUN

To be continued...

とある科学の一方通行

とある魔術の禁書目録(インデックス)
外伝

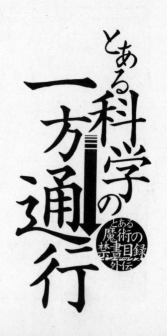

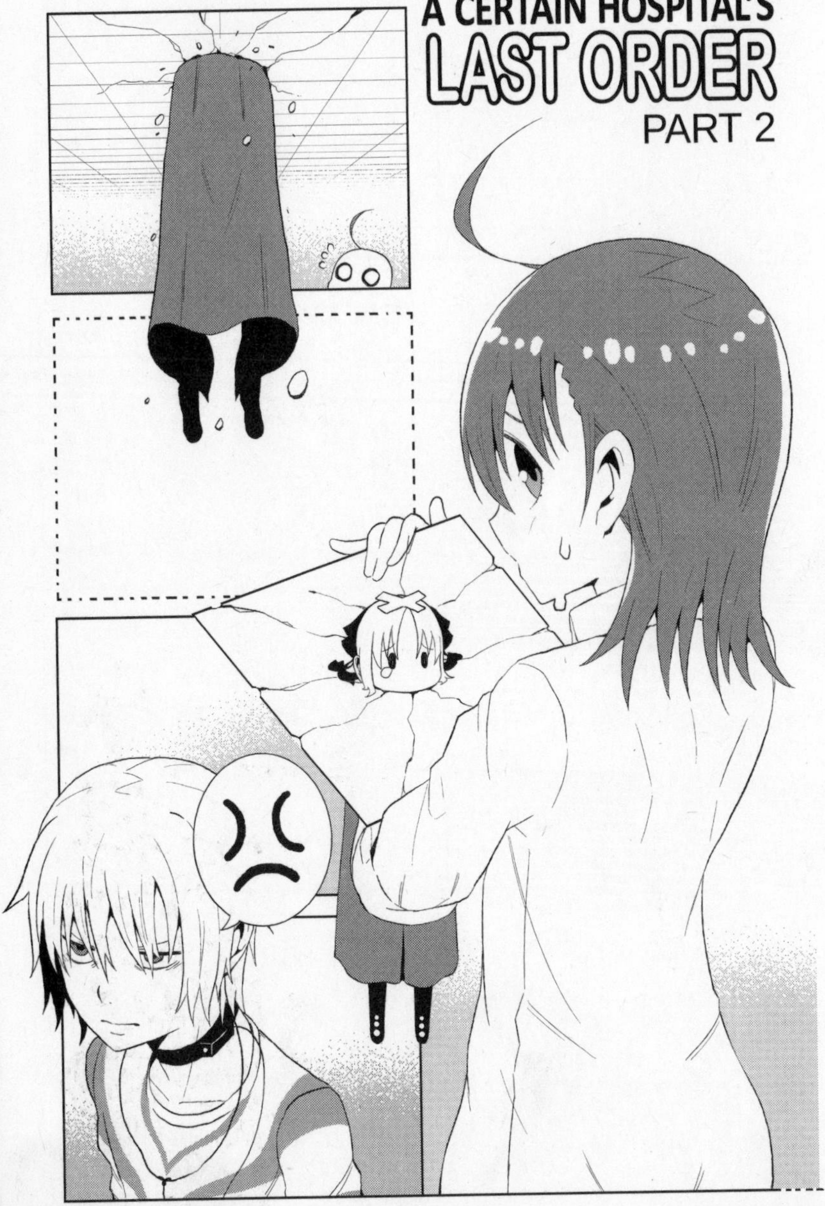
A CERTAIN HOSPITAL'S
LAST ORDER
PART 2

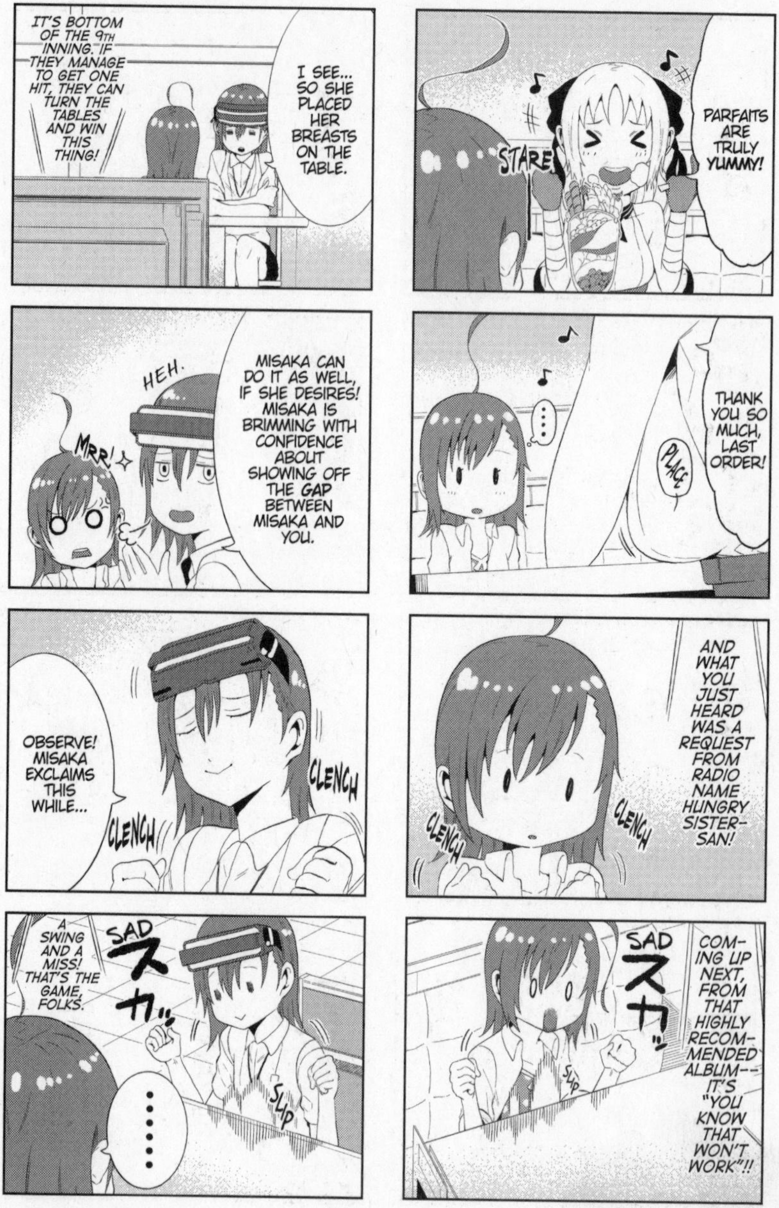
PARFAITS ARE TRULY YUMMY!
STARE
THANK YOU SO MUCH, LAST ORDER!
PLACE
...
AND WHAT YOU JUST HEARD WAS A REQUEST FROM RADIO NAME HUNGRY SISTER-SAN!
CLENCH
CLENCH
COMING UP NEXT, FROM THAT HIGHLY RECOMMENDED ALBUM-- IT'S "YOU KNOW THAT WON'T WORK"!!
SAD
スカッ
SLIP
I SEE... SO SHE PLACED HER BREASTS ON THE TABLE.
IT'S BOTTOM OF THE 9TH INNING. IF THEY MANAGE TO GET ONE HIT, THEY CAN TURN THE TABLES AND WIN THIS THING!
MISAKA CAN DO IT AS WELL, IF SHE DESIRES! MISAKA IS BRIMMING WITH CONFIDENCE ABOUT SHOWING OFF THE GAP BETWEEN MISAKA AND YOU.
HEH.
MRR!
OBSERVE! MISAKA EXCLAIMS THIS WHILE...
CLENCH
CLENCH
A SWING AND A MISS! THAT'S THE GAME, FOLKS.
SAD
スカッ
SLIP
......

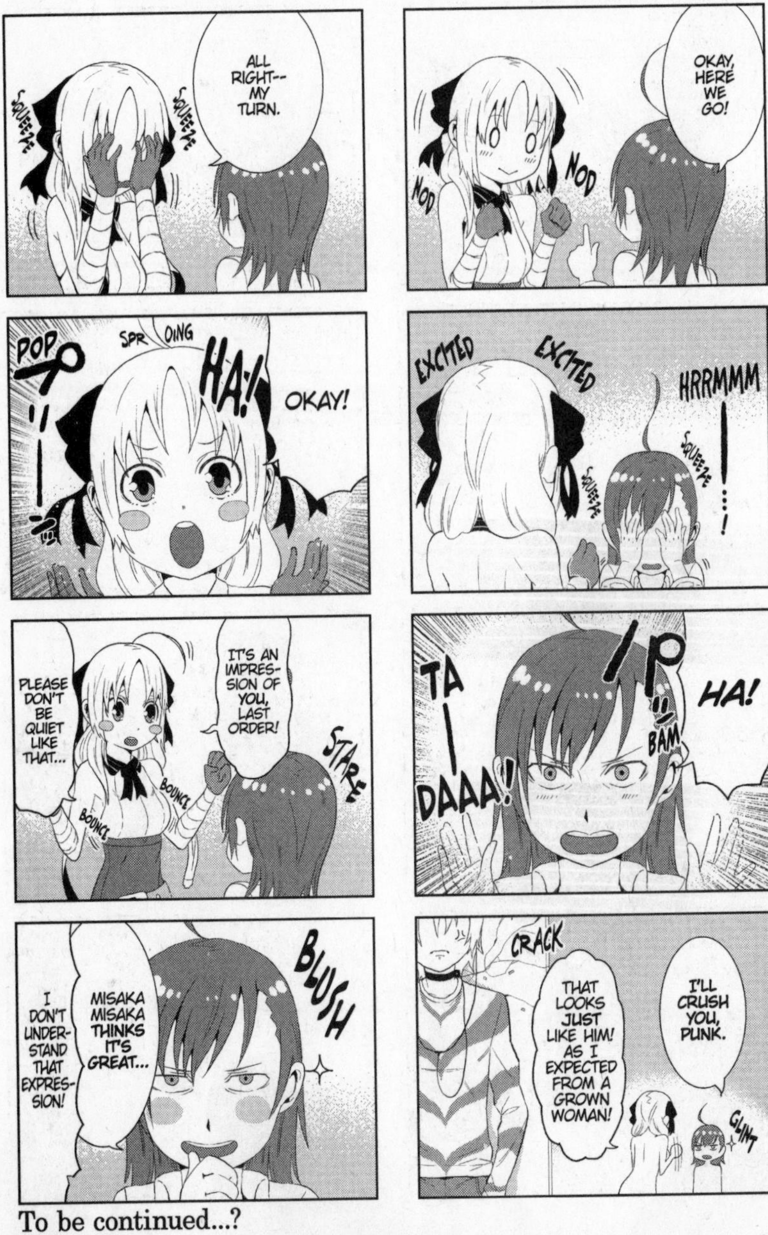
OKAY, HERE WE GO!
NOD
NOD
HRRMMM...!
SQUEEZE
SQUEEZE
EXCITED
EXCITED
HA!
BAM
TA-DAAA!
I'LL CRUSH YOU, PUNK.
THAT LOOKS JUST LIKE HIM! AS I EXPECTED FROM A GROWN WOMAN!
CRACK
GLINT
ALL RIGHT-- MY TURN.
SQUEEZE
SQUEEZE
OKAY!
HA!
SPROING
POP
IT'S AN IMPRESSION OF YOU, LAST ORDER!
PLEASE DON'T BE QUIET LIKE THAT...
STARE
BOUNCE
BOUNCE
MISAKA MISAKA THINKS IT'S GREAT...
I DON'T UNDERSTAND THAT EXPRESSION!
BLUSH

To be continued...?

Those who hatch a plan to use the Sisters...

YOU TAKE THAT MUCH OF A BEATING AND STILL DEFY US?

HA HA HA HA HA!

DA

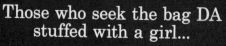

over the "Sisters"!!

IS MISAKA #10046?!

Those who seek the bag DA stuffed with a girl...

屍喰部隊
SCAVENGERS

COMING SOON!